SHORT COURSE SERIES

WORLD TRADE PRESS®

Professional Books for International Trade

THE SHORT COURSE IN INTERNATIONAL TRADE SERIES

A Short Course in International Business Culture

A Short Course in International Business Ethics

A Short Course in International Business Plans

A Short Course in International Contracts

A Short Course in International Economics

A Short Course in International Intellectual Property Rights

A Short Course in International Joint Ventures

A Short Course in International Marketing

A Short Course in International Marketing Blunders

A Short Course in International Negotiating

A Short Course in International Payments

A Short Course in International Trade Documentation

A SHORT COURSE IN

International Contracts

3rd Edition

Drafting the international sales contract—
for attorneys and non-attorneys

Karla C. Shippey, J.D.

Published in arrangement with World Trade Press by

ATLANTIC
PUBLISHERS & DISTRIBUTORS (P) LTD
7/22, Ansari Road, Darya Ganj, New Delhi-110 002
Tel: 40775252, 23273880, 23275880, 23280451; Fax: +91-11-23285873
E-mail: orders@atlanticbooks.com; Web: www.atlanticbooks.com

World Trade Press
800 Lindberg Lane, Suite 190
Petaluma, California 94952 USA
Tel: +1 (707) 778-1124
Fax: +1 (707) 778-1329
USA Order Line: +1 (800) 833-8586
E-mail: sales@worldtradepress.com
www.WorldTradePress.com
www.WorldTradeREF.com (international trade and logistics)
www.BestCountryReports.com (business travel, communications and culture)
www.GiantMapArt.com (Giant maps for building lobbies, conference rooms and education)

A Short Course in International Contracts, 3rd Edition
By Karla C. Shippey, J.D.
Short Course Series Concept: Edward G. Hinkelman
Cover Design: Ronald A. Blodgett
Text Design: Seventeenth Street Studios, Oakland, California USA
Desktop Publishing: Steve Donnet

ISBN 978-81-269-1246-9
First Indian Reprint 2009

Library of Congress Cataloging-in-Publication Data
Shippey, Karla C., 1957–
A short course in international contracts : drafting the international sales contract for attorneys and non-attorneys / Karla C. Shippey. -- 3nd ed.
p. cm. — (The short course in international trade series)
1. Export sales contracts—United States. 2. Export sales contracts.
I. Title: International contracts. II Title. III. Series.
KF915.Z9S53 2009
343.73'0878--dc21 2009037150

Printed in India at Chaman Enterprises, 1603, Pataudi House,
Darya Ganj, New Delhi-110 002

INTRODUCTION

A SHORT COURSE IN INTERNATIONAL CONTRACTS is intended to give you an understanding of commercial agreements between parties trading across country borders. For the most part, you will face the same issues in negotiating domestic contracts as you will when you make agreements with traders in other countries. For example, parties to any commercial contract, whether domestic or international, must consider quality control, compliance with government regulations, protection of intellectual property rights, and dispute resolution. The international aspect of the contract adds a level of complexity to negotiations, performance, and enforcement because the parties are distant, have diverse cultural backgrounds, and are subject to the laws of different countries.

THE LAWYER'S POINT OF VIEW

International contracts must be understood within the context of the legal profession. If you should be so unlucky as to be in a crowd of practitioners of the legal profession, there are two words that you will hear spoken over and over again. Without a doubt, it is those two words that have led to the development of the complex language known to the general public as "legalese." No matter what the culture, regardless of the country, legal professionals from around the world live by this two-word creed. Ask them a question, and their eyes will take on a thoughtful gaze, their brow will furrow intently, and they will declare, "It depends" (or the equivalent in their own tongue).

Legal practitioners are trained to consider all options, and therefore they strive to state explicitly every possibility, leaving no room for argument or doubt. For example, if a sales contract requires a buyer to inform a seller that the goods being purchased must meet certain specifications, a question may arise as to the meaning of the word "inform." An attorney for the buyer might say, "it depends." In this case, the seller should have known that the buyer had particular specifications because the seller previously filled five orders for the buyer for the same goods. Then an attorney for the seller might say, "it depends." In this case, the buyer should have given written instructions because the buyer wrote the specifications on the previous five order forms. Thus, the attorneys might turn the simple phrase "the buyer must inform the seller of any particular specifications for the goods" into legalese: "the buyer, regardless of whether he or she has previously ordered any of the seller's goods to conform with any specifications whatsoever, shall inform, whether in writing, orally, or otherwise, the seller of any and all specifications with which the buyer demands conformance of the goods that are the subject of this contract."

SIMPLE VS. COMPLEX CROSS-BORDER TRANSACTIONS

The author of this book has made every effort to avoid "legalese" and to recognize the extent to which different customs and laws will affect the creation, interpretation, and enforcement of cross-border contracts. To this end, the author has provided examples throughout the text to illustrate the effects of various regional business practices, a special section to explain how contracts are viewed in different legal systems, and a glossary to define the technical legal meaning of common legal terms.

Nevertheless, you are forewarned that the author starts from a biased platform: she is a lawyer, and an American one at that. For this reason, the author must admit to a strong belief in the "contract-happy" American tradition that every commercial relationship is best defined in a written contract because, while the contracting parties offer each other mutual benefits, they also have at least potentially adverse interests in securing the best deal. Written contracts take on added significance when parties from different cultures and countries have different expectations and customs and are subject to contrary laws. Increasingly, parties who are trading internationally have begun to recognize the advantages of entering into written contracts. There is a distinct trend among parties to cross-border transactions to operate on something more than a handshake.

In answer to the question of how simple an international commercial contract may be, the author is compelled to answer in the tradition of her chosen profession, "it depends." On the one hand, any contract can be written in plain terms. On the other hand, the complexity of the relationship, rights, and obligations of the parties should be reflected in the length and intricacy of the contract provisions. When parties first meet and agree, they usually prefer not to think of what might go wrong and a simple contract is enticing. But if something does go wrong, parties who have fully set out their rights and obligations will be prepared for, if not protected against, the failure to complete the contract terms. While the author has presented "plain term" contract provisions, she has also included cautionary notes to alert you to the potential pitfalls in an effort to develop your awareness of whether a contract term states your intent. You should keep in mind that, while contract provisions should be as clear and definite as possible, when it becomes necessary to interpret the meaning of a contract provision—well, yes once again—*it depends* on the interpreter.

SAMPLE CONTRACTS

Finally, a few comments must be made about the sample contracts included in this book. You may find these forms quite useful in your own transactions. However, you will most certainly need to change the provisions to fit your own special situation. The author has dealt with the common issues and has tried to bring to your attention the problems that frequently arise because of imprecise or missing contract terms. Always be careful that your contract covers the rights and risks of your particular transaction, and seek the assistance of a lawyer to draft or review the contract in light of your specific circumstances. If you decide to use any of the forms, you should be certain to note the conventions used to indicate alternative phrasing in the forms. The conventions are not part of the forms. Alternative phrasing is shown in brackets, and inside the brackets, by parentheses. The brackets contain both instructions (in italics) and actual text (in roman). A slash between words that are enclosed in brackets indicates that you must select one of the words, again, depending on your specific situation.

Karla C. Shippey, J.D.
Orange, California

TABLE OF CONTENTS

CHAPTER 1

The Role of Contracts in International Commerce

CONTRACTS ARE SO MUCH a part of living in a society that you are probably unaware of how many contracts you make every day. In the broadest sense, a *contract* is simply an agreement that defines a relationship between one or more parties. Two people exchanging wedding vows enter into a contract of marriage; a person who has a child contracts to nurture and support that child; shoppers selecting food in a market contract to purchase the goods for a stated amount. A *commercial contract*, in simplest terms, is merely an agreement made by two or more parties for the purpose of transacting business.

Any contract may be oral or written. Written terms may be recorded in a simple memorandum, certificate, or receipt. Because a contractual relationship is made between two or more parties who have potentially adverse interests, the contract terms are usually supplemented and restricted by laws that serve to protect the parties and to define specific relationships between them in the event that provisions are indefinite, ambiguous, or even missing.

When one party enters into a commercial contract with an unfamiliar and distant party across a country border, a contract takes on added significance. The creation of an international contract is a more complex process than the formation of a contract between parties from the same country and culture. In a cross-border transaction, the parties usually do not meet face-to-face, they have different societal values and practices, and the laws to which they are subject are imposed by different governments with distinct legal systems. These factors can easily lead to misunderstandings, and therefore the contracting parties should define their mutual understanding in contractual, and preferably written, terms. The role of a contract in an international commercial transaction is of particular importance with respect to the following aspects.

Balance of Power

The essence of a contract is the mutual understanding reached by two parties who hold adverse positions against each other. In most contractual situations, one party will have a stronger position than the other. For example, a large corporation that offers goods for sale may be able to insist on contract terms that are highly favorable to the corporation while restricting the rights of individual buyers. The corporation may offer a standard form sales contract with nonnegotiable terms—take it or leave it—to the buyer.

THE PARTY WHO DRAFTS THE CONTRACT

The balance of power between contracting parties usually tips in favor of the party who drafts the written contract. Even if the essential contract terms have already been negotiated and agreed by both parties, the drafting party will typically include provisions that are more skewed to his or her favor. To illustrate, a seller who drafts a sales contract may provide trade terms by which the risk of loss passes to the buyer at the first possible moment of the transfer.

THE PARTY FAMILIAR WITH WRITTEN CONTRACTS

In cross-border transactions, the balance of power may tip toward the party who is most familiar with written contracts and whose country has a more highly developed system of contract enforcement. This party may insist on terms that are common in his or her domestic contracts, and the other party, with less or no understanding of those terms, may simply acquiesce. As an example, a clause that is commonly inserted into contracts in the United States is, "Time is of the essence." If such a clause is included, failure to perform the contract within the time allowed is considered a material breach of the contract, entitling the other party to claim damages or other remedies. In cultures that place more emphasis on continuing business relationships, this clause has little meaning because contract terms are commonly renegotiated to allow for a party's difficulties in performing the contract—the ongoing relationship is more important than the one-time deal.

ENFORCEMENT OF ONE-SIDED CONTRACTS

In the context of enforcement, the balance of power can work against the stronger party in a contract negotiation. Courts and arbitrators often refuse to enforce terms that unreasonably burden one party or that are otherwise unconscionable. Furthermore, contract provisions are typically given a strict interpretation against the party who drafted the terms, since that party had the opportunity to draft a clear and definite contract.

TIP: Because of the problem with enforcement, parties to cross-border transactions should avoid taking unfair advantage. A contract that is in accord with fair business practices will encourage both parties to perform their obligations, and therefore the need for enforcement—and the need to outlay the costs attendant to enforcement—may be avoided.

Cross-Border Rights and Obligations

In any contractual arrangement, it is important to establish clearly the rights and obligations of each party. If these terms are absent or ambiguous, the parties will probably not be able to perform the contract without first modifying the terms. Moreover, enforcement will be unpredictable, because a court will have to imply terms based on what the court believes would have been the intent of the parties.

DIFFERENCES IN BUSINESS PRACTICES

For contracts made between parties within the same country, missing or indefinite terms may be filled in by local laws or practices. The rationale is that the parties likely intended to follow the local laws and practices with which they were familiar. If the parties are from different countries, their intentions cannot be so easily implied because they herald from different legal systems and no doubt utilize dissimilar business practices. For this reason, it is essential for your international contract to spell out in definite terms the rights and obligations of each party.

INTERNATIONAL LAWS

In recognition of the difficulties that parties face in contracting across country boundaries, the international community has begun to adopt systems of laws and rules to be applied instead of local laws in transactions between parties located in different countries. The intent behind adopting uniform, international laws is to ensure that all parties to a cross-border transaction are subject to the same set of rules, regardless of whether the laws of their home countries are dissimilar. If parties to an international sales contract are nationals of countries that have acceded to an international treaty or pact, such as the United Nations Convention on the International Sale of Goods (CISG), they may rely on international law to determine at least some of their rights and obligations.

In general, it is unwise to rely on the law, even international law, for implied contractual terms. The application of international laws to the interpretation of a contract can lead to unexpected and even unfavorable results. Thus, if an international contract of sale fails to provide a delivery time and the buyer sues for breach when the seller fails to deliver within one month, the contract may be deemed invalid under the local law of the buyer's country because of the absence of an essential term. But if a court applies international law, it may imply a reasonable delivery time of two months in accordance with the practice of the industry and therefore may enforce the contract.

PRECISENESS AND PREDICTABILITY

To avoid an unfavorable and uncertain result, it is best to define your rights and obligations in a written contract when you are dealing across country borders. Hopefully your contract terms will be sufficiently explicit that both parties will understand what they are supposed to do and what they are entitled to receive. In the event of a breach, there is a greater chance that a court will enforce explicit terms (unless the provisions are unconscionable), and thus the parties can more closely predict the outcome.

Cross-Cultural Expectations

Well-drafted contracts can help to ensure that parties who have diverse cultural backgrounds reach a mutual understanding with regard to their rights and obligations. All contracting parties come to the table with individual expectations, which in turn tint their understanding of the terms. What is reasonable to one may not be to the other, in which case mutual understanding—an essential element in the creation of an enforceable contract—is lacking.

The key is in the drafting of the agreement. You should write the provisions to reflect the culture of the foreign party, while at the same time keeping in mind your own requirements. Such drafting requires that you have an understanding of the other party's culture and the extent to which it differs from your own. Your contract provisions may need to be simplified so that they can be clearly understood, particularly if the contract will have to be translated into the other party's own language. You should review the provisions for shorthand phrases, legalese, and slang familiar to you but not to the other party—these provisions should be written in plain terms to ensure mutual understanding.

Further, you will need to determine the extent to which the other party is familiar with international business. If the other party has been trading internationally for some time, he or she is more likely to have gained an understanding of cross-cultural transactions. During your negotiations, you should explore the business history of the other party so that you can draft your contract to the appropriate level of sophistication.

A contract that reflects the cultural expectations of each party is more likely to be performed to the satisfaction of both. Mutual understanding means not only that each party knows its rights and obligations before signing the contract, but that the parties are in complete agreement as to each other's rights and obligations. Disputes typically arise when one party interprets a right or obligation differently than the other party. A contract drafted to ensure mutual understanding of culturally diverse parties will help to avoid, or at least to settle, subsequent disagreements over performance.

10 TIPS TO CULTURAL SUCCESS

- Follow your host's lead
- Practice fundamental politeness and business courtesies
- Listen attentively and with interest
- Keep hand motions and body movement to a minimum
- Speak firmly, with conviction, and in a warm tone that invites the other party's comments; avoid boisterous talk and slang
- Personally sign all correspondence
- Respond promptly to inquiries and orders
- Ask what language is spoken and arrange for a translator if necessary
- Avoid generalities and preconceived expectations
- Laugh at yourself, and be serious when it counts

See *A Short Course in International Business Culture*, also by World Trade Press.

Personal Commitment

When dealing with a distant party in another country, you may be uncertain of the extent to which that party is making a commitment to perform the contract. While you are no doubt serious about the bargain, you have no evidence as to whether the other party has equal resolve. Does timely delivery of your order have the same importance to the other party as it does to you? Is the other party committed to producing quality products that meet or even exceed your expectations? Trust is built on the personal commitment that each party demonstrates to the transaction, and therefore this aspect of any transaction whether domestic or international is especially significant.

Gaining evidence of commitment in cross-border transactions, in which parties usually operate by different business practices, can be more difficult than in domestic transactions, in which parties typically share the same business practices. A party who orally agrees to become obligated has made a commitment to the other party, but the terms of that commitment depend exclusively on the word of one party against the other. In many cultures, bargains are struck only when the parties meet personally; a handshake seals the promise. Other cultures insist on the signing of written informal or formal contracts before a final commitment is made.

In transacting business with a person of another culture, you should keep in mind the way in which they are likely to show their commitment. You will need to decide in advance of negotiating the bargain whether to accept the other party's evidence of commitment, insist on your own, or reach a compromise. If you meet the other party personally, shake hands, and gain that parties respect and trust, you may decide that an oral agreement is sufficient to express commitment to the transaction.

If you do not feel comfortable with an oral arrangement, consider the other party's culture before you act. The other party may be from a culture where contracts are usually in writing, and thus without much fuss, you may simply mention that you will put the contract in writing and send it for signing. On the other hand, the other party's common practice may be to operate on a handshake, and that party may be insulted if you insist on a written contract. In that event, you may have to find an indirect approach. For example, you might tactfully explain the custom of your country, and ask the custom of your host's country. Then, if your host seems open to the idea, you might suggest an informal letter or memorandum as a compromise. If not, you may take or leave the handshake bargain, depending on whether you want the business and whether you can afford the risk.

If you have previously done business with the other party, you might well be willing to accept a handshake to seal the bargain, but such practice should be the exception not the rule. When dealing internationally, it is always best to insist on written evidence of personal commitment, even if you simply exchange a memorandum. In relative terms, there is more cost—in time and money—involved in cross-border transactions than in domestic ones. When you agree to sell or buy goods internationally, you are also responsible for complying with import, export, customs, consumer product, marking, transport, and other trade-regulating laws of two or more countries. It is wise to ensure that the other party shares the same commitment.

Governing Law

When trading internationally, parties frequently assume that they can operate in accordance with their own domestic laws and practices. This assumption is erroneous and can lead to grave misunderstandings. When you trade across country borders, you are subject to not only the laws of your own country but to the laws of other countries where you do business. You need not physically enter another country to become subject to its laws—merely selling goods by mail or electronic means may establish a sufficient connection to bring you within the jurisdiction of another country's courts.

To a certain extent, you may control the application of a country's laws to your particular transaction by expressly setting forth the law that will govern the contract. However, parties do not have complete freedom of contract in choosing the governing law. Most countries have laws that mandate domestic jurisdiction over particular types of contractual arrangements, such as those involving land transactions.

Even in the absence of a statute, the determination as to which law will be applied is nearly always left to the discretion of the court, which may or may not respect the choice you have made. In practice, courts tend to uphold the expressed intent of the parties provided it is not contrary to statute. An express provision on governing law therefore has a significant effect on which laws will be employed to interpret contractual rights and obligations in international transactions.

Enforcement

As you move from a domestic to an international setting, enforcement issues increase in complexity. Local laws and practices will usually determine the evidence required to prove contract terms. An oral contract may be sufficient in one country, while another may require a written and even notarized agreement.

TIP: You should always try to secure the best possible proof of your agreement—which is a precisely drafted, written contract—in the event that enforcement becomes necessary. Remember, even if you avoid a court action, you will have more power in negotiating amended terms if you have clear and definite proof of your agreement.

Most jurisdictions require certain contracts to be written to be enforceable. Typically, contracts for the sale of goods with a total value exceeding the amount specified by law must be in writing to be enforceable. Contracts for the sale or lease of real property may have to be written to be enforced. Although parties may make such contracts orally and may voluntarily agree to perform the terms to completion, their contractual rights will not be involuntarily enforced if a dispute should arise.

Choice of Remedies

Most contracting parties expect that all will go smoothly and that both parties will mutually benefit from the transaction. These positive expectations are more likely to be realized if you have provided for contingencies. Even in the simplest of transactions, you must think about the possible problems that may develop later.

TIP: The first rule of a successful international business transaction is also the last: decide how to resolve disputes before they happen.

The best time to decide how to handle a conflict is at the time the contract is made when both parties are feeling positive toward the bargain. The contract should include provisions as to which remedies a party may seek in the unlikely event that the other party fails to perform the requisite obligations. If you are unable to reach an agreement on the choice of remedies when drafting the contract, you are even less likely to do so after a problem arises. By selecting a mutually acceptable remedy in the beginning, both parties will know what to expect should performance fail.

Necessary Terms

In most countries, parties to commercial transactions may make their own bargains free of legal restraints. However, in most jurisdictions, the courts will enforce a contract only if the parties have agreed to four basic terms:

1. The description of the goods in terms of type, quantity, and quality
2. The time of delivery
3. The price
4. The time and means of payment

These terms are considered essential because they cannot be easily implied by law—they are the necessary parameters to the contractual relationship. Every international contract should provide for these terms.

INTERNATIONAL TRENDS

As a brief aside, a current trend in the law of several nations—and eventually, no doubt, in international law among nations—is to recognize contracts that are the basis of commercial transactions even if they fail to provide the essential terms. If a dispute arises and any of the essential terms are missing or ambiguous, the intent of the parties may be implied from customary trade or financial practices. The bottom line is that judges, arbitrators, rule makers, and law makers prefer to uphold a bargain made by business folks—who are presumed to know what they are doing. In comparison, private individuals and consumers are given more protection against bad bargains that do not cover all of the essential agreement terms because there is a presumption that they are at the mercy of the business folks. In any event, it is best not to rely on trends or implied contract terms. You should always state your intent in clear and definite written terms.

PAYMENT AND DELIVERY TERMS

Two of the essential terms take on further significance in international contracts: the payment terms and the delivery terms. In international transactions, it is essential to establish the payment terms. It may be assumed in a domestic transaction that the traders intend to exchange goods for domestic currency. When dealing cross-border, there will probably be a choice of currencies. You may also be subject to foreign exchange restrictions on the currency. Payment terms should be clearly defined to ensure that the contract will be enforceable.

In an international contract, a clear definition of the transport and delivery term is also essential. This term can have different meanings in domestic as opposed to international contracts. If each party interprets this provision differently, a breach of the contract is quite likely, and there is a greater risk of incurring a loss on the sale. Mutual agreement on the meaning of the transport and delivery term is extremely important.

CHAPTER 2

Issues Affecting International Contracts

Cultural Issues

Your success in foreign trade will depend on how flexible you are in recognizing and respecting the culture of other people. Cultural differences will affect not only your negotiations with foreign traders, but also the acceptance of your goods or services in foreign markets. In a business context, culture is a set of rules that govern the way in which commercial transactions are conducted between nationals of particular nations. These rules dictate the etiquette, traditions, values, communication, and negotiating styles of a group of people. You must be aware and sensitive to other cultures, and you must adapt your products and services to the preferences of the foreign market.

Culture should be considered as applying to people, not to nations. Although it may be possible to identify an overall culture for a particular country, many subcultures are likely to exist. Even if you have identified a foreign trader's country and have learned the rules that you think will apply, you should avoid clinging to preconceived notions. In today's world, people are on the move, and even more importantly, cultures are crossing country borders and cultural rules are constantly evolving.

Cultural awareness will be most important in the initial contact and negotiation, since in subsequent contacts you will have figured out many of the rules. In making initial contact, you should first establish whether the general protocol in the country tends to be rigidly applied. The next step is to determine what that protocol is, especially for the issues that will arise at the first stage of contract negotiations. These issues include greetings, courtesies, business ethics, decision making, gender, meeting formalities, and business attire.

The final step should be to ensure that you are approaching cultural issues with the proper attitude. Once you have researched the rules, learned what you believe is the proper protocol, and made an attempt to practice it, be willing to laugh at yourself. Cultural missteps are inevitable and will be made on both sides. Humor will usually ease even the tensest situation. Pull out your cultural pocket guide, show the rules and illustrations to your host, and have a good laugh together.

Trends Toward Globalization and Uniformity

Doing business with the world is the theme for the decade. The 1990s has seen a multitude of trade agreements spring up between nations all around the world. The Uruguay Round of the General Agreement on Tariffs and Trade (GATT), signed by 117 nations in 1993, went into effect in 1995. Regional agreements encouraging trade have included the North American Free Trade Agreement (NAFTA) of 1993 and the United States Andean Trade Preference Act (ATPA) of 1991. These have added to the trade agreements already in force, among which some of the most important have been the earlier GATT treaties.

Cultural Dos and Don'ts of Negotiating Contracts

WHEN YOU MEET A FOREIGN TRADER

DO use a title to show respect and wait for the other party to initiate informality. Reply to inquiries immediately, preferably by telephone. Be enthusiastic but not overbearing. Allow the other trader equal speaking time.

DON'T be in a hurry. Determine in advance whether it is common business practice in the other party's country to "grow" deals over time. If not, make your deal. If so, plan to establish a professional relationship before you sign a contract. If you are seeking more than a one-time sale, you may need months or even a year to reach a long-term arrangement.

WHEN YOU CONFRONT GENDER OR RACE BIAS

DO keep your appearance subdued, your demeanor professional, and your approach formal. Present a business card, speak quietly with knowledge and authority, and take a firm attitude. If possible, bring a business partner or coworker who is of the same race or gender as the foreign trader and who is prompted in advance to acknowledge your authority and aptitude. Find out whether you can deal with a different representative of the company.

DON'T try to make a statement about rights. If the deal is important, try not to take personal offense and refrain from lecturing the other party. Do not assume that others from the same company or even the same country share the same bias.

WHEN YOU ARE AT THE NEGOTIATING TABLE

DO show firm authority. Be aware of your host's level of eye and physical contact and remain within the bounds established. Research common cultural traits and business practices of the foreign trader. Determine in advance the points on which you can be flexible so that you start the negotiations above your bottom line. Insert humor when appropriate, balanced with reserve when the discussion is serious.

DON'T appear inflexible on all points. Avoid overt conflict or belaboring a point. Don't jump to fill every conversation gap; silence can yield golden results. Refrain from sudden shifts in your tone of voice or changes in your demeanor.

WHEN YOU ARE FACED WITH LEGAL ISSUES

DO find out whether negotiations will be merely preliminary or whether the other party intends to make a deal. Ask your host for a list of who will be present at the meeting, and if legal counsel for your host plans to attend, consider bringing your own attorney. Consult an attorney if negotiations are serious and you are uncertain of the risks.

DON'T agree to any deal or sign any contract unless you are absolutely certain that you fully understand and agree to all rights and obligations of both parties to the agreement.

WHEN YOU SOCIALIZE

DO accept an invitation if your host graciously extends it. Go prepared with several conversational topics that might be of interest to your hosts other than the business at hand. Research the cultural norms of gift exchanging, and consider a gift that is representative of your country.

DON'T offer to socialize if your host sticks to business and places time constraints on the meetings. Avoid criticizing your host's country, and do not raise sensitive topics such as politics, personal inquiries, or religion. Be careful not to consume too much alcohol.

When you begin to research the global marketplace, you will find an expanding horizon. Although some countries continue a self-imposed isolation, most have come to recognize that development and refinement of a global economic strategy is important to the growth and maintenance of a strong economy. Trade barriers among countries are being reduced and infrastructures for foreign transportation and communication are improving. Trade and business journals are devoting more and more space to international news, governments are revising laws to provide more uniformity for cross-border transactions, and dispute and enforcement systems are being improved.

Much of the pressure toward globalization is bubbling up from the private business sector. Underlying the trends in government policies are the needs and demands of the populace, and in particular of businesses, which have the means to be influential. Large companies and individual traders alike are seeking cross-border opportunities, and they are finding ways to make deals within the evolving international marketplace. In turn, their activities are encouraging the trend toward a uniform international law of commerce in recognition of the difficulties of applying national laws across country borders.

UNITED NATIONS CONVENTION ON CONTRACTS FOR THE INTERNATIONAL SALE OF GOODS (CISG)

■ ADOPTION OF THE CISG

In the area of international sales transactions, one of the most important developments has been the adoption by member nations of the United Nations of the Convention on Contracts for the International Sale of Goods (CISG).

The CISG was finalized at the United Nations convention in Vienna on April 11, 1980. However, it has gone into effect at different times in each of the various member countries, depending on when the country acceded to the CISG. Thus, in New Zealand the CISG entered into force as of October 1, 1995, while in the United States the CISG took effect as of January 1, 1988.

Member countries are entitled to accede to the CISG with reservations, and many of them have chosen to exclude the application of certain CISG provisions. The most commonly excluded CISG provisions are those that allow a sale contract, offer, acceptance, other indication of intention, or modification or termination of a sale contract, to be made in any form other than in writing. For example, in Argentina, Chile, Hungary, and Russia, contracts for the international sale of goods should be written to be enforceable, despite the CISG provisions.

■ OBJECTIVES

The CISG was adopted by members of the United Nations with the following objectives:

1. To adopt uniform rules governing contracts for the international sale of goods
2. To adopt uniform rules that account for different social, economic, and legal systems
3. To contribute to the removal of legal barriers in international trade
4. To promote the development of international trade

■ APPLICATION

Unless contracting parties specifically exclude its application, the CISG may be applied to interpret contracts for the sale of goods between parties with business places in different countries, provided the countries are signatories to CISG or the law of a signatory country would be applied to determine a dispute. The CISG is intended to clarify points related to the formation of a contract and the rights and obligations of the parties, but its provisions do not determine the validity of a contract, the effect of a contract with respect to ownership of the goods sold, or the liability of a party for injury or death caused by the goods.

■ PROVISIONS

The CISG provisions primarily delineate the elements that must be present to prove formation of a contract for the sale of goods and supply implied terms if the parties have otherwise failed to state their obligations in full. A number of provisions also concern the application of various remedies for breach of contract, including specific performance, damages, modification or termination by agreement, avoidance of the contract, and mitigation of damages.

Examples of when the CISG provisions might be applied include the following:

1. A seller makes a proposal and the buyer accepts it. The seller claims that the proposal was not an offer, and therefore no contract was formed. The buyer claims that the acceptance created a contract. A court may apply the CISG, which provides that a proposal constitutes an offer if it is communicated to the buyer and it indicates the goods, fixes a means for determining the quantity and price, and expresses the seller's intent to be bound by the terms if the buyer accepts. Thus, the outcome of the case will depend on the content of the seller's proposal.

2. A seller makes an offer and the buyer agrees but only on condition that two of the contract provisions are modified in the buyer's favor. The buyer claims that a contract was formed, but the seller refuses to acknowledge the agreement. If a court applies the CISG to resolve the dispute, the seller would win because the CISG defines an acceptance as an assent made at the time the offer is still outstanding, communicated timely to the buyer, and made on the same terms as the offer without material modification.

3. The parties to a cross-border contract fail to specify a place of delivery. Reference may be made to the CISG to complete the contract terms.

4. The seller is not obligated to insure the goods up to the point of delivery to the buyer. If the parties agree to application of the CISG, the seller must disclose before shipping sufficient information to allow the buyer to obtain insurance.

5. A contract omits the time for delivery. Three months elapse, and the buyer sues for breach. If the CISG is applied, the result of the case will depend on what is considered to be a reasonable time for delivery after the contract was made.

6. The seller ships goods that are not in conformance with the contract specifications. The buyer refuses the shipment and sues for breach. In applying the CISG, the court will consider whether the nonconformance was immaterial or material to the contract. If the nonconformance was minor and of no consequence to the value or quality of the goods, the contract is likely to be enforced.

7. The contract requires that the buyer accept or refuse the goods on delivery. No period for inspection is given. The goods are delivered, stacked in the buyer's warehouse, and returned to the seller four days later. The seller sues for breach. Pursuant to the CISG, a reasonable inspection period is allowed before acceptance of the goods if the parties have not otherwise provided for inspection.

8. A sale contract is signed, but no price for the goods is stated. The parties cannot later agree on a price, and the seller refuses to ship the goods claiming that no contract was in fact formed. The buyer sues for breach. The court applies the CISG and enforces the contract, implying a price at which similar goods would have been sold under comparable circumstances in the trade.

9. No provision is made in an international sales contract for the time at which the buyer is to remit payment for the goods. The seller demands payment on delivery, but the buyer accepts the delivery without remitting the payment. Under the CISG, the seller has a right to be paid at the time and place of the delivery if no other provision is made.

10. The parties to an international sales contract fail to provide for the transfer of the risk of loss between them. The goods are destroyed in transit, and the buyer sells for breach. A court may apply the CISG to establish when the risk passed from the seller to the buyer.

■ EXCLUSIONS

The mere fact that the parties to a cross-border transaction are located in countries that have acceded to the CISG does not mean that the CISG applies to the transaction. There are many exclusions, and the member countries themselves are permitted to limit the application of this treaty with respect to their own nationals. In this regard, you should consult a legal professional in your own country to find out if application in your country or in the foreign trader's country has been limited at the time of accession.

The CISG allows parties who would otherwise be subject to its provisions to opt out. Thus, parties may restrict the application of the CISG to any particular contract or may eliminate its application completely. To invoke this exclusion, the parties must expressly provide in writing that the CISG will not apply or will apply in limited terms.

Finally, the CISG does not apply to a number of contracts for sale, even if the parties are located in different member states. Specifically, the CISG is inapplicable to contracts for the following:

1. The sale of goods for personal, family, or household use, unless the seller did not know or have reason to know that the goods were bought for this use,
2. The sale of goods that are to be made substantially from materials supplied by the buyer,
3. An obligation that is primarily for the supply of labor or other services,
4. A sale by auction,
5. A sale pursuant to a legal remedy, such as execution or foreclosure,
6. The sale of stocks, shares, investment securities, negotiable instruments, or money,

7. The sale of ships, vessels, hovercraft, or aircraft,
8. The sale of electricity.

If your contract could be subject to the CISG and is not within one of the exclusions to the CISG, you should familiarize yourself with the CISG provisions. Although you can expressly provide that the CISG will not apply to your contract, you may find that its provisions in fact are useful for protecting your rights and limiting your risks when dealing with foreign traders. Moreover, the CISG reflects the growing trend in international law to develop uniform legal systems to ensure the fair treatment of nationals from different countries with diverse local laws and rules. Its provisions may appear more reasonable and inviting to a foreign trader, and therefore by agreeing to its application, you may further encourage the other party's trust in your good faith, which is essential to the foundation of a successful business deal.

Role of Politics

Political events have a major impact on the economy of a country. Instability can be devastating to a country's markets, while a stable government can be a great asset. A strong and growing economy will in turn have a calming effect on political turmoil. Although some would argue that politicians should take less of a role in regulating the commercial affairs of private traders, the influence of politics will no doubt always be a major factor because these two forces are so entwined.

International trade plays such a significant role in a country's economy that governments throughout history have used direct and indirect trade barriers to force changes in the governments and policies of other countries. Trade barriers include boycotts, quotas, tariffs, import and export prohibitions, licenses, consumer and labeling requirements, and environmental regulations. Trade sanctions are often used to influence another country's domestic policies or practices and to protest a country's aggressive actions toward its neighbors. Favorable trade preferences are granted to countries that implement the changes thought to be desirable.

As an international trader, you must stay in touch with political trends. The stability or instability of a region will indicate whether you will succeed in establishing long-term arrangements there.

TIP: As regulations and trade barriers are relaxed in a particular country, look for new opportunities. Take advantage of your own government's incentives for trading with other countries. Before making a commitment to do business in a particular market, you should consider whether the country's political past and current political climate are conducive to your trade.

Regulatory Laws

It is your responsibility to know the law. Lack of knowledge is not a defense to a criminal charge, penalty proceeding, or civil lawsuit. It is essential that you know and understand the legal implications and boundaries of trading in your own country and abroad. An attorney with international legal experience can advise you on the issues that you should know.

Countries are exploding with laws regulating the import, export, and sale of goods. Developing countries are taking their cues from the laws of developed countries. New and revised laws are being introduced throughout the world as countries come under pressure to join the globalization trend. To compete in the world economy, most countries are recognizing that they have to offer domestic and foreign traders a business-oriented environment. At the same time, they are striving to protect the rights of their own nationals. Wherever you transact or plan to transact business, you should be aware of existing laws and regulations governing import, export, antitrust, antibribery, consumer protection, intellectual and industrial property rights, and environmental issues. You must also keep watch for changes in those laws and regulations.

Internet Issues

The potential of the Internet, a new electronic marketplace, is an exciting concept for traders today. In just a few minutes, you can find a particular populace by search criteria and send off your advertisement. You can develop your own web site to improve customer access to your company. Sales can be made at electronic speed, suppliers can be sought worldwide, and classified advertising has taken on a global meaning.

Traders on the Internet must beware of the pitfalls. Security of the information that passes through electronic channels remains a problem. Before using the Internet for confidential information, you should be certain to encode that information. The Internet is a public domain. If you place your intellectual property—trademarks, copyrighted or patented materials, designs, etc.—on the Internet, you should first ensure its protection from infringement.

Use of the Internet to advertise and transact business in countries far from home might be a sufficient minimum contact to subject you to the jurisdiction of the courts in those other places. You could also become subject to business, income, and sales taxation in those countries, and your activities may be regulated by local country laws such as those governing antitrust, consumer fraud, and unfair trading practices. Similarly, you may be required to comply with business and profession licensing requirements in jurisdictions where you do business. Be certain that you understand the legal implications of using the Internet before you take the plunge.

CHAPTER 3

Parties to the Transaction, Part 1

SALES TRANSACTIONS occur between two parties: buyer and seller. Sometimes transactions involve more than several parties who are jointly buying or selling goods, but the individual interests of parties acting jointly become melded as a single interest in the sales contract. Thus, for purposes of the sales contract, there is a buyer and a seller. In addition, the buyer and seller may each be represented by legal counsel.

Other interests of third persons, and the individual interests of parties acting jointly, are not directly controlled by the sales contract between buyer and seller. These outside interests may be indirectly affected by whether the buyer and seller perform the sales transaction to the letter of the sales contract, but generally the rights and risks of these third persons and individual parties depend on contracts separate from the sales agreement. Thus, if parties are acting jointly in a sale of goods, the goods are shipped and accepted by the buyer, the buyer makes payment pursuant to the contract terms, but one of the sellers absconds with the payment, the other seller's recourse is against the absconding party for breach of their joint arrangement, not against the buyer for a second payment. Similarly, if a buyer in a sales transaction in turn promises to sell the goods to a third-party retailer by a certain date, the retailer then arranges to resell those goods accordingly, but the goods are delivered two months late and the resales are lost, the third party's recourse is against the buyer. Of course, the buyer (but not the third-party retailer) may also have recourse against the seller for damages caused by the late delivery.

TIP: If you ask legal counsel for further explanation of this concept, you are likely to hear the term "privity of contract" bandied about, i.e., the rights of the third party are not protected because he or she is not in privity of contract. This simple term is a shorthand expression for a fairly complex set of legal rules derived from English common law to determine who may enforce contractual rights. The very basic answer is: any person who is directly a party to the contract. Whether a third party has a right to enforce the contract is an issue best left to the advice of your attorney in light of the particular circumstances involved.

Buyer

THE BUYER AS CONSUMER

A buyer consumes goods or services in return for compensation to the seller. The buyer may be in the middle of the consuming chain, in which case goods or services are purchased and resold to other buyers who in turn consume or utilize them to produce other goods or services, which may then be sold to other buyers. Alternatively, the buyer may be the ultimate consumer, who uses the goods or services without selling them to other buyers.

THE BUYER'S GOALS

A buyer's goal, whether the buyer is a "middleman" or ultimate consumer, is to obtain the best quality and most quantity for the least cost. To attain this goal, you must have an understanding of the market for the goods or services that you want to buy. The primary factors that will affect the market are supply and demand. If there are many suppliers but only a few buyers, you will have a strong negotiation position because the suppliers will be in competition for your business. If there are many suppliers and many buyers, your position will be weaker because you will face competition from other buyers, and yet you will have an advantage in that the suppliers are also in competition. If there are few suppliers, you will also have the weakest negotiating position because you will have fewer purchase options.

THE BUYER'S SAFEGUARDS

As a buyer, you should seek assurances of quality and protection against defective or damaged goods or unsatisfactory services. It is wise to do a background or reference check on the seller who is unknown to you. Whether you are buying goods or services, you might ask to meet the seller at his or her place of business. If the transaction is substantial, you should request a tour of your seller's facilities.

TIP: Seek proof of your seller's claimed capabilities, whether you test a sample of the goods, observe the seller's services in action, check references, or agree to a low-risk contract as a trial run.

THE BUYER'S HIDDEN COSTS

When considering the cost of the transaction, remember to add in the hidden expenses before you agree to a price. What are the goods or services actually costing you? Will you be able to recoup the entire cost of the goods, plus make a profit? Will the services increase your profitability by a sufficient percentage beyond the real cost of the services? These hidden expenses might include the following items.

- INTERNATIONAL SHIPPING If the seller is not responsible for transporting goods to your door, you will have to arrange and pay for at least part of the shipping, which may include a switch between modes of transport with the attendant costs and delays of unloading, reloading, inspecting, and administering by two or more shippers.
- CUSTOMS CLEARANCE If the seller is not responsible for clearing goods through customs, you will be. Customs clearance must usually be obtained twice: first, to export the goods from the seller's country; second, to import the goods into your country. Clearance costs may involve costs for preparation of the documents to satisfy customs authorities, for temporary holding or storage of the goods while awaiting clearance, and for making the goods available for inspection. You will probably have to pay someone to clear the goods through customs, and you may have to hire an import-export broker to assist you in the process. In addition, there are the fees charged by the various government authorities that control the import and export of the particular goods you are buying, which may include special license or permit fees, customs processing charges, and value added taxes (VATs).

- **INSURANCE** You should consider obtaining insurance against the risk of loss or damage to the goods in transport, particularly if a substantial amount of money is involved. Although it may be difficult to obtain insurance on goods until the risk of loss passes from the seller before or during the transport, if this insurance is available, you should balance the losses you are likely to incur if a shipment does not arrive in satisfactory condition against the cost of the insurance. Be certain that you can afford the risk.

  A separate insurance issue involves the question of product liability. If you will be reselling the goods and if product liability is a recognized legal claim in your country, you may become liable to a consumer who is injured when using the product. Such claims have been made and won for millions of dollars. You should consider whether your product could cause injury if defectively designed or made, and if so whether you can afford the risk of a product liability claim. Although the seller is likely to be held primarily responsible for a design or manufacturing defect, if you sell a product that you know or should have reasonably known is defective or likely to cause injury without the proper cautionary warnings to the consumer, you will probably be ordered to share in the liability.

- **INTERRUPTION OF BUSINESS** You should consider whether you will have any interruption in your own business when the goods arrive, whether for training, installation, testing, maintenance, or otherwise. How much will it cost to put one of your top managers at the convenience of a supplier to ensure proper handling of the goods?

- **HOSPITALITY COSTS** Whether you are buying goods or services, you may incur costs for entertaining a visiting seller. For goods that must be installed or otherwise handled under the seller's supervision, you may be expected to provide meals, transportation, and housing costs for the seller's representative. These charges may be added into the price of the goods, but check your contract to see if separate reimbursements are expected.

- **THIRD-PARTY EXPENSES** When goods or services are being delivered across borders, the risk of delay, and even nonperformance, is increased because of factors that cannot be controlled by either party, such as national and international political events, customs clearance, national laws, and transport over lengthy distances. If there is a delay in the seller's performance, whether avoidable or not, you will probably incur resulting costs outside the contract.

- **LOST SALES OR PRODUCTION DELAYS** If satisfactory goods do not arrive or services are inadequate, you may lose your own sales or you may have to delay your own production.

- **TEMPORARY FACILITIES** If a shipment is late, you may have to retain an empty storage facility for the imminent but uncertain arrival of the goods. If services are delayed, you may have to hire temporary assistance.

- **REPLACEMENT GOODS OR SERVICES** A delay in performance may require you to pay for replacement goods or services, and because you will probably need the replacements quickly to avoid further delay and resulting costs, you will probably have to pay a premium.

Seller

A seller is the individual or entity that places goods or services into the consuming chain and receives compensation in return. The seller may be at the beginning or in the middle of the consuming chain.

THE SELLER'S GOALS

A seller's goal—whether the seller is at the start or in the middle of the chain—is to obtain the best price while keeping the cost of production or distribution minimal. To turn a profit, a seller must know the market for the goods or services offered—just like the buyer—but the factors of supply and demand will work in reverse. Thus, if there are many suppliers and only a few buyers, you will have a weak negotiation position because you will have strong competition from other suppliers. If there are many suppliers and many buyers, your position will be stronger because the buyers will be in competition, and yet you have the disadvantage of competing against other suppliers. If there are few suppliers, you will have the strongest negotiating position because the buyer has limited purchase options.

THE SELLER'S PROMOTION

As seller, you will have to promote the quality and distinctiveness of your goods and services to command the price that you desire. You may have to take on at least some of the costs of shipping and custom clearance to make the deal attractive. You will gain recognition—leading to increased goodwill and sales—if you are able to offer high-quality customer service, which is at a premium internationally because sellers and buyers frequently transact business at a distance, making the practicalities of on-site or fast service more difficult.

THE SELLER'S HIDDEN COSTS

Competition is especially vigorous in international markets, and you will have to prove that your goods or services are worth top dollar. To remain competitive, you will need to meet market demands while controlling your costs. Like the buyer, you must consider the hidden costs when pricing your goods or services. Hidden costs could cut your profits significantly.

- PRODUCT ADAPTATIONS International markets may require modification of your goods or services to follow national laws or consumer cultural preferences. You may need to meet legal labeling, marking, and advertising requirements, and if your customers speak another language, you will infiltrate the market more successfully if you have translated your promotional brochures, product brand names, instruction manuals, and warning labels. It will be essential to find cost-effective means of adapting your products or services to the market.
- INTERNATIONAL SHIPPING If you have sweetened the deal by agreeing to be responsible for transporting the goods at least part of the way, you will have to arrange and pay for those shipping costs.
- CUSTOMS CLEARANCE Depending on the deal you are able to make, you may be responsible for clearing goods through customs in your own country and possibly through customs in the country of importation. If the buyer has agreed to clear the goods through customs, you will still need to provide sufficient

documentation to the buyer for purposes of customs clearance. Clearance costs may include costs for preparation of the documents to satisfy customs authorities, for temporary holding or storage of the goods while awaiting clearance, and for making the goods available for inspection. You may need to pay someone to clear the goods through customs, and you may need to hire an import-export broker to assist you in the process. In addition, the various government authorities that control the import and export of the goods impose fees and taxes, which may include special license or permit fees, customs processing charges, and value added taxes (VATs).

- INSURANCE You should consider obtaining insurance against the risk of loss or damage to the goods in transport, at least until the goods are delivered to the buyer. If you do not insure the goods, be certain that you can afford the risk. A separate insurance issue involves the question of product liability. As a manufacturer of goods, you may become liable to a consumer who is injured when using the product. If you are merely selling goods made by another company, you could still be held liable for selling a product that you know or should have reasonably known is defective or likely to cause injury without the proper cautionary warnings to the consumer. Such claims have been made and won for millions of dollars. Even if product liability claims are not recognized by the laws of your own country, you could be sued and forced to defend in the consumer's country because courts generally take a broad view of jurisdictional requirements in these cases. You should consider whether your product could cause injury if defectively designed or made, and if so whether you can afford the risk of a product liability claim. If product liability insurance is unavailable to you in your own country, consider whether you can obtain it in the jurisdictions where you sell your goods.

- THIRD-PARTY EXPENSES The complexities of trading over international distances increases the potential expenses that you might incur if the buyer delays performance or fails to perform, whether the breach is avoidable or unavoidable. You should consider the risks involved and make your bargain keeping in mind the following costs.

  - TEMPORARY FACILITIES If the buyer is unable to take delivery of goods or services at the time set in the contract and requests a short delay, you may have to arrange temporary storage or rearrange the schedule of your service providers.

  - MITIGATION EXPENSES If a contract for the sale of goods fails completely, you will have to find a new buyer. You may have to arrange for a return shipment of the goods, and you may have to modify the goods to sell them to another buyer. If the contract is for services, you may be obliged to cancel travel arrangements for a penalty.

Attorney for Buyer

As a buyer, you know your business and you have a thorough understanding of your market. You can quickly list the products that you want to buy, you have in mind the quality and quantity that would be the most desirable, and you have located at least one if not several overseas resources for those products.

WHY SHOULD THE BUYER CONSULT AN ATTORNEY?

The bottom line answer to this question is, you still do not know everything, and you can end up in a lot of financial and legal trouble because of your ignorance or innocence. When you buy internationally, your transaction will be subject to the laws and regulations of more than one country—the seller's nation and your own. What you don't know can hurt you.

More significantly, you will become subject to the government authorities of that foreign nation. If you take delivery of the goods before they are exported, you will have to satisfy a customs officer of the seller's country. If you buy goods that are illegal to export, you could become criminally liable. If you breach the contract, you may be brought before a court in the seller's country where you will have to answer to a foreign judge.

An attorney will offer you general advice—necessary advice, in fact—regarding your rights, obligations, risks, and options when buying internationally, and then the attorney will point out the issues that should be of particular concern within your specific set of circumstances. As a buyer, you should ask your attorney about all of the following topics:

- **THE LEGAL SYSTEMS** Very few businesspeople fully understand the legal system in their own country, let alone their business partner's. This is where an experienced attorney can prove an invaluable source.

  - Is the legal system of the seller's country similar to the legal system in your own country? What are the similarities? How do the two systems differ?
  - Does the government in your country heavily regulate trade, whether domestic or international? What about the government in the seller's country? What types of regulations are you going to encounter?
  - Are there any treaties or bilateral agreements that affect trade between the seller's country and your own? Do they apply in your industry? How can you take advantage of them?
  - What types of taxes are imposed by your country on importation or sale of the goods or services? By the seller's country on exportation or sale of the goods or services?

- **IMPORTING AND EXPORTING** Aside from outlining the legal systems, an attorney can provide you with useful and necessary information concerning the journey through customs clearance.

  - Can you freely import the goods or services that you want? What are the restrictions?
  - Are there any permits or licenses required for importing or selling the goods or services in your country? What agencies must approve the import and sale?
  - Are there export restrictions imposed by the seller's country?

- **CONTRACTS** Even the simplest transaction can have a complicated contract. It takes the expertise of an attorney to understand the nuances and implications of most contracts.

  - Is there freedom of contract in your own country? In the seller's country? What are the limits?
  - What types of contractual relationships should you consider? One-time sale? Installment purchase? Agency or distributorship?

- Why should you sign a written contract? Will a memorandum, purchase order, or similar form be sufficient evidence of the transaction?
- If you do make a written contract, why should you pay legal fees to have it reviewed by your own attorney? Why not simply rely on the seller's attorney?
- When does an agreement become binding on you? What does mutual understanding mean?

■ PROTECTION AGAINST LIABILITIES AND LOSSES The sale and purchase of a product involves risk, which can translate into a loss. To lessen the risk and fight against the loss, advice from an attorney is usually necessary.

- If the goods or services are defective and cause injury, whether to you or to a third person, what remedy will you have against the seller? What will be your own liability and how can you protect yourself and your business? How enforceable is an indemnity clause?
- What does the protection of intellectual or industrial property rights mean? What are these rights, and why are they significant? If you do not take steps to protect these rights for the seller, what recourse will the seller have against you?
- If the seller breaches the contract, what remedies are available in your own country? In the seller's country?
- What are the various options for protecting yourself against loss if the seller breaches?
- What does mitigation of damages mean, and are you obligated to mitigate your damages?
- If you breach the contract, what rights does the seller have?
- What is an illegal contract? When is a contract considered void? When is it voidable?

WHEN TO CONSULT AN ATTORNEY

■ IN THE BEGINNING The most important time to seek legal advice is before you need legal advice. You should consult your attorney before you begin buying internationally because the answers to your questions will affect your course of action. If you have not yet made a contract, you are still on the offensive. You have bargaining power, and you can insist on the protection of your rights, provided you know and understand your rights and obligations. Once you have entered into a contract, your attorney can only provide you with defensive advice—how to renegotiate, repudiate, or otherwise avoid the contract or at least minimize your losses from a bad deal.

The first meeting with your attorney should provide you with the background information that you will need to negotiate your contract with the seller. Your attorney's advice will be most helpful if it is relevant to your specific situation. You should be certain to present to your attorney a well-rehearsed business plan, complete with information about your industry, your domestic business, and your foreign inquiries and potential sources. Adequate preparation for this meeting is to your benefit, as your attorney's time will cost you money.

■ DURING A TRANSACTION Whether you consult your attorney during a transaction depends on many factors. If each transaction is identical and no new issues are presented, you probably do not need to consult your attorney while negotiating the deal. When the situation changes, you should seek legal advice.

In complex transactions, the wisest course of action may be to have your attorney conduct the negotiations or at least to be present to advise you during the negotiations.

- FINALIZING YOUR PURCHASE For the first purchase you make internationally, it is wise to have your attorney review and comment on the contract before you agree to it. Your attorney will be able to point out the obligations and liabilities that you should avoid and will advise you on how to renegotiate the terms to better protect your rights. Once you have been through this procedure with your attorney, you may find that further legal advice is not necessary unless the terms of new contracts substantially differ or your circumstances change.
- ENFORCING OR RENEGOTIATING THE PURCHASE If you are faced with enforcing or renegotiating a purchase, the first step you should take is to call your attorney to discuss your options. Consulting with an attorney does not necessarily mean that you will sue the other party. The attorney can review the situation in terms of your strengths and weaknesses in renegotiating the deal and can explain what your risks and liabilities might be under various scenarios should you decide to enforce or breach the contract.

  After you have consulted with your attorney, you may choose to renegotiate or settle with the other party on your own, or you may ask the attorney to represent you through the entire process. In making this decision, you should consider such factors as the strength of your bargaining position, the legal system of the seller's country and your own, the extent to which you have developed a trusting relationship with the seller, and whether the other party is acting with legal representation. In any event, if the rift becomes irreparable, you should resort to assistance of counsel.

HOW TO SELECT AN ATTORNEY

Finding an attorney is as easy as consulting a telephone or legal directory, calling an attorney referral service, asking friends or family for a recommendation, or seeking out a relative who just happens to have a law office in your home town. Once you have narrowed your choices, pick the attorney who is:

1. Knowledgeable about business and your country's laws regulating business,
2. Knowledgeable about international business law, or at least willing to learn the relevant international aspects without costing you too much extra for the research involved,
3. Knowledgeable about importing and exporting issues,
4. Connected to business resources in your own jurisdiction and abroad, or at least willing to make those connections,
5. Frank in advising you to contact other professionals, such as foreign legal counsel, bankers, accountants, appraisers, and customs brokers, for assistance with issues that are not legal, and who is willing to liaise with those professionals on your behalf, and

6. Diplomatic, culturally aware, understanding of the difficulties involved in negotiating across country borders, and excited to be part of the international trade arena.

As a note of caution, never use the seller's attorney. Even if the seller is your best friend, the seller's interest is adverse to your own. The seller wants the highest price at the lowest production and delivery cost, while you want the lowest price for the best quality, quantity, and delivery terms. If a single attorney represents both of you, there is a distinct potential for conflict of interest because the attorney is bound ethically and morally not to give conflicting advice to parties within the same transaction.

ADVICE AN ATTORNEY TYPICALLY WILL NOT PROVIDE

You may certainly ask your attorney about subjects that are usually outside the realm of the attorney's advice. However, an attorney's time is extremely valuable, and you will pay the price. Most likely the attorney will inform you that you should contact other service providers for this advice.

- CUSTOMS Attorneys do not provide information regarding specific procedures for customs clearance, including necessary forms, types of entry, availability of preshipment inspections, pre-entry filings, and expedited clearance. Some customs attorneys can assist you in these areas, but you should consider consulting a customs broker or freight forwarder if your import or export is complex.
- TRANSPORT Attorneys are not experts on modes of transport available and the means of arranging it. For this type of information, you should consult a freight forwarder.
- BANKING A banker should be consulted for specific information about foreign exchange, loans, letters of credit, and other instruments of payment.
- ACCOUNTS AND TAX FILINGS Lawyers rarely create and maintain your business and personal records of account. Attorneys can advise you on tax liabilities, and some attorneys prepare income tax returns for their clients. It is best to consult an accountant for advice on keeping financial records at least, if not for preparation of your tax returns.

Attorney for Seller

As a seller, you have researched your market and you have developed a line of products or services that you know are, or will be, in demand in foreign markets. You have studied the business aspects and have determined the most efficient means of producing the goods or providing the services. You have added incentives and customer support to enhance the uniqueness of what you are selling and to rise above your competitors. Why should you consult an attorney?

WHY SHOULD THE SELLER CONSULT AN ATTORNEY?

The bottom line answer is the same for the seller as it is for the buyer: you still do not know everything and you can end up in a lot of financial and legal trouble because of your ignorance or innocence. Your international sales transaction will be subject to the laws and regulations of more than one country, the buyer's nation and your own. What you don't know can hurt you.

More significantly, you too will become subject to the government authorities of a foreign nation. If you agree to deliver the goods to the buyer, you will have to satisfy a customs officer of the buyer's country. If your goods are prohibited imports, they may be seized and even destroyed by the importing customs officer. If you breach the contract or if a defective product causes harm to a consumer in the chain, you may be sued in a court in the buyer's country. Your indiscretions could come to the attention of agencies that regulate antitrust or bribery, with resulting criminal penalties if you are found in violation of such laws.

You need to have a thorough understanding of your rights, obligations, risks, and options in selling internationally and of the issues that are most likely to arise in your particular situation. An attorney will offer you general advice for selling internationally and will explain the issues relevant to your own situation. As a seller, you should ask your attorney about the following topics.

- THE LEGAL SYSTEMS Very few businesspeople fully understand the legal system in their own country, let alone in their business partner's country. This is where an experienced attorney can prove an invaluable source.
  - Is the legal system of the buyer's country similar to the legal system in your own country? What are the similarities? How do the two systems differ?
  - Does the government in your country heavily regulate trade—whether domestic or international? What about the government in the buyer's country? Are there special requirements for selling the goods in the buyer's country?
  - Are there any treaties or bilateral agreements that affect trade between the buyer's country and your own? Do they apply in your industry? How can you take advantage of them?
  - What types of taxes are imposed by your country on exportation or sale of the goods or services? By the buyer's country on importation or sale of the goods or services?
- IMPORTING AND EXPORTING Aside from reviewing the legal systems for you, an attorney can provide useful and necessary information concerning the requirements for shipping across country borders.
  - Can you freely export the goods or services? What are the restrictions?
  - Are there any permits or licenses required for exporting or selling the goods or services to a foreign buyer? What agencies must approve the export and sale?
  - Are there import restrictions imposed by the buyer's country?
- CONTRACTS Even the simplest transaction can have a complicated contract. It takes the expertise of an attorney to understand the nuances and implications of most contracts.
  - Is there freedom of contract in your own country? In the buyer's country? What are the limits?
  - What types of contractual relationships should you consider? One-time sale? Installment purchase? Agency or distributorship? How can you ensure that the relationship you intend to create is the one that you in fact create?

- Why should you sign a written contract? Will a memorandum, invoice, or similar form be sufficient evidence of the transaction?
- If you do make a written contract, why should you pay legal fees to have it reviewed by your own attorney? Why not simply rely on the buyer's attorney?
- When does an agreement become binding on you? What does mutual understanding mean?
- What types of warranties are recognized in your own country? In the seller's country? Will warranties be implied in the seller's country even if they are not expressly included in the contract? Are there any warranties that will be implied by law even if the contract expressly excludes them?
- What other contract terms might be implied by the law of your country? Of the buyer's country?

- **PROTECTION AGAINST LIABILITIES AND LOSSES** Any transaction involves a risk, which could mean a loss. An attorney's advice can be useful in avoiding or lessening the losses.

- If the goods or services are defective and cause injury to a consumer, what will be your liability? How can you protect yourself and your business?
- How can you best protect your intellectual or industrial property rights? What are these rights, and why are they significant? Can they be protected in the buyer's country, and what is the procedure? What recourse do you have against a buyer who does not protect your intellectual or industrial property rights?
- What regulatory problems might you face? Are there antitrust, anti-bribery, consumer protection, environmental, or other similar laws by which you might become subject to civil or criminal sanctions?
- If the buyer breaches the contract, what remedies are available in your own country? In the buyer's country?
- What are the various options for protecting yourself against loss if the buyer breaches?
- What does mitigation of damages mean and are you obligated to mitigate your damages?
- If you breach the contract, what rights does the buyer have?
- What is an illegal contract? When is a contract considered void? When is it voidable?

WHEN TO SEEK LEGAL ADVICE

- **IN THE BEGINNING** As the seller, you have the negotiating advantage of holding goods or services that a buyer desires, and therefore you can often make the deal that you want. But you can lose your negotiating edge if you do not know your rights, obligations, and options, and therefore you should seek legal advice before you begin negotiations. Your attorney's advice will influence the decisions you make regarding how, what, where, when, and to whom you sell internationally. If you have not consulted your attorney first, you probably will not know whether you have made a bad deal, a good deal, or a great deal unless someone breaches the contract. Assuming contract performance flows smoothly—which it does 95 times out of 100—you will have to be satisfied with what you get, and you probably will not know whether you had a stronger bargaining position from which you could have made an even better deal. If there is a breach, and it might even be your own, your attorney will most likely be able to get you out of a tough spot and will also advise you on how to avoid paying so many legal fees in the future by making a better deal in the beginning.

It is up to you to make your first meeting with your attorney as productive as possible. You should summarize the history of your own business, describe the trade or industry generally, and explain the international opportunities that you are exploring. Your attorney will then be able to tailor the legal advice to your special circumstances. Adequate preparation for this meeting is to your benefit, as your attorney's time will cost you money.

- DURING A TRANSACTION Whether to consult your attorney during a transaction depends on factors similar to those considered by the buyer: the uniqueness and complexity of the transaction. For contracts that do not vary significantly, ongoing legal advice may not be necessary. If the terms of the sale are substantially different or complex, you would be wise to consult legal counsel during the negotiations.

- FINALIZING YOUR SALE Before you close your first international deal and sign the sale contract, be certain that your attorney has reviewed the provisions. Your attorney will explain which provisions are enforceable, which are burdensome, which carry hidden risks, and which need modification to ensure protection of your rights and limits on your liability. Each time you make a new contract of sale that substantially differs from any you have made previously, you should seek advice of legal counsel before you sign on the bottom line.

- ENFORCING OR RENEGOTIATING THE SALE If the buyer breaches or you cannot complete the contract, call your attorney. In addition to the obvious remedy of "sue or be sued," your attorney will be able to present various alternatives and will assist you in evaluating your position. You may be able to renegotiate, seek an accord and satisfaction, avoid the contract altogether, or you may decide to force the other party's performance.

  In any event, your attorney should be there with you—whether in the background, if you choose to renegotiate or settle with the other party on your own, or as your direct representative during the entire process. You may need less legal assistance if the buyer is willing to compromise. But if you are forced to seek redress through the foreign legal system of the buyer's country, your attorney's presence will be a significant advantage.

HOW TO SELECT AN ATTORNEY

Sellers typically find attorneys by the same means as buyers—through directories, referrals, or recommendations of friends or family. You should select an attorney who is:

1. Knowledgeable about business and your country's laws regulating business,
2. Knowledgeable about international business law, or at least willing to learn the relevant international aspects without costing you too much extra for the research involved,
3. Knowledgeable about importing and exporting issues,
4. Connected to business resources in your own jurisdiction and abroad or at least willing to make those connections,
5. Frank in advising you to contact other professionals—such as foreign legal counsel, bankers, accountants, appraisers, and customs brokers—for assistance with issues that are not legal, and who is willing to liaise with those professionals on your behalf, and
6. Diplomatic, culturally aware, understanding of the difficulties involved in negotiating across country borders, and excited to be part of the international trade arena.

Representation by the buyer's attorney is taboo. The buyer's interests are, at least potentially, adverse to your own. The buyer wants the lowest price for the most products of the highest quality at favorable delivery terms. There is a definite potential for conflict of interest, and attorneys have an ethical and moral obligation to avoid advising two parties on opposite sides of the same transaction.

ADVICE AN ATTORNEY TYPICALLY WILL NOT PROVIDE

You may certainly ask your attorney about subjects that are usually outside the realm of the attorney's advice. However, an attorney's time is extremely valuable, and you will pay the price. Most likely the attorney will inform you that you should contact other service providers for this advice.

- **CUSTOMS** Attorneys do not provide information regarding specific procedures for customs clearance, including necessary forms, types of entry, availability of preshipment inspections, pre-entry filings, and expedited clearance. Some customs attorneys can assist you in these areas, but you should consider consulting a customs broker or freight forwarder if your import or export is complex.
- **TRANSPORT** Attorneys are not experts on modes of transport available and the means of arranging it. For this type of information, you should consult a freight forwarder.
- **BANKING** A banker should be consulted for specific information about foreign exchange, loans, letters of credit, and other instruments of payment.
- **ACCOUNTS AND TAX FILINGS** Lawyers rarely create and maintain your business and personal records of account. Attorneys can advise you on tax liabilities, and some attorneys prepare income tax returns for their clients. It is best to consult an accountant for advice on keeping financial records at least, if not for preparation of your tax returns.

CHAPTER 4

Drafting the International Contract for Sale of Goods

WHEN DEALING INTERNATIONALLY, you must consider the business practices and legal requirements of both the buyer's and the seller's country. Parties to a commercial transaction generally have the freedom to agree to any contract terms that they desire, but the laws of your country or the foreign country may require a written contract. In some transactions, the laws may even specify all or some of the contract terms.

Terms Necessary for Enforcement

Whether a contract is valid in a particular country is mainly of concern if you have to seek enforcement. Otherwise, you have fairly broad flexibility in negotiating contract provisions. However, you should always be certain to come to a definite understanding with the other party on four basic issues: the goods (quantity, type, and quality); the time of delivery; the price; and the time and means of payment.

Implied Terms

If you leave terms out of your contract, the gaps will be filled in by application of the law. To the extent that the terms are vague, open to interpretation, or left to implication or custom, you will have to rely on the law to determine your rights and obligations should a dispute arise. For cross-border contracts, the implied terms will vary depending on which country's law is applied. Disputes will be resolved according to the laws of the country with jurisdiction. Jurisdiction is largely at the discretion of the court, which may agree to follow the expressed intent of the parties as to the governing laws or may apply another test, such as the place where the contract was signed or where the parties have the most significant contacts.

Accordingly, the best way to control the results of your contract is to clarify each party's responsibility in the agreement by paying close attention to every contract term. Always be specific. Plan for each contingency. For instance, you may agree to buy a certain quantity of a specific product, but how are you going to pick up the goods? Is someone going to box them? Do you want the entire order at once? When do you want them?

Checklist

The following provisions are for a complete, simple, international contract for the one-time sale of goods. Not every provision listed is applicable to every contractual arrangement. The purpose for referring to the following checklist is to ensure that you have defined your relationship with the other party as clearly as possible and that you have considered and provided for as many contingencies as may be anticipated in advance.

Regardless of whether you draft the terms of your contract by yourself, you need to be aware of the key provisions because it is up to you to insist on the protection of your own interests. Although the law of many countries will imply certain terms to encourage fair dealing, this law is generally applied through costly and time-consuming legal processes, whether court, arbitration, or mediation proceedings. Moreover, the application of provisions implied by law is up to disinterested third persons, and the end result may not be what you want. The best course of action is to define all of the provisions of your contract in writing at the time you enter into it. These provisions should include

1. Contract date ❑
2. Identification of parties ❑
3. Goods—description ❑
4. Goods—quantity ❑
5. Goods—price ❑
6. Payment—method of payment ❑
7. Payment—medium of exchange ❑
8. Payment—exchange rate ❑
9. Costs and charges—duties and taxes ❑
10. Costs and charges—insurance ❑
11. Costs and charges—handling and transport ❑
12. Packaging arrangements ❑
13. Delivery—date ❑
14. Delivery—place ❑
15. Delivery—transfer of title ❑
16. Transportation—carrier ❑
17. Transportation—storage ❑
18. Transportation—notice provisions ❑
19. Transportation—shipping time ❑
20. Transportation—insurance or risk of loss protection ❑
21. Import/export documentation ❑
22. Invoice preparation and delivery ❑
23. Re-exportation prohibition ❑
24. Inspection rights ❑
25. Indemnities ❑
26. Intellectual property rights ❑
27. Warranties ❑
28. Enforcement and remedies ❑
29. Arbitration provisions ❑
30. Time is of the essence ❑
31. Modification of contract ❑
32. Cancellation ❑
33. Liquidated damages ❑
34. Attorneys' fees ❑
35. Force majeure ❑
36. Inurement and assignment ❑
37. Conditions precedent ❑
38. Governing law ❑
39. Choice of forum ❑
40. Severability of provisions ❑
41. Integration of provisions ❑
42. Notices ❑
43. Authority to bind ❑
44. Independent counsel ❑
45. Acceptance and execution ❑

Simple vs. Complex Transactions

For a small, one-time sale, an invoice or a simple contract may be acceptable. These are the most common commercial relationships. The seller manufactures or represents one or more products and has a number of buyers. The buyer has no exclusive rights to purchase the products.

For a more involved business transaction or an ongoing relationship, a formal written contract is preferable to define clearly the rights, responsibilities, and remedies of all parties. Contracts that involve capital goods, high credit risks, or industrial or intellectual property rights will require special protective clauses. In preparing such contracts, it is essential to obtain legal advice from a professional who is familiar with the laws and practices of both countries.

TIP: In drafting international contracts, it is extremely wise to go through each contract provision with each party and expressly ask them to indicate their comprehension, such as: "Do you understand that you are assuming the responsibility for packing these goods according to our shipper's instructions?" If you are concerned that misunderstandings over performance are likely, you may want to have the each party initial all or some paragraphs, and it is common practice to have each party initial every page. Some multinational contracts have every paragraph initialed after the parties have spent weeks negotiating the contract through interpreters.

Specific Contract Provisions Explained

CONTRACT DATE

■ PROVISION:

This Agreement is made on [*date*].

COMMENT: The date when the contract is signed is usually also the date when it becomes effective unless the contract provides otherwise. This date is particularly important if payment or delivery times will be fixed in reference to it. For example, a contract may provide for "shipment within 30 days after the contract date."

When dealing internationally, you should remember that the conventional format for dates differs from country to country. In some, the day is stated before the month; in others, the month is given before the day. To avoid confusion, it is highly recommended that you spell out the month when dating your contract.

IDENTIFICATION OF PARTIES

■ PROVISION:

This Agreement is made between [*full name of party A*] of [*address of party A*], a/an [*description and nationality of party A*] ("Seller"), and [*full name of party B*] of [*address of party B*], a/an [*description and nationality of party B*] ("Buyer").

COMMENT: The agreement is binding on the parties who sign it, and these parties should be identified in this clause. To ensure that there is no misunderstanding, the full name of each party to the contract should be given. If a party is an entity, the type of entity (partnership, corporation, limited liability company, nonprofit corporation, and so forth) should be disclosed here. Any question as to whether the entity or the person representing the entity has authority to make the contract should be resolved before the contract is executed.

The common practice is to include the address of each party in this provision, although sometimes the addresses are included at the end of the agreement with the signatures of the parties. The address given should be the business address for the party. If a party has more than one business address, the address given should be for the registered office or the principle place of business. Unless otherwise specified in the contract, this address is where the party will receive the goods, the payment for the goods, and any notices related to the transaction.

In international contracts, the description of each party includes the party's nationality. Examples of descriptions: "a Société Anonyme organized and existing under the laws of France" or "a partnership organized and existing under the laws of the State of California in the United States of America" or "an individual who is a citizen of Singapore."

GOODS—DESCRIPTION, QUANTITY, AND PRICE

■ PROVISION:

SALE AND PURCHASE OF GOODS. The Seller agrees to sell to the Buyer, and the Buyer agrees to purchase from the Seller, goods (the "Goods") that are *[specify either* as described in the attached Exhibit A, which is incorporated into this Agreement *or* of the following type for the price and quantity stated:
Model Number:
Description:
Quantity:
Price:
Item:
Total Price:]

COMMENT: The provision for goods contains two terms that are essential to all contracts, whether international or domestic: a description of the goods and the price. For the contract to be enforceable, the parties must usually agree to both of these terms. Although a few jurisdictions will allow these terms to be implied in commercial transactions, the general rule is that these terms cannot be implied.

If a description of the goods is missing or is not specific, enforcement of the contract may be impossible because the goods cannot be identified. A clause is considered sufficiently specific if it is so clear that both parties fully understand the specifications and have no discretion in interpreting them. The goods may be described by model numbers, shown in plans or drawings, or defined by other specifications. For multiple goods, you should provide a detailed list attached as an exhibit to the agreement.

If the parties fail to agree to a price or to a means for determining the price, the courts are unlikely to enforce the contract. You may indicate a total price for all goods or a price per unit or other measure, such as per pound or ton, and the extended price. Even if the quantity of the goods is not fixed at the time the contract is made, a means of determining the price must nevertheless be stated (refer to Chapter 8: Drafting Precise Contract Provisions). In an international contract, it is wise to state the price using an abbreviation of the currency in which payment is to be made, such as HK$ (Hong Kong dollars) or US$ (United States dollars), to avoid any misunderstandings.

The quantity of goods is important. If the contract covers goods of more than one type, the quantity of each type should be given. You may specify a number of units or any other measure of quantity. If the goods are measured by weight, be certain to specify net weight, dry weight, or drained weight.

PAYMENT TERMS

■ PROVISION:

TERMS OF PAYMENT. The Buyer will pay the purchase price [*specify e.g.*, on or before (*date*) *or* not later than (*number*) days before the Delivery Date]. The payment must be remitted to the Seller at [the address stated above *or* specify other address]. The payment must be made in [currency] by means of [*instrument of transfer*].

COMMENT: In a one-time transaction, the seller will typically seek the most secure form of payment before committing to shipment, while a buyer will want the goods cleared through customs and delivered in satisfactory condition before remitting payment. The parties will need to negotiate a compromise between these two positions, and each should insist on certain protective clauses to alleviate some of the risk (refer to Chapter 8: Drafting Precise Contract Provisions).

In international contracts, you should always specify the acceptable currency and the instrument of payment. The currency selected should be strong and stable to allow some protection against fluctuating exchange rates, and the means of payment should be secure. For example, the payment may be made by delivery of a documentary letter of credit or documents against payment, by advance payment in cash or wire transfer, or by a line of credit for a specified number of days.

COSTS AND CHARGES

■ PROVISION:

COSTS AND CHARGES. The buyer is responsible for the following costs and charges incurred in the sale and transport of the goods: [*list*]. The seller is responsible for the following costs and charges incurred in the sale and transport of the goods: [*list*].

COMMENT: You should specify which party is to pay any additional costs and charges related to the sale. Even if you use a trade term in your contract to indicate one party's responsibility for the payment of costs and charges, you should elaborate on the obligations of both parties. The items to be considered include import, export, and other customs and shipping fees, ad valorem and other taxes, and expenses for obtaining requisite licenses.

PACKAGING ARRANGEMENTS

■ PROVISION:

PACKAGING ARRANGEMENTS. The Seller has discretion in packaging the goods, provided that the packaging must withstand transportation, prevent damage to the goods during transport, and comply with the following requirements: [*specify, e.g.,* product warning and origin marking laws of the Buyer's country, as set forth in Exhibit A annexed to this Agreement]. The Seller will endeavor to complete all packaging within time for the Delivery Date. If there is any delay, the Seller will immediately notify the Buyer of the delay, the expected time for completion, and the reason for the delay. The Buyer will then have the option to renegotiate with the Seller for a new Delivery Date, which the parties will confirm in writing as a modification to this Agreement, or to notify the Seller that the Agreement is terminated.

COMMENT: At a minimum, this provision should require the seller to package the goods in such a way as to withstand transportation. If special packaging requirements are necessary, you should specify them also. Special packaging may be required to meet both legal requirements and market expectations in the buyer's country. Thus, products may be subject to importation, transportation, health, agricultural, environmental, navigation, construction, and consumer laws and regulations. Compliance may involve getting a license or permit, arranging for inspections, using proper packaging and labeling, providing proof of insurance, and presenting proper entry documents for customs clearance.

The parties may decide that the buyer will be responsible for conforming the packaging for sale in the buyer's country. In this case, the seller should insist on protective provisions for intellectual property and third-party liability (refer to Chapter 8: Drafting Precise Contract Provisions).

TRANSPORTATION AND DELIVERY OF GOODS

- PROVISION:

DELIVERY AND TRANSPORT OF GOODS. The Goods will be delivered [*trade term, e.g.,*F.O.B.] [*place*] on or before [*date*] ("Delivery Date"). The Seller will deliver the Goods in a single shipment. The mode of transport to the point of delivery is at the Seller's discretion. The Seller will make every effort to commence transport of the Goods so that they will arrive by the Delivery Date. If there is any delay, the Seller will immediately notify the Buyer of the delay, the expected time for delivery, and the reason for the delay. The Buyer will then have the option to renegotiate with the Seller for a new Delivery Date, which the parties will confirm in writing as a modification to this Agreement, or to notify the Seller that the Agreement is terminated.

COMMENT: Contracts for the sale of goods most commonly use international trade terms—usually Incoterms as defined by the International Chamber of Commerce in Paris—to assign responsibility for the risks and costs of transport. Although international trade terms have been standardized, in practice their meanings can vary. Precise definitions of these terms are important to your contract because these terms can determine such items as which party is responsible for insuring the goods at any one time, the time at which title to the goods will transfer from seller to buyer, and the party responsible for paying certain transportation costs.

If you do not use an Incoterm, the delivery and transport provision may simply state the name of the carrier who will handle the freight shipment, designate the point at which and the date on which the goods will be delivered to the buyer, and identify the party who will pay for transportation from point A to point B.

If more than two or three carriers are involved or your goods require special treatment, you will have to add extra details to this provision.

It is often wise to name a preferred carrier for transporting the goods. You should designate a particular carrier if, for example, a carrier offers you special pricing or is better able than others to transport the product. If the carrier is designated, however, you may be locked into using that carrier under unfavorable terms. Therefore, the choice of carrier should remain flexible, even if a preference is stated. Another alternative is to describe a type of carrier, particularly if special handling of the goods is required. The transport clause should also specify any particular requirements for storage of the goods before or during shipment, such as security arrangements, special climate demands, and weather protection needs.

The parties may include notice provisions, particularly if goods are not ready for immediate transfer. Thus, a seller may be required to notify the buyer when the goods will be ready for delivery or pickup, particularly if the goods are perishable or fluctuate in value. If your transaction is time sensitive, you could even provide for several notices, which will allow you to track the goods and to take steps to minimize costs and damages if delivery is delayed.

INSURANCE

■ PROVISION:

INSURANCE. The [*Buyer/Seller*] will obtain and pay, on its own account, for all insurance on the Goods while in transit, provided that the insurance obtained will include for the protection of the [*Seller/Buyer*] coverage for the following: [*specify*]. Evidence of this insurance, in the form of a copy of the policy or other statement provided by the insurer, will be provided to the [*Seller/Buyer*] before the Goods are shipped. Each party is responsible for obtaining on its own account any other insurance coverage for the Goods that he/she may desire.

COMMENT: You should specify the insurance required, the beneficiary of the policy, the party who will obtain the insurance and who will pay for it, and the date by which it must be obtained. You should also agree on which documents will be considered satisfactory evidence of insurance.

TITLE TO GOODS

■ PROVISION:

TITLE TO GOODS. Title to the Goods will pass to the Buyer at the time the Goods are delivered to [*place*], provided the Buyer has transmitted payment to the Seller by that time.

COMMENT: This is a critical provision because, if the goods are lost during transit, the party with title generally bears the risk. The general rule is that title transfers at the point when the seller delivers the goods to the buyer. Thus, if the buyer picks up the goods at the seller's place of business and carries them off, title has transferred and the buyer bears the risk of loss or damage during transport. If the seller ships the goods, title may transfer at any point during transit, even right up to the buyer's door, depending on the agreement of the parties.

Each party should be certain to insure "their" goods for at least the time they have possession, hold title, or have responsibility for the goods. If Incoterms are used, each term defines the time and place of transfer of responsibilities and title.

IMPORT/EXPORT DOCUMENTATION

■ PROVISION:

IMPORT/EXPORT DOCUMENTATION. The Seller will be responsible for obtaining, completing, and presenting to [*country*] customs all export documentation and fees required for clearance, including the following: [*list*].The Buyer will be responsible for obtaining, completing, and presenting to [*country*] customs all import documentation and fees required for clearance, including the following: [*list*]. The Buyer must notify the Seller that all import requirements have been met. The Seller is not required to ship the Goods until the Buyer furnishes the Seller with proof that the import requirements and fees have been or will be timely met. If shipment is delayed because the Buyer fails to furnish such proof timely, the Seller will not be deemed to have breached the contract.

COMMENT: Shipment of the goods, and even the contract itself, may be made contingent on a party's having obtained or arranged in advance the proper licenses, inspection certificates, and other authorizations. Always make complete import and export documentation—that is, documentation that is satisfactory for customs clearance and entry—a requirement of your contract for the purchase of products or commodities.

As written, this provision is intended to split the responsibility for customs clearance between the parties in accordance with the requirements most familiar to each—the seller for the exporting country, the buyer for the importing country. The clause may be amended to provide that one party will make all arrangements for customs clearance.

INVOICES

■ PROVISION:

INVOICES. The Seller will issue provisional invoices and final invoices for the shipment of the Goods. The invoices must specifically describe the Goods, the quantity of the Goods, and the price of the Goods.

COMMENT: In international transactions, invoices serve to confirm the shipment, notify the buyer of shipment, and furnish documentary evidence for customs clearance. The contract should also require that the invoice be in compliance with any specific requirements imposed by the laws or regulations of the buyer's or seller's country, and it is wise to append those requirements to the contract to facilitate compliance.

RE-EXPORTATION PROHIBITION

■ PROVISION:

RE-EXPORTATION. The Buyer covenants that the Goods will be shipped to and delivered in [*country*] and that the Buyer will not ship or deliver the Goods to any other country, nor will the Buyer re-export the Goods after delivery in [*country*].

COMMENT: This clause is especially important if the goods might be subject to import or export restrictions, including trade embargoes, in any particular country. Under the laws of some countries, such as the United States, a sale to a buyer who in turn ships the goods to another country where a sale from the first exporting country would otherwise have been prohibited may subject the first seller to criminal penalties in that seller's own country. Penalties may be imposed if the seller knew or should have reasonably known of the subsequent export and sale. Thus, if the seller has any suspicion that the buyer may be delivering or re-exporting the goods to a prohibited country, the seller should avoid the transaction entirely. This clause may be amended to allow re-export to one or more designated countries to which re-exports are permissible.

INSPECTION RIGHTS

■ PROVISION:

INSPECTIONS. The Buyer is entitled to inspect, or to have its agent inspect, the Goods at the [Seller's place of business *or* point of shipping]. The Seller will pay return freight charges and will replace Goods that the Buyer or its agent rejects with Goods that meet the description and specifications set forth in this Agreement. On completion of the inspection and acceptance of the Goods, the Buyer or its agent will execute a certificate of inspection and acceptance. The inspection and execution of the certificate will be at the Buyer's cost. The Buyer's failure to inspect the Goods will constitute a waiver of the right of inspection, and the Buyer will be deemed to have accepted the Goods as delivered.

COMMENT: The buyer should insist on a right of inspection of the goods before taking delivery to determine whether the goods meet the contract specifications. This clause should specify who will do the inspection—the buyer, an agent, a neutral third party, or a licensed inspector; where the inspection will occur (for example, at the seller's plant, the buyer's warehouse, or a receiving dock) and when the inspection will occur.

WARRANTIES

■ PROVISION:

EXPRESS AND IMPLIED WARRANTIES. The Seller expressly warrants that the Goods are free from all defects of material, workmanship, or installation. Within [*number*] days after delivery, the Seller will replace free of all charges, including the cost of transportation, any part of the Goods found defective. EXCEPT AS EXPRESSLY STATED IN THIS AGREEMENT, THE SELLER DOES NOT WARRANT THE GOODS IN ANY MANNER AT ALL. IMPLIED WARRANTIES OF FITNESS FOR A PARTICULAR PURPOSE OR OF MERCHANTABILITY ARE DISCLAIMED. THE GOODS ARE SOLD "AS IS" AND THE BUYER UNDERSTANDS AND AGREES THAT NO RELIANCE HAS BEEN PLACED ON THE SELLER'S SKILL AND JUDGMENT TO SELECT OR FURNISH GOODS FOR ANY PARTICULAR PURPOSE.

COMMENT: The seller may agree to offer extended or limited warranties, or no warranties at all, as to fitness or quality of the goods. The exact terms of the warranties should be given in the contract. In some countries, the law will imply warranties unless the seller expressly disclaims them. Implied warranties also arise under the UN Convention on International Sale of Goods. Because of enforcement difficulties, it may be wise to have both parties initial the warranties paragraph.

INDEMNITY

■ PROVISION:

INDEMNIFICATION OF BUYER. Provided the Buyer has not altered the Goods or the packaging of the Goods in any manner before sale, the Seller will defend any suit for damages brought against the Buyer based on a defect in the materials, design, or manufacturing of the Goods or on patent or trademark infringement in connection with the sale or use of the Goods. If an action is brought against the Buyer, it will promptly notify the Seller. The Seller will indemnify the Buyer against any liability, damage, or expenses incurred in connection with any such suit and will pay any judgment entered against the Buyer in such suit.

COMMENT: An indemnification clause is optional. In international contracts, the seller will sometimes agree to hold the buyer harmless from damages that arise from specific causes, such as a design flaw or manufacturing defect, in order to encourage the buyer to debut the seller's products in a new market. If an indemnity is given, the seller should always insist that there is no change in the goods, packaging, labeling, or markings before the sale; any alteration by the buyer should cancel the indemnity, unless the alteration was approved by the seller.

INTELLECTUAL AND INDUSTRIAL PROPERTY RIGHTS

■ PROVISION:

INTELLECTUAL PROPERTY PROTECTION. The Buyer understands that the Seller owns the exclusive rights in the designs, patents, trademarks, trade names, and company names (the "Intellectual Property") used in connection with the Seller's Goods. The Buyer is given no rights in any of the Seller's Intellectual Property. The Buyer will not use the Seller's Intellectual Property as if it were the Buyer's own property, nor will the Buyer register the Seller's Intellectual Property in any country as if it were the Buyer's own. The Buyer acknowledges that its unauthorized use or registration of the Seller's Intellectual Property, or of any intellectual property that is confusingly or deceptively similar to the Seller's Intellectual Property, will be deemed an infringement of the Seller's exclusive rights.

COMMENT: The infringement of rights in intellectual property, trademarks, service marks, trade names, patents, designs, and similar rights, should be prevented if at all possible from the outset of the relationship between the parties. All too often, a company will make a small sale to a foreign buyer, who never places another order. Then, five or ten years later, the company decides to expand into that same foreign market only to find that it cannot register its intellectual property there because the foreign buyer has acquired registration of the same or nearly identical trademarks, trade names, or patents. If the company tries to sell in that country, it will be charged with infringement. Its only remedy is to buy out the infringer or expend substantial time and costs in fighting the infringement through the courts. The value of intellectual property rights should not be underestimated—even for a one-time sale—and they should be protected. The legal remedies available against infringers are often inadequate relative to the harm caused, and therefore a liquidated damages clause is recommended.

TIMELY PERFORMANCE

■ PROVISION:

TIME. The parties agree that [*specify, e.g.*, time is of the essence *or* timely performance of this Agreement is important, provided that if a party fails to perform on time, the parties will strive to renegotiate the terms].

COMMENT: In the United States, the parties to a contract often stipulate that timely performance is essential. The inclusion of this clause allows a party to claim breach simply because the other party fails to perform within the time prescribed in the contract. In other countries, a clause of this type is considered less important because contracting parties often waive or renegotiate terms, rather than sue for damages on breach of the contract. An optional provision is included here in case you prefer to amend this clause to more closely reflect the international practice.

CONDITIONS PRECEDENT

■ PROVISION:

CONDITIONS PRECEDENT. This Agreement is subject to [*specify, e.g.*, the issuance of an import license to the Buyer by the appropriate agency of (*country*) government and the issuance of an export license to the Seller by the appropriate agency of (*country*) government].

COMMENT: You should specify any events that must occur before a party is obligated to perform the contract. For example, you may agree that the seller has no duty to ship goods until the buyer forwards documents that secure the payment for the goods. Another condition precedent might be receipt of advance payment. If the contract is contingent on the occurrence of certain conditions, it is best to repeat all of the contingencies for termination to ensure that your intent is clear. In general, conditions that could result in termination are not considered desirable and therefore are strictly construed by the courts in most jurisdictions.

CANCELLATION

■ PROVISION:

RIGHT TO CANCEL. The Buyer has a right to cancel this Agreement if the Seller fails [*specify, e.g.*, to ship all or any of the Goods on time]. The Seller has a right to cancel this Agreement if the Buyer fails [*specify, e.g.*, to make any payment required by this Agreement within (*number*) days of its due date]. If either party notifies the other party that it will not, or is unable to, perform this Agreement, the party receiving notice is entitled to cancel the Agreement. To make the cancellation effective, the party seeking to cancel must give notice to the other party that the Agreement is deemed canceled. The date of the cancellation will be the date on which the party receives the notice of nonperformance.

COMMENT: If either party has a right to cancel the contract, the grounds for exercising that right should be specified, and there should be a requirement for notice of cancellation. The provision of a right to cancel furnishes a party with a remedy that can be utilized without having to seek satisfaction through legal proceedings.

FORCE MAJEURE

■ PROVISION:

FORCE MAJEURE. This Agreement will be deemed canceled, and neither party will have any liability to the other for losses resulting from nonperformance, if delivery is prevented by causes beyond the control of the Seller. Such causes include, but are not limited to, acts of nature, labor disputes, failure of essential means of transportation, or changes in policy with respect to exports or imports by the [*country*] government or the [*country*] government.

COMMENT: A common clause in all contracts, the force majeure clause merely expresses what is no doubt the intent of the parties: if performance is prevented by a natural disaster or other catastrophic event beyond the control of the parties, the agreement is canceled.

LIQUIDATED DAMAGES

■ PROVISION:

LIQUIDATED DAMAGES. Each party understands that a breach of this Agreement will cause the nonbreaching party damages that will be difficult to calculate in terms of sales, markets, and goodwill lost. It is agreed that the parties have considered what would be a reasonable estimate of the damages each would suffer if the other were to breach this Agreement. If the Seller cannot deliver the Goods for any reason other than by fault of the Buyer, the Seller will pay to the Buyer as liquidated damages the sum of [*currency and amount*]. If the Buyer fails to furnish shipping instructions, wrongfully refuses to accept the Goods, or fails to pay the amount due on time, the Buyer will pay to the Seller as liquidated damages the sum of [*currency and amount*]. If the Buyer infringes the Seller's Intellectual Property, the Buyer will pay to the Seller as liquidated damages the sum of [*currency and amount*] for each day of continued use. Payment of liquidated damages will not, in any way, affect the Seller's rights to enjoin the Buyer's continued use of the Seller's Intellectual Property.

COMMENT: The parties may provide for a specific amount of damages payable on breach of the agreement, and that provision will usually be enforceable as long as it is a reasonable estimate of the damages. The estimate must be reasonable in relation to the anticipated or actual harm caused by the breach. In general, proof of damages must also be difficult or impracticable, or damages must be an inadequate remedy because the harm will continue to occur unless it is enjoined.

ARBITRATION

■ PROVISION:

ARBITRATION. Except when liquidated damages apply, if a dispute arises between the parties to this Agreement with regard to any of the provisions or the performance of any terms and conditions of this Agreement, the dispute will be settled by [*binding/nonbinding*] arbitration to be conducted in accordance with the [*name of arbitration rules*] in [*location*].

COMMENT: You might provide for arbitration as an alternative to litigation for resolving contract disputes. Arbitration is less formal procedurally than a court trial but still allows the parties to present their claims before a neutral person or panel for an objective decision. This remedy is increasing in popularity in commercial disputes, largely because it is less adversarial, less costly, and faster than litigation. However, be certain that you seriously intend to settle disputes in this way. If you agree to arbitrate but later file suit, the court is likely to uphold the arbitration clause and force you to settle your dispute as you agreed under the contract.

An arbitration clause should specify whether arbitration is binding or nonbinding on the parties; the country where arbitration will be conducted; the procedure for enforcement of an award; the rules governing the arbitration, such as the U.N. Commission on International Trade Law Model Rules; the institute that will administer the arbitration, such as the International Chamber of Commerce (Paris); the law that will govern procedural issues or the merits of the dispute; any limitations on the selection of arbitrators (for example, a national of a disputing party may be excluded from being an arbitrator); the qualifications or expertise of the arbitrators; the language in which the arbitration will be conducted; and the availability of translations and translators if needed.

Arbitration is not used in all countries. For example, disputes in Mexico are rarely settled by arbitration, and throughout Asia, arbitration is frowned on nearly as much as litigation in court. Moreover, some countries do not recognize arbitration awards from other jurisdictions. You should consult an attorney familiar with the law of the country of your supplier before assuming that you will be able to arbitrate potential contract disputes.

GOVERNING LAW AND CHOICE OF FORUM

- PROVISION:

FORUM AND GOVERNING LAW. The parties understand and agree that the laws of [*location*] will be applied to interpret this Agreement. This Agreement [is/is not] to be interpreted by application of the United Nations Convention on International Sale of Goods. Any action filed to resolve a dispute between the parties must be brought in [*location*].

COMMENT: Choose the law of a specific jurisdiction to control any interpretation of the contract terms. The law that you choose will usually affect where you can sue or enforce a judgment and what laws, rules, and procedures will be applied. If you file suit in your own country, where domestic counsel and commercial laws are familiar to you, your experience will be different than if you litigate in a foreign country, where you will be subject to unfamiliar laws, rules, and procedures and will have to rely on foreign counsel. You should also identify the place where a dispute may be settled—for example, the country of origin of the goods, the country of destination, or a third country that is convenient to both parties.

AMENDMENTS TO CONTRACT

- PROVISION:

MODIFICATIONS AND WAIVERS. All modifications of this Agreement must be in writing and signed by the parties or their authorized agents. If a party waives any of its rights under this Agreement to make a claim for breach, that waiver will have no effect with regard to the party's right to enforce the Agreement as to any subsequent breach.

COMMENT: Require the parties to make all changes to the contract in advance and in a signed written modification. This provision is common to all contracts. It is a wise protection against oral alterations and, if there is an oral or written waiver of a right, against the expectation that other rights are also waived. You should insist on this clause in contracts with foreign traders to avoid misunderstandings that can arise from oral modifications—when it's your word against that of the other trader.

INUREMENT AND ASSIGNMENT

■ PROVISION:

INUREMENT AND ASSIGNMENT. This Agreement binds, and inures to the benefit of, the parties, their successors, and assignees, subject to the limitations of any assignment. Neither party may assign the rights or delegate the performance of its duties under this Agreement without the prior written consent of the other party.

COMMENT: In a one-time sale, it is unlikely that a party will have time to assign the contract to another person. Nevertheless, the potential exists, and when dealing overseas in a country where the economy or the government is unstable, an assignment clause can become significant.

SEVERABILITY

■ PROVISION:

SEVERABILITY OF PROVISIONS. If any provision of this Agreement is held invalid or unenforceable for any reason, that provision is fully separable, and will be deemed separated from, the rest of this Agreement. The remaining provisions will be valid and enforceable as if the invalid or unenforceable provision were not part of this Agreement.

COMMENT: You should include this standard provision that individual clauses can be removed from the contract without affecting the validity of the contract as a whole. This clause is important because it provides that, if one clause is declared invalid and unenforceable for any reason, the rest of the contract remains in force.

INTEGRATION

■ PROVISION:

ENTIRE AGREEMENT. This Agreement is the entire understanding between the parties. The Seller is not bound by any statements, representations, promises, or inducements, regardless of whether made by the Seller, an agent, or employee, unless it is set forth in this Agreement. The Buyer specifically agrees that no reliance has been placed on any representations other than the provisions contained in this Agreement.

COMMENT: Contract negotiations may last for some time and through several meetings. In overseas contracts, traders often meet in various settings from business to social to ferment their relationship before cementing it. This clause then becomes particularly significant in emphasizing to the parties that the written words constitute their entire final agreement, regardless of what representations were made during the negotiations.

NOTICES

■ PROVISION:

NOTICES. To give notice pursuant to this Agreement, a party must send written notice to the other party at the address stated in this Agreement. Notice is deemed to be given at the time it is received. A party must notify the other party in writing of any change in address within [*number*] days of the effective date of the change.

COMMENT: Although not an essential term, the notice provision is important to clarify the acceptable procedure. This term requires written notice, and thus an oral notice must be confirmed in writing before the notice becomes effective.

AUTHORITY TO BIND PARTY TO CONTRACT

■ PROVISION:

BINDING AUTHORITY. The parties warrant to each other that each has legal capacity to enter into and be bound by the terms of this Agreement.

COMMENT: This clause should be added regardless of whether a party is an individual or an entity because it gives some assurance to each party that the person signing the contract has authority to do so. If a signer had no authority, a contract may subsequently be voidable. If the party is an individual, he or she must be legally capable of making the contract (i.e., of adult age and mentally fit). If the party is an entity, the signer must be an authorized representative.

If performance of the agreement extends beyond a single transaction, the person's authority to act for the foreign company should be established additionally by a copy of a statement of capacity certified by a government official in that country. If the foreign company is a corporation or similar entity, authority to act should also be established by a corporate resolution of the company's governing body, such as its board of directors. The foreign company may require similar certified proof of authority from you. Your contract should describe documents that will be considered satisfactory evidence of authority.

INDEPENDENT COUNSEL

■ PROVISION:

INDEPENDENT LEGAL ADVICE. Each party acknowledges that it has been advised and has been given the opportunity to obtain independent advice regarding the legal, tax, and accounting issues and consequences of this Agreement. The parties further acknowledge that they have been given the opportunity to make their own separate judgments, and each is relying solely on its own review and that of its own advisors regarding the rights, obligations, liabilities, and consequences of this agreement.

COMMENT: International agreements are made between parties who are subject to different laws, and one party is often more sophisticated in business than the other party. For purposes of enforcing this Agreement, it is wise to include this provision to show that the parties are acting with due regard to their right to receive separate legal advice about their rights and obligations under the agreement.

LEGAL COSTS AND FEES

■ PROVISION:

COSTS AND ATTORNEYS' FEES. Costs and attorneys' fees may be sought by the prevailing party in a legal action if (1) either party to this Agreement is required to employ legal counsel, to incur other expenses to enforce any obligation of the other party, or to defend against any claim, demand, action, or proceeding because the other party fails to perform any obligation imposed by this Agreement; (2) a legal action is filed by or against a party to this Agreement; and (3) the action or its settlement establishes the default of the other party. In such event, the prevailing party is entitled to recover from the other party the amount of all reasonable attorneys' fees and all other expenses incurred in the enforcement or defense. These fees and expenses are recoverable regardless of whether they were incurred prior to, in preparation for, in contemplation of, during, or after the filing of the action.

COMMENTS: The law on the recoverability of legal costs and attorneys' fees varies from country to country. In some countries, the prevailing party is entitled to recover from the other party in most actions. In other countries, recovery is available only in certain types of actions, such as suits based on negligent, wrongful, or fraudulent conduct. The courts will usually enforce an express agreement for the recovery of legal costs and fees, even in the absence of a law that implies this right.

ACCEPTANCE AND EXECUTION

■ PROVISION:

ACCEPTANCE. To accept this offer, the Buyer must sign and return it without any modifications to the Seller, who must receive it no later than [*date*]. The Seller is entitled to revoke this offer at any time before receipt of acceptance.

Signed this [*date*]
By: [*signature of officer or agent*]
Seller/ [*title of seller's representative*] for Seller

Accepted on [*date*]
By: [*signature of officer or agent*]
Buyer/ [*title of buyer's representative*] for Buyer

COMMENT: If the terms of an offer specify the means for acceptance, the acceptance must be in compliance or no contract will arise. This provision requires acceptance without modification, which means that any modification by the "accepting" party will in fact result in a counteroffer.

The full name of each person who is signing the contract should be typed below his or her signature to avoid any question as to who represented each party to the transaction. For any party who is not an individual, the relationship of the party and the signer should be stated.

CHAPTER 5

Trade Terms and Incoterms

IN INTERNATIONAL BUSINESS transactions, you will use different methods of payment, and possibly different currencies, than you do in domestic transactions. In addition, while the terms of sale in international business often sound similar to those commonly used in domestic contracts, they often have different meanings in global transactions. Confusion over these terms can result in a lost sale or a financial loss on a sale. Thus, it is essential that you understand what terms you are agreeing to before you finalize the contract.

Incoterms 2000[1]

DEVELOPMENT OF INCOTERMS

By the 1920s, commercial traders had developed a set of trade terms to describe their rights and liabilities with regard to the transport of goods. These trade terms consisted of short abbreviations for lengthy contract provisions, and therefore they were commonly used for convenience. Unfortunately, there was no uniform interpretation of them in all countries, and therefore misunderstandings often arose in cross-border transactions.

To improve this aspect of international trade, the International Chamber of Commerce (ICC) developed rules for the interpretation of international commercial terms. First published in 1936, these rules have been periodically revised to account for changing modes of transport and document delivery, and they have become popularly known as *Incoterms*.

"Incoterms 2000" is a set of uniform rules codifying the interpretation of trade terms defining the rights and obligations of buyers and sellers in international transactions. Developed and issued by the International ICC, the current version is publication No. 560 from 2000.

USE OF INCOTERMS

Incoterms are not implied into contracts for the sale of goods. If you desire to use Incoterms, you must specifically include them in your contract. Further, your contract should expressly refer to the rules of interpretation as defined in the latest revision of Incoterms, for example, *Incoterms 2000*, and you should ensure the proper application of the terms by additional contract provisions. See Chapter 4: Drafting the International Contract for Sale of Goods and Chapter 6: Key Issues in International Sales Contracts.

Incoterms Do. . .

Incoterms 2000 may be included in an international sales contract if the parties desire the following:

1. To complete a sale of goods
2. To indicate each contracting party's obligations with regard to delivery of the goods as follows:
   a. When is the delivery completed?
   b. How does a party ensure that the other party has met that standard of conduct?
   c. Which party must comply with requisite licenses and other government-imposed formalities?
   d. What are the mode and terms of carriage?
   e. What are the delivery terms and what is required as proof of delivery?
   f. When is the risk of loss transferred from the seller to the buyer?
   g. How will transport costs be divided between the parties?
   h. What notices are the parties required to give to each other regarding the transport and transfer of the goods?
3. To establish basic terms of transport and delivery in a short format

Incoterms Do Not. . .

Incoterms 2000 are not sufficient on their own to express the full intent of the parties. These terms will not:

1. Apply to contracts for services
2. Define contractual rights and obligations other than for delivery
3. Specify details of the transfer, transport, and delivery of the goods
4. Determine how title to the goods will be transferred
5. Protect a party from his or her own risk of loss
6. Cover the goods before or after delivery is made
7. Define the remedies for breach of the contract

TIP: Incoterms can be quite useful, but their use has limitations. If you use them incorrectly, your contract may be ambiguous, if not impossible to perform. It is therefore important to understand the scope and purpose of Incoterms—when and why you might use them—before you rely on them to define such important terms as mode of delivery, customs clearance, passage of title, and transfer of risk.

Incoterms 2000

1. Ex Works (EXW)
2. Free Carrier (FCA)
3. Free Alongside Ship (FAS)
4. Free On Board (FOB)
5. Cost and Freight (CFR)
6. Cost, Insurance and Freight (CIF)
7. Carriage Paid To (CPT)
8. Carriage and Insurance Paid To (CIP)
9. Delivered At Frontier (DAF)
10. Delivered Ex Ship (DES)
11. Delivered Ex Quay (DEQ)
12. Delivered Duty Unpaid (DDU)
13. Delivered Duty Paid (DDP)

1) EX WORKS . . . [*NAMED PLACE*] (EXW)

In Ex Works, the seller/exporter/manufacturer merely makes the goods available to the buyer at the seller's "named place" of business. This trade term places the greatest responsibility on the buyer and minimum obligations on the seller.

The seller does not clear the goods for export and does not load the goods onto a truck or other transport vehicle at the named place of departure.

The parties to the transaction, however, may stipulate that the seller be responsible for the costs and risks of loading the goods onto a transport vehicle. Such a stipulation must be made within the contract of sale.

If the buyer cannot handle export formalities the Ex Works term should not be used. In such a case Free Carrier (FCA) is recommended. The Ex Works term is often used when making an initial quotation for the sale of goods. It represents the cost of the goods without any other costs included. Normal payment terms for Ex Works transactions are generally cash in advance and open account.

2) FREE CARRIER . . . [*NAMED PLACE*] (FCA)

In Free Carrier, the seller/exporter/manufacturer clears the goods for export and then delivers them to the carrier specified by the buyer at the named place.

If the named place is the seller's place of business, the seller is responsible for loading the goods onto the transport vehicle. If the named place is any other location, such as the loading dock of the carrier, the seller is not responsible for loading the goods onto the transport vehicle.

The Free Carrier term may be used for any mode of transport, including multimodal. The "named place" in Free Carrier and all "F" terms is domestic to the seller.

"Carrier" has a specific and somewhat expanded meaning. A carrier can be a shipping line, an airline, a trucking firm, or a railway. The carrier can also be an individual or firm who undertakes to procure carriage by any of the above methods of transport including multimodal. Therefore, a person, such as a freight forwarder, can act as a "carrier" under this term. In such a case, the buyer names the carrier or the individual who is to receive the goods.

The Free Carrier term is often used when making an initial quotation for the sale of goods. Normal payment terms for Free Carrier transactions are generally cash in advance and open account.

3) FREE ALONGSIDE SHIP . . . [*NAMED PORT OF SHIPMENT*] (FAS)

In Free Alongside Ship, the seller/exporter/manufacturer clears the goods for export and then places them alongside the vessel at the "named port of shipment." [The seller's clearing the goods for export is new to Incoterms 2000.]

The parties to the transaction, however, may stipulate in their contract of sale that the buyer will clear the goods for export.

The Free Alongside Ship term is used only for ocean or inland waterway transport.

The "named place" in Free Alongside Ship and all "F" terms is domestic to the seller. The Free Alongside Ship term is commonly used in the sale of bulk commodity cargo such as oil, grains, and ore. Normal payment terms for Free Carrier transactions are generally cash in advance and open account, but letters of credit are also used.

4) FREE ON BOARD . . . [*NAMED PORT OF SHIPMENT*] (FOB)

In Free On Board, the seller/exporter/manufacturer clears the goods for export and is responsible for the costs and risks of delivering the goods past the ship's rail at the named port of shipment. The Free On Board term is used only for ocean or inland waterway transport. The Free On Board term is used only for ocean or inland waterway transport. The "named place" in Free On Board and all "F" terms is domestic to the seller. Normal payment terms for Free On Board transactions include cash in advance, open account, and letters of credit.

The Free On Board term is commonly used in the sale of bulk commodity cargo such as oil, grains, and ore where passing the ship's rail is important. However, it is also commonly used in shipping container loads of other goods.

The key document in FOB transactions is the "On Board Bill of Lading."

Sellers and buyers often confuse the Free On Board term with Free Carrier. Free On Board (FOB) does not mean loading the goods onto a truck at the seller's place of business. Free On Board is used only in reference to delivering the goods past a ship's rail in ocean or inland waterway transport. Free Carrier, on the other hand, is applicable to all modes of transport.

5) COST AND FREIGHT . . . [*NAMED PORT OF DESTINATION*] (CFR)

In Cost and Freight, the seller/exporter/manufacturer clears the goods for export and is responsible for delivering the goods past the ship's rail at the port of shipment (not destination).

The seller is also responsible for paying for the costs associated with transport of the goods to the named port of destination. However, once the goods pass the ship's rail at the port of shipment, the buyer assumes responsibility for risk of loss or damage as well as any additional transport costs.

The Cost and Freight term is used only for ocean or inland waterway transport.

The "named port of destination" in Cost and Freight and all "C" terms is domestic to the buyer. Normal payment terms for Cost and Freight transactions include cash in advance, open account, and letters of credit.

The Cost and Freight term is commonly used in the sale of oversize and overweight cargo that will not fit into an ocean freight container or exceeds weight limitations of such containers. The term is also used for LCL (less than container load) cargo and for the shipment of goods by rail in boxcars to the ocean carrier.

6) COST, INSURANCE, FREIGHT . . . [*NAMED PORT OF DESTINATION*] (CIF)

In Cost, Insurance and Freight, the seller/exporter/manufacturer clears the goods for export and is responsible for delivering the goods past the ship's rail at the port of shipment (not destination).

The seller is responsible for paying for the costs associated with transport of the goods to the named port of destination. However, once the goods pass the ship's rail at the port of shipment, the buyer assumes responsibility for risk of loss or damage as well as any additional transport costs.

The seller is also responsible for procuring and paying for marine insurance in the buyer's name for the shipment. The Cost and Freight term is used only for ocean or inland waterway transport.

The "named port of destination" in Cost and Freight and all "C" terms is domestic to the buyer. Normal payment terms for Cost and Freight transactions include cash in advance, open account, and letters of credit.

7) CARRIAGE PAID TO . . . [*NAMED PLACE OF DESTINATION*] (CPT)

In Carriage Paid To, the seller/exporter/manufacturer clears the goods for export, delivers them to the carrier, and is responsible for paying for carriage to the named place of destination. However, once the seller delivers the goods to the carrier, the buyer becomes responsible for all additional costs.

In Incoterms 2000 the seller is also responsible for the costs of unloading, customs clearance, duties, and other costs if such costs are included in the cost of carriage such as in small package courier delivery. The seller is not responsible for procuring and paying for insurance cover. The CPT term is valid for any form of transport including multimodal The "named place of destination" in CPT and all "C" terms is domestic to the buyer, but is not necessarily the final delivery point.

The Carriage Paid To term is often used in sales where the shipment is by air freight, containerized ocean freight, courier shipments of small parcels, and in "ro-ro" (roll-on, roll-off) shipments of motor vehicles. A "carrier" can be a shipping line, airline, trucking firm, railway or also an individual or firm who undertakes to procure carriage by any of the above methods of transport including multimodal. Therefore, a person, such as a freight forwarder, can act as a "carrier" under this term. If subsequent carriers are used for the carriage to the agreed destination, the risk passes when the goods have been delivered to the first carrier.

8) CARRIAGE AND INSURANCE PAID TO . . . [*NAMED PLACE OF DESTINATION*] (CIP)

In Carriage and Insurance Paid To, the seller/exporter clears the goods for export, delivers them to the carrier, and is responsible for paying for carriage and insurance to the named place of destination. However, once the goods are delivered to the carrier, the buyer is responsible for all additional costs.

In Incoterms 2000 the seller is also responsible for the costs of unloading, customs clearance, duties, and other costs if such costs are included in the cost of carriage such as in small package courier delivery. The seller is responsible for procuring and paying for insurance cover. The CIP term is valid for any form of transport including multimodal The "named place of destination" in CIP and all "C" terms is domestic to the buyer, but is not necessarily the final delivery point.

The Carriage and Insurance Paid To term is often used in sales where the shipment is by air freight, containerized ocean freight, courier shipments of small parcels, and in "ro-ro" (roll-on, roll-off) shipments of motor vehicles.

A "carrier" can be a shipping line, airline, trucking firm, railway or also an individual or firm who undertakes to procure carriage by any of the above methods of transport including multimodal. Therefore, a person, such as a freight forwarder, can act as a "carrier" under this term. If subsequent carriers are used for the carriage to the agreed destination, the risk passes when the goods have been delivered to the first carrier.

9) DELIVERED AT FRONTIER . . . [*NAMED PLACE*] (DAF)

In Delivered At Frontier, the seller/exporter/manufacturer clears the goods for export and is responsible for making them available to the buyer at the named point and place at the frontier, not unloaded, and not cleared for import.

In the DAF term, naming the precise point, place, and time of availability at the frontier is very important as the buyer must make arrangements to unload and secure the goods in a timely manner. Frontier can mean any frontier including the frontier of export. The DAF term is valid for any mode of shipment, so long as the final shipment to the named place at the frontier is by land. The seller is not responsible for procuring and paying for insurance cover.

10) DELIVERED EX SHIP . . . [*NAMED PORT OF DESTINATION*] (DES)

In Delivered Ex Ship, the seller/exporter/manufacturer clears the goods for export and is responsible for making them available to the buyer on board the ship at the named port of destination, not cleared for import.

The seller is thus responsible for all costs of getting the goods to the named port of destination prior to unloading.

The DES term is used only for shipments of goods by ocean or inland waterway or by multimodal transport where the final delivery is made on a vessel at the named port of destination. All forms of payment are used in DES transactions.

11) DELIVERED EX QUAY . . . [*NAMED PORT OF DESTINATION*] (DEQ)

In Delivered Ex Quay, the seller/exporter/manufacturer clears the goods for export and is responsible for making them available to the buyer on the quay (wharf) at the named port of destination, not cleared for import.

The buyer, therefore, assumes all responsibilities for import clearance, duties, and other costs upon import as well as transport to the final destination. This is new for Incoterms 2000. The DES term is used only for shipments of goods arriving at the port of destination by ocean or by inland waterway. All forms of payment are used in DEQ transactions.

12) DELIVERED DUTY UNPAID . . . [*NAMED PLACE OF DESTINATION*] (DDU)

In Delivered Duty Unpaid, the seller/exporter/manufacturer clears the goods for export and is responsible for making them available to the buyer at the named place of destination, not cleared for import.

The seller, therefore, assumes all responsibilities for delivering the goods to the named place of destination, but the buyer assumes all responsibility for import clearance, duties, administrative costs, and any other costs upon import as well as transport to the final destination.

The DDU term can be used for any mode of transport. However, if the seller and buyer desire that delivery should take place on board a sea vessel or on a quay (wharf), the DES or DEQ terms are recommended. All forms of payment are used in DDU transactions. The DDU term is used when the named place of destination (point of delivery) is other than the seaport or airport.

13) DELIVERED DUTY PAID . . . [*NAMED PLACE OF DESTINATION*] (DDP)

In Delivered Duty Paid, the seller/exporter/manufacturer clears the goods for export and is responsible for making them available to the buyer at the named place of destination, cleared for import, but not unloaded from the transport vehicle. The seller, therefore, assumes all responsibilities for delivering the goods to the named place of destination, including all responsibility for import clearance, duties, and other costs payable upon import.

The DDP term can be used for any mode of transport. All forms of payment are used in DDP transactions. The DDP term is used when the named place of destination (point of delivery) is other than the seaport or airport.

For a book fully describing responsibilities of the seller and the buyer in each term, contact: ICC Publishing, Inc., 156 Fifth Avenue, New York, NY 10010; tel: [1] (212) 206-1150; fax: [1] (212) 633-6025, or the International Chamber of Commerce (ICC), 38, Cours Albert 1er, 75008 Paris, France; tel: [33] (1) 49-53-28-28; fax: [33] (1) 49-53-29-42.

Other Trade Terms

Incoterms are not the only trade terms in use in the world. In the US, for example, some firms still use the outdated Revised American Foreign Trade Definitions. Also, some industries have developed specialized trade terms to deal with issues specific to their commodity and industry (e.g., steel, grain). In other cases antiquated trade terms have survived for hundreds of years in regional trade.

Finally, some firms use supplimental terms in combination with Incoterms. This is an incorrect use of Incoterms and can present many problems for both the buyer and seller. For example, a contract may stipulate that Incoterms are to be used. However, there is no provision in Incoterms for use of supplimental terms. Also, many firms use supplimental terms that are in direct conflict with the formal definition of the Incoterm used.

One example of an incorrect use of a supplimental term added to an Incoterm is "FOB our warehouse." The contradiction is that FOB can only be used for ocean or inland waterway shipments of goods. We strongly suggest conformity with the formal definitions and use of Incoterms 2000.

Other trade terms that are in common use as abbreviated versions of lengthier contract provisions include:

ADDITIONAL SERVICES

Commonly used with Incoterm FOB port of shipment or DAF place, this term indicates that the seller will contract for carriage of the goods on usual terms and at the buyer's risk and expense. The seller might agree to this term when "liner service" is available from the seller's country or when the mode of transport will result in physical delivery of the goods after they cross the border of the buyer's country.

CLEARED FOR EXPORT

This term requires that the seller clear the goods for export when the goods are made available to the buyer before reaching the border. It is often used with Incoterm EXW or FAS.

CLEARED FOR IMPORT

If the buyer takes delivery before the goods reach customs, this term will nevertheless obligate the seller to clear the goods for import. It is often used with Incoterm DDU.

DUTY UNPAID

Sometimes used with Incoterm DEQ, this term obligates the seller to pay the costs of discharge exclusive of duties imposed.

DUTY UNPAID NOT CLEARED FOR IMPORT

This is the short-hand version for requiring the seller to pay the costs of discharge exclusive of duties and the costs of import clearance. It can be used with Incoterm DEQ.

EX DOCK OR EX QUAY

Pursuant to this term, the buyer takes title to the goods only after they are unloaded on the dock designated by the buyer.

EX FACTORY

Similar to Ex Works, this term changes the passage of risk slightly to require the buyer to take title to the goods after they leave the vendor's dock.

FOB VESSEL

For transport by sea, this term makes the seller responsible for all transportation costs to the vessel that the buyer designates and for costs of loading the goods onto the vessel. Risk of loss transfers to the buyer when the goods have been loaded. FCA is used for the same purpose and is not limited to a particular mode of transport.

FOR (FREE ON RAIL)

If transport is by rail, the parties may make the seller responsible for all transportation costs to the train that the buyer designates and for costs of loading the goods onto the train. Risk of loss transfers to the buyer when the goods are aboard. Many sellers use Incoterm FCA, which is used for the same purpose and which is not limited to a particular mode of transport.

FOT (FREE ON TRUCK)

A similar term to FOR, but FOT is used for truck transports. Many sellers use Incoterm FCA, which is used for the same purpose and which is not limited to a particular mode of transport.

FREIGHT COLLECT

By this term, the buyer is responsible for the payment of freight charges at the time the goods are delivered to the buyer, and risk of loss remains with the seller until that time.

FREIGHT PREPAID

This term means that the sales price quoted includes the costs of shipping to a named destination.

FREIGHT PREPAID AND CHARGED

Use of this term indicates that the sales price quoted includes the costs of shipping to a named destination, and the costs are charged by adding them to the invoice furnished to the buyer.

RELOADED ON CARRYING VEHICLE

If goods must be reloaded onto the carrier providing transport after the place of delivery, this term will require the seller to arrange and pay for reloading. It is often used with Incoterm DDP.

STOWED AND TRIMMED

Frequently used with Incoterm FOB, this term obligates the seller to load the goods on board the ship in the port of shipment. If you do not know the custom of the port where the goods are delivered and transferred to the buyer, you should specify which party will be responsible for payment of the loading costs and which will bear the risk of loss or damage. Thus, your contract term could expressly require "FOB stowed, costs and risks in connection with loading on the seller."

UNLOADED FROM ARRIVING VEHICLE

Pursuant to this term, the seller is responsible for unloading the goods at the place of delivery. It is most often added to Incoterm DDP.

VAT PAID

This is a short-hand term requiring the seller to pay the value added tax charged on importation of the goods. It is often used with Incoterm DDW.

VAT UNPAID

Often used with Incoterm DEQ, this term shifts the obligation to pay value added tax on importation of the goods from the seller to the buyer.

CHAPTER 6

Key Issues in International Sales Contracts

THERE ARE MANY ISSUES that need concern only one of the parties to a sales transaction, but a number of key issues must be taken into account by both parties. At first glance, the key issues may seem relevant to one party or the other only. However, the success of the entire transaction, as well as the profit for both parties, tend to hinge on these key issues. Regardless of whether you are the buyer or the seller, you must at the least become aware of export and import requirements, international payment methods, foreign exchange rules, intellectual property rights, and choice of governing law and jurisdiction.

Export Issues

When entering into a cross-border transaction, both parties must consider the issues related to exporting. These issues do not arise in purely domestic contracts and therefore are probably unfamiliar, especially to the first-time exporter. A party who has no understanding of these issues may well find that performance of the contract is impossible, or disadvantageous at best. Rather than renegotiate the terms of your contract later, you should take export issues into account up front.

ADAPTATIONS TO IMPORTING COUNTRY

The first issue to consider when exporting is whether your products will be acceptable in the foreign market. Before a product can be considered ready for export, the seller will have to ensure that the product is adapted for the market of the importing country. The costs of adaptation, whether to meet cultural preferences or regulatory laws, typically fall on the seller because a buyer is unlikely to make a deal unless the products can be used or sold in the buyer's country. Your contract may need to cover one or more of the following points.

■ COMPLIANCE WITH LAWS

Which party is obligated to adapt the goods such that they are in compliance with consumer laws, any other quality standard regulations, and environmental laws of the importing country?

The seller often agrees to provide goods that comply with the laws and regulations of the importing country so that the seller can ensure that the same standards of quality are maintained when the goods are adapted. However, if the seller is unfamiliar with the requirements, the contract may require the buyer to supply specifications sufficient to meet the requirements. If alterations are minimal, such as the addition of labels or stamps, the buyer may agree to make the changes because the cost is minor and the seller can then ship immediately.

■ MARKET ADAPTATIONS

Which party is obligated to adapt the goods to allow for local languages, cultural, or religious preferences; climatic differences; preferences for metric measurements; differences in electrical, water, wire, telephone, and other systems; and variations in the standard of living of the consumers?

The same considerations apply to adaptations of the goods to account for cultural, societal, and economic conditions as for government requirements.

If the buyer will be allowed to adapt the products, what protections will the seller have for its rights in patents, designs, trademarks, trade names, and other similar intellectual property associated with the products?

To the extent that the buyer is permitted to alter goods for sale in the importing country, the contract should expressly protect the seller's intellectual property rights. The fact that the contract permits alteration of the goods, packaging, or labeling by the buyer could be deemed a waiver of the right to exclusive ownership and use of the seller's intellectual property rights.

■ WARRANTIES

Will customer service or warranties be provided, and if so, how will reliable service be ensured?

Customer service and warranties are significant aspects of contracts. Whether selling high-tech machinery or consumer appliances, customer goodwill will be greatly enhanced if customer service is offered, but only so long as it is helpful to the customer. The contract should specify the extent to which warranties and customer service are available. If these benefits are to be provided through the buyer as a local representative for the seller in the importing country, the contract should further specify the standards to be met and other requirements for the protection of the seller's goodwill in the products.

GOVERNMENT REGULATIONS OF EXPORTING COUNTRY

It is wise to research the government requirements for exporting before formalizing the contract. The requirements will vary depending on the goods being exported, and you can simplify your contract terms if you provide for the requirements specific to the goods being exported. Many goods can be freely exported, others are subject to minimal regulation, while still others can be exported only if considerable restrictions are met. Some goods cannot be exported at all, and therefore a contract to export them will be impossible to perform and will be considered void or voidable.

As a contracting party, you need to know who will be responsible for complying with the government requirements for exporting the products from the seller's country. Your contract should identify whether you or the other party will be responsible for compliance and for the payment of costs. Depending on what your preliminary research has revealed, the terms of your contract should cover the following issues.

■ LICENSE PROCUREMENT

Which party will procure any necessary export licenses?

Typically, the seller is given this responsibility because the seller is likely to be the most familiar with the export requirements of his or her own country. However, the buyer may need to assist if the seller is unsophisticated or is financially unable to procure an export license.

■ LICENSE COSTS

Which party will pay for the export license?

If the export license is a one-time deal and must be obtained for each shipment exported, the cost of the license is usually negotiable between the parties. One party may agree to pay the cost as an incentive toward the foreign purchase. As another alternative, the parties may agree to share the cost. If the export license can be reused for more than one shipment, the cost is usually borne by the seller who will benefit from the reuse.

■ COMPLIANCE WITH EXPORT RESTRICTIONS

If the goods are subject to export restrictions—including packaging, labeling, marking, quarantine, fumigation, other pest control treatments, or inspections—which party will be responsible for making the arrangements?

The seller is usually responsible for arranging compliance with export restrictions or inspections because the seller is more familiar with the requirements, and compliance will often need the seller's cooperation in making the goods available.

■ COSTS OF COMPLYING WITH RESTRICTIONS

Which party will be obligated to pay the costs of complying with export restrictions or inspections?

There is no hard rule as to which party will pay the compliance costs. It is negotiable. If the export and import costs are comparable, the seller may pay for exporting and the buyer may pay for importing. If these costs are imbalanced, the parties may consider totaling the costs and splitting them. As another option, one party may pay all of the costs as part of the incentive for making the deal.

■ EXPORT FEES AND TAXES

Which party will be obligated to pay export duties or other government-imposed fees or taxes for exporting?

Again, there is no "typical" arrangement for payment. The same considerations apply for these exporting costs as for the costs of complying with export restrictions or inspections.

RISK OF DELAY OR FAILURE

An extremely important export issue that is often neglected in international contracts is the risk involved if export requirements are not met, whether timely or at all. Both parties are at risk if the export fails—the seller may have to absorb costs for in preparing the goods for export, shipment, and sale overseas, and the buyer may have to assume amounts spent in presale promotion, importing and receiving arrangements, and consumer sale compliance, unless the buyer can obtain replacement goods, often at additional cost. If the export is delayed, both parties are likely to incur additional labor, storage, shipping, and other costs.

The issue of failure or delay in exporting is made more complex by the question of fault. Did the seller use the wrong labels? Did the buyer change the order just before shipment? Was the failure or delay caused by factors beyond the control of either party? In international contracts, there is a significant political risk involved. Governments and economies are intertwined, and the right to export is therefore dependent on the relationships between the governments of the exporting and importing countries. Your contract should anticipate the risks involved and should establish the rights and obligations of the parties accordingly. Be sure to consider provisions for the following issues.

■ TIMELINESS

What is considered a "timely" export?

Your contract should provide a time for export or a means for determining that time. If no time is provided, a reasonable time may be implied, but "reasonableness" is a subjective standard that may result in a dispute because one party is dissatisfied with the other's choice of a "reasonable" time. Moreover, if a reasonable time is implied by a court, both parties may be dissatisfied by the court's opinion of reasonableness.

■ DEFAULT

If failure or delay in exporting is caused by one party, what will be that party's obligations and what will be the other party's rights?

Most contracts take a hard approach to a failure or delay in exporting caused by one party: it is usually a ground for termination of the contract, and the party at fault owes damages, actual or liquidated, to the other party. The hard approach may be softened a bit by requiring the party not at fault to mitigate the damages by taking reasonable steps, such as by diligently seeking a replacement sale or purchase. Assuming that the parties would rather complete the sale than negate the transaction, most contracts also give the party at fault a short extension of time within which to rectify the problem and to complete the contract, perhaps with a comparable allowance for costs caused by the delay.

■ GOVERNMENT INTERFERENCE

What will be the rights and obligations of the parties if, before the goods clear customs, there is a sudden change in export laws such that performance of the contract becomes overly burdensome on one party or impossible?

The effect of uncontrollable factors is commonly covered in a contract provision known as a *force majeure clause*. However, a force majeure clause usually provides for termination of the contract if performance becomes impossible because of natural catastrophies. If man-made events cause performance to become more burdensome (for example because export duties are imposed or increased) or impossible but only for an unknown time (for example, because trade sanctions are imposed by the government), the parties may still want to complete the contract—in which event they should provide for renegotiation or termination only if export remains impossible after a certain period has elapsed.

Exporting Around the World

Most countries favor exports, since foreign capital flows into the exporting country. The following sampling of countries illustrates some of the common restrictions on exports generally and certain goods in particular. For any one country, you can learn the export requirements from various sources, such as government agencies that regulate the country's trade or customs, shippers, freight brokers, international business lawyers, and books on trading worldwide or with the particular country of interest.

ARGENTINA

- CONTROLS: Minimal export controls are imposed and documentary requirements have been simplified. Exporters must register. Export subsidiaries are available.

AUSTRALIA

- CONTROLS: Approximately 40 percent of exports are subject to restrictions. Controls include permits, licenses, and export clearance numbers.
- GOODS SUBJECT TO SPECIFIC CONTROLS: Food, animals, plants, exports to Libya and Iraq, and protected wildlife and cultural goods.

BELGIUM

- CONTROLS: The European Union export control and tax scheme applies. Minimal documentation is required for exports to EU countries; complete documentation is required for exports to non-EU countries. Exports are actively promoted, although no direct export subsidies are offered.
- GOODS SUBJECT TO SPECIFIC CONTROLS: Weapons.

BRAZIL

- CONTROLS: Export licenses are required. Quotas and other controls are applied to some commodities.
- GOODS SUBJECT TO SPECIFIC CONTROLS: Coffee, timber, and some other commodities.

BULGARIA

- CONTROLS: Export licenses are required for some products. A customs tax is imposed on exports. The government sets base export pricing for live animals, meat, dairy products, and striped sunflower seeds.
- GOODS SUBJECT TO SPECIFIC CONTROLS: Pharmaceuticals, tobacco, explosives and other dangerous substances, and precious metals.
- PROHIBITED EXPORTS: Crude oil, raw cattle hides, vegetable oils, motor petrol, gas oil for engine and industrial application, fuel oil, and raw materials with strategic importance for domestic industries.

CANADA

- CONTROLS: Export permits are required for a few goods, depending on supply and distribution within Canada. Products on the Export Control List require permits for export. Permits are also required before exporting to certain countries, as listed on the Area Control List.
- GOODS SUBJECT TO SPECIFIC CONTROLS: Products of wood and other natural resources.

CHINA

- CONTROLS: Exporters and foreign trade corporations (FTCs) must be authorized and licensed by a government ministry. Export policies have been liberalized, but controls remain in effect. Restrictions on exports vary depending on shortages in China and may include prohibitions or quotas. Approvals for restricted exports may have to be sought from multiple local and state authorities.
- GOODS SUBJECT TO SPECIFIC CONTROLS: Goods that threaten national security or public interest, cultural relics, wild animals, plants and plant products, and textiles.

EGYPT

- GOODS SUBJECT TO SPECIFIC CONTROLS: Scrap metal, hide, alpaca fibers, and metal and agricultural commodities.

FINLAND

- CONTROLS: Export controls are in line with the European Union. Most exports require no license.
- GOODS SUBJECT TO SPECIFIC CONTROLS: High technology goods and scrap metal.

GERMANY

- CONTROLS: Export licenses are not required, and customs procedures are relatively efficient.

GREECE

- CONTROLS: Few export controls exist. Exports are encouraged and subsidies are available, particularly for agricultural products.

INDIA

- CONTROLS: Exports are handled through export houses, trading houses, and star trading houses depending on the value of the goods. Documentation is complicated and customs procedures vary at each port. Export subsidies are available for certain products.

ISRAEL

- CONTROLS: Few controls exist on exports. Licenses are required for internationally controlled substances and goods considered to threaten national security. Export proceeds must be received within one year of the export date. Some exports must have certificates of origin.

ITALY

- CONTROLS: Most goods can be exported under a general license that does not require formal approval.
- GOODS SUBJECT TO SPECIFIC CONTROLS: Gas products and high-tech products.

JAPAN

- CONTROLS: Most exports are handled by large trading companies. Export licenses are required for some products. Most export restrictions are adopted in response to pressure from Japan's trading partners to address balance of payment problems with Japan.

MALAYSIA

- CONTROLS: Export licenses are required for only a few sectors. Incentives are offered for import of raw materials, machinery, and equipment used for the production of exports. Export subsidies are also available.
- GOODS SUBJECT TO SPECIFIC CONTROLS: Textiles, rubber, petroleum, pepper, palm oil, and tin.

MEXICO

- CONTROLS: Most exports do not require permits or licenses. A permit may be required for goods that must meet safety standards, that must comply with international conventions, or are important to state security.

PAKISTAN

- CONTROLS: Most goods can be exported freely, but some are subject to export quotas and some are prohibited because of shortages in the country. Exporters must be registered with Ministry of Commerce.
- GOODS SUBJECT TO SPECIFIC CONTROLS: Rice, cotton, surgical instruments, cinematographic film, exotic captive birds, horses, wheat flour, bran, soda, and dry red chilies.

PHILIPPINES

- CONTROLS: Exports are encouraged and procedures have been simplified. There are few export controls. Subsidies are available.

RUSSIA

- CONTROLS: Export duties ranging up to 30 percent are levied on various goods. Some goods require export licenses, particularly those that are considered a threat to national security.
- CONTROLS ON SPECIFIC GOODS: Commodities, weapons, military equipment, dual-use materials, and technology.

SOUTH AFRICA

- CONTROLS: Incentives in the form of tax benefits and other privileges are significant for exporters.

SOUTH KOREA

- CONTROLS: Parties who wish to export must register with the Ministry of Trade and Industry and must obtain a license. Most exporting is accomplished through general trading companies known as *chaebol*. The export of some goods requires approval of various ministries or industry associations. Product inspection may be required.

SPAIN

- CONTROLS: Certificates and licenses are required for a few products, but most goods can be freely exported. Some exports are subject to statistical control and require the submission of notices of export.
- GOODS SUBJECT TO SPECIFIC CONTROLS: Pharmaceuticals, illicit drugs, explosives, firearms, weapons, defense equipment and materials, tobacco, and gambling materials.

TAIWAN

- CONTROLS: The export process is being liberalized, and it is particularly efficient in the export processing zones. Approximately 70 percent of products that can be exported require no export license. Exporters must register before engaging in a trading business.

UNITED KINGDOM

- CONTROLS: Export controls are minimal. Preferences are given to traders within the European Union.
- GOODS SUBJECT TO SPECIFIC CONTROLS: Antiques, metal wastes.

UNITED STATES

- CONTROLS: Most goods can be exported without formal approval. Some goods require special licenses, primarily those that could be a threat to national security or that are in short supply within the country.
- GOODS SUBJECT TO SPECIFIC CONTROLS: Weapons, high-tech products, strategic goods.

Import Issues

All countries process imports, and the requirements vary from country to country. International traders must consider the import process as part of their transaction. Before goods can pass through customs, a trader will probably need to file proof of source and destination, to complete entry certificates and other forms, and to satisfy local customs officials that the goods meet the regulatory laws of the importing country. The trader may also have to pay fees and taxes. If international traders fail to understand and account for importing issues they may well find that performance of the contract is impossible or disadvantageous at best. It is best to cover import issues in your initial contract so you do not have to renegotiate and amend the contract later.

GOVERNMENT REGULATION OF IMPORTS

Most countries regulate their imports more rigorously than their exports. The encouragement of imports will indirectly improve a country's economy by vitalizing the economies of other countries, which in turn can lead to increased demand for exports among all countries. Countries tend to be more concerned with the direct impact of imports on their domestic economy. Regulation of imports is considered an essential means of protecting domestic industries from destruction by sales of more competitive foreign-made products and of ensuring that more revenue from exports is flowing into the country than is flowing out from imports.

Your contract may contain a vague clause requiring one party to comply with all import requirements, but you may find that the burden imposed on a party by such a clause far outweighs the benefit of the contract. Therefore, it is advisable to determine in advance of making the contract exactly what import regulations will be applicable to the specific goods you are trading. If import regulations are minimal, a vague clause may suffice. However, if there are heavy import restrictions, the cross-border sale may be feasible only if the parties negotiate to share the burden of compliance.

Both the buyer and seller should verify that the contract clearly expresses their intentions with respect to compliance with import requirements. Your contract should identify which party must meet the import regulations and which will pay the duties, taxes, fees, and other costs involved. The terms of your contract should reflect your research into the import requirements for the goods that you are selling or buying. You should consider terms to cover the following issues.

■ LICENSE PROCUREMENT

Which party will procure the necessary import licenses?

Typically, the buyer is responsible because the buyer is likely to be the most familiar with the import requirements of his or her own country. If more than one license is required, such as one for trading and one for each transaction, you should make the clause more specific to refer to licenses for import trading and for the import transaction.

■ LICENSE COSTS

Which party will pay for the import license(s)?

If the import license is a one-time deal and must be obtained for each shipment imported, the cost of the license is usually negotiable between the parties. One party may agree to pay the cost as an incentive toward the foreign purchase. As another alternative, the parties may agree to share the cost. If an import license authorizes the importer to trade in imports for a fixed time and covers all shipments within that time, the cost is usually borne by the buyer, who will benefit from the reuse.

■ COMPLIANCE WITH IMPORT RESTRICTIONS

If the goods are subject to import restrictions—including packaging, labeling, marking, quarantine, fumigation, other pest control treatments, or inspections—which party will be responsible for making the arrangements?

There is no set custom with regard to which party will be obligated to comply with import restrictions or inspections. Often, the buyer will make the arrangements because the buyer is more familiar with the requirements. However, the goods generally have to be prepared for import clearance at the time they are shipped by the seller, in which case the seller will make the arrangements. The seller may want to require in the contract that the buyer is responsible for informing the seller of all necessary arrangements to meet import regulations.

■ COSTS OF COMPLYING WITH RESTRICTIONS

Which party will be obligated to pay the costs of complying with import restrictions or inspections?

Again, there is no customary practice as to which party will pay the compliance costs. It is negotiable. If the import and export costs are comparable, the seller may pay for exporting and the buyer may pay for importing. If these costs are very unequal, the parties may consider totaling the costs and splitting them. As another option, one party may pay all of the costs as an incentive for making the deal.

■ IMPORT FEES AND TAXES

Which party will be obligated to pay import duties or other government-imposed fees or taxes for importing?

The import duties and fees can be substantial because most countries impose tariffs, VAT taxes, customs processing fees, and other taxes, often based on the value of the goods imported. No "typical" arrangement is customary for payment. The same considerations apply for importing costs as for the costs of complying with import restrictions or inspections.

■ CUSTOMS REGULATIONS

Which party will provide the necessary import documentation for purposes of valuing the goods, meeting statistical requirements, and otherwise complying with customs regulations for clearance?

Import documentation, including the papers required to establish valuation for purposes of taxation, is often complex and should be completed by persons familiar with the process to ensure an efficient import. The parties should agree which of them will be responsible for complying with these requirements.

RISK OF DELAY OR FAILURE

All international contracts carry the risk that import requirements will not be met—whether timely or at all. Both parties are at risk if the import fails—the seller may have to absorb costs for preparing the goods for export, shipment, and sale overseas, and the buyer may have to assume amounts spent in presale promotion, importing and receiving arrangements, and consumer sale compliance unless they can obtain replacement goods, often at additional cost. A delay in clearing customs of the importing country is likely to cause both parties to incur additional labor, storage, shipping, and other costs.

The issue of failure or delay in importing is made more complex by the question of fault. Did the seller use the wrong labels? Did the buyer change the order just before shipment? Was the failure or delay caused by factors beyond the control of either party? In international contracts, there is a significant political risk involved. Governments and economies are intertwined, and the right to import is therefore dependent on the relationships between the governments of the exporting and importing countries. Your contract should anticipate the risks involved and should establish the rights and obligations of the parties accordingly. Be sure to consider provisions for the following items.

■ TIMELINESS

What is considered a "timely" import?

Your contract should provide a time for import or a means for determining that time. If no time is provided, a reasonable time may be implied, but "reasonableness" is a subjective standard that may result in a dispute when one party is dissatisfied with the other's choice of a "reasonable" time. Moreover, if a reasonable time is implied by a court, both parties may be dissatisfied by the court's opinion of reasonableness.

■ DEFAULT

If failure or delay in importing is caused by one party, what will be that party's obligations and what will be the other party's rights?

Most contracts take a hard approach to a failure or delay in importing caused by one party: it is usually a ground for termination of the contract and the party at fault owes damages, actual or liquidated, to the other party. The hard approach may be softened a bit by requiring the party not at fault to mitigate the damages by taking reasonable steps—such as by diligently seeking a replacement sale or purchase. Assuming that the parties would rather complete the sale than negate the transaction, most contracts also give a party at fault a short extension of time within which to rectify the problem and to complete the contract, perhaps with a comparable allowance for costs caused by the delay.

■ GOVERNMENT INTERFERENCE

What will be the rights and obligations of the parties if, before the goods clear customs, there is a sudden change in import laws such that performance of the contract becomes overly burdensome on one party or impossible?

The effect of uncontrollable factors is commonly covered in a contract provision known as a *force majeure clause*. However, a force majeure clause usually provides for termination of the contract if performance becomes impossible because of natural causes. If man-made events cause performance to become more burdensome (for example because import duties are imposed or increased) or impossible but only for an unknown time (for example because trade sanctions are imposed by the government), the parties may still want to complete the contract—in which event they should provide for renegotiation or termination only if import remains impossible after a certain period has elapsed.

Importing Around the World

Governments control imports more rigorously than exports, primarily in an effort to stem the flow of domestic capital into foreign countries and to protect domestic industries from what is considered unfair competition by foreign producers with access to cheaper labor and better technology. The following are simply illustrative of some of the import controls that you might encounter when trading on any of the world's continents. To learn about the import controls of a certain country, you should seek assistance from the government agency in charge of trade or imports for that country, shippers, freight forwarders or customs brokers, or international trade lawyers.

ARGENTINA

- CONTROLS: Temporary quotas are imposed on some imports and government approvals are required for a few types of products. Documentary procedures have been simplified, and licenses are not required for most imports.
- GOODS SUBJECT TO SPECIFIC CONTROLS: Automobiles, paper, pulp, pharmaceuticals, foodstuffs, and defense materials.

AUSTRALIA

- CONTROLS: Tariffs are imposed on certain goods, including manufactured goods. Import quotas are in effect only for a few products. Certain types of products must meet government standards before being imported.
- GOODS SUBJECT TO SPECIFIC CONTROLS: Manufactured goods, textiles, automotive products, cheese and curd, drugs, weapons, heritage items, cordless telephones, CB radios, food, plants, animals, and protected wildlife.

BELGIUM

- CONTROLS: The European Union common external tariff applies to goods imported from non-EU countries. Imports are subject to VAT tax. Certain goods and products from certain countries may be imported only with a license. Quotas are also imposed on some imports.
- GOODS SUBJECT TO SPECIFIC CONTROLS: Strategic goods.

BRAZIL

- CONTROLS: Import duties, taxes, and fees are charged, and permits are required for nearly all imports.
- GOODS SUBJECT TO SPECIFIC CONTROLS: Used materials, computer software, petroleum products, arms and ammunition, soft drinks, flammables, airplanes, dangerous substances, chlorinated pesticides, insecticides, agricultural chemicals, and animal foodstuffs.

BULGARIA

- CONTROLS: Imports are subject to duties and VAT taxes. A limited number of products require import permits. Certain items must meet product standards set by the government.
- GOODS SUBJECT TO SPECIFIC CONTROLS: Agricultural goods, pharmaceuticals, nuclear materials, weapons, precious metals, and electrical appliances.

CANADA

- CONTROLS: Most imports are subject to a VAT tax. No license is required for most imports, but some are subject to restriction and can be imported only after obtaining a permit or certificate.
- GOODS SUBJECT TO SPECIFIC CONTROLS: Alcoholic beverages, food products, clothing, drugs, medical devices, hazardous products, certain weapons and firearms, endangered species, and motor vehicles.
- PROHIBITED IMPORTS: Oleomargarine, reprints of Canadian copyrighted works, and certain game birds.

CHINA

- CONTROLS: Licenses are required for many product categories, although licenses are being phased out. Duties and taxes are imposed on imports, and some imports require approval of local and central government authorities.
- GOODS SUBJECT TO SPECIFIC CONTROLS: Consumer goods, raw materials, production equipment.

EGYPT

- CONTROLS: Except for commodities specifically banned, all goods are freely imported. Tariffs are imposed on imports, but they are being reduced.
- GOODS SUBJECT TO SPECIFIC CONTROLS: Certain textile and apparel goods.

FINLAND

- CONTROLS: Many goods are subject to import duties and taxes. Permits or licenses are required for only a few items and for imports from Taiwan and North Korea.
- GOODS SUBJECT TO SPECIFIC CONTROLS: Cars, motorcycles, tobacco, candy, beer and other alcoholic beverages, sugar, fertilizers, live animals, and animal products.
- PROHIBITED IMPORTS: PCB and PCT chemicals, alcoholic beverages containing 60 percent or more alcohol, home wine manufacturing kits, whale meat, and certain halogenated derivatives.

GERMANY

- CONTROLS: Safety standards are zealously enforced, and testing and certification are required for many products. No licenses are required, but tariffs are imposed on many goods.

GREECE

- CONTROLS: Imports from European Union countries are duty-free. Other goods are subject to the EU common external tariff. Quotas are applied to some products from low-cost countries, and special approval of government agencies is required for a few imports.
- GOODS SUBJECT TO SPECIFIC CONTROLS: Raw materials, textiles, agricultural products, and pharmaceuticals.
- PROHIBITED IMPORTS: Firearms, weapons, and illegal drugs.

INDIA

- CONTROLS: Tariffs and excise taxes are imposed on goods. A large number of imports require licenses. Customs procedures are complex and vary from port to port. Some commodity imports must be channeled through public sector companies.
- GOODS SUBJECT TO SPECIFIC CONTROLS: Consumer goods, seeds, plants, animals, insecticides, pesticides, electronics, chemicals, pharmaceuticals, petroleum products, and bulk agricultural products.
- PROHIBITED IMPORTS: Addictive drugs, weapons, explosives, ivory, animal fats, and some apparel and fabric items.

ISRAEL

- CONTROLS: Tariffs, VAT taxes, and luxury taxes are imposed on various imports. Licenses and quotas are imposed, primarily for food and agricultural products.
- GOODS SUBJECT TO SPECIFIC CONTROLS: Automobiles, consumer electronics, wine, other alcoholic beverages, food, agricultural products, fresh fruit, and vegetables.

- PROHIBITED IMPORTS: Certain agricultural products and items that threaten national security or public morals, or human, animal or plant health.

ITALY

- CONTROLS: Tariffs follow the European Union requirements, and stamp and administrative taxes may be levied. A few goods require licenses or are restricted by quotas.
- GOODS SUBJECT TO SPECIFIC CONTROLS: Apparel and textile products, arms and munitions, agricultural products, gas products, high-tech products.
- PROHIBITED IMPORTS: Foodstuffs, food colorings, drugs, narcotics, animal products, plants, seed grains, alcohol, cosmetics, and toiletries.

JAPAN

- CONTROLS: Large trading companies handle the imports, which are largely unrestricted. Licenses are required for only a few products. Tariffs are applied to some products, and quotas limit certain goods, primarily agricultural commodities.
- GOODS SUBJECT TO SPECIFIC CONTROLS: Agricultural commodities.

MALAYSIA

- CONTROLS: A few imports require permits, and many are subject to duties. Quotas exist for certain products, and technical licenses are necessary for a few items.
- GOODS SUBJECT TO SPECIFIC CONTROLS: Arms, explosives, motor vehicles, dangerous drugs, chemicals, plants, soil, tin ore, slag or concentrates, certain essential foodstuffs, plastic resins, tobacco, and rice.

MEXICO

- CONTROLS: Most imports are subject to tariffs, and a few require an import license. Import quotas and permits are applied in trade sensitive areas. Government quality and safety standards must be met.
- GOODS SUBJECT TO SPECIFIC CONTROLS: Agricultural goods, petrochemicals, footwear, vehicles, electronic equipment, household appliances, and medical instruments.

PAKISTAN

- CONTROLS: Duties and taxes are imposed on imports.

PHILIPPINES

- CONTROLS: Quotas and licensing are imposed on some goods. Tariffs and VAT taxes are applied to many imports.
- GOODS SUBJECT TO SPECIFIC CONTROLS: Corn, corn substitutes, hogs, pork products, meat, meat products, rice, coconut oil, sugar, fruits, liquor, wines, processed fruits and vegetables, snack foods, tobacco, candy, and leather goods.
- PROHIBITED IMPORTS: Dynamite; gunpowder; ammunition; explosives; firearms; weapons; written or printed articles advocating or inciting treason, rebellion, insurrection, deception, or subversion; obscene or immoral articles; negatives or film; items for production of unlawful abortion; gambling items; gold; silver; other precious metals; misbranded food products; and narcotics, marijuana, and opium.

RUSSIA

- CONTROLS: Import licenses are required for dangerous or hazardous items. Tariffs and VAT taxes are imposed on most goods.
- GOODS SUBJECT TO SPECIFIC CONTROLS: Combat and sporting weapons; self-defense articles; explosives; military and ciphering equipment; radioactive materials and waste; poisons; narcotics; precious metal alloys; precious stones; alcohol; cigarettes; and automobiles.

SOUTH AFRICA

- CONTROLS: Many goods enter duty-free, but a VAT is payable on nearly all imports. Some products require import permits.
- GOODS SUBJECT TO SPECIFIC CONTROLS: Beverages, tobacco, mineral waters, petroleum products, motor vehicles, office machinery, photographic film, cosmetics, home entertainment products, motorcycles, automobiles, consumer goods, wood, paper, and motor and aviation fuels.

SOUTH KOREA

- CONTROLS: Parties who wish to import must register with the Ministry of Trade and Industry and must obtain a license. A license is also required for each transaction. If items are not restricted, the import license is automatically granted. Tariffs are imposed on many products.

SPAIN

- CONTROLS: Licenses are required for importing, and they are valid for six months at a time. Quotas and tariffs are in place to control imports.

TAIWAN

- CONTROLS: Importers must be registered. Tariffs and various taxes are imposed on imports, and some goods require certifications for import.
- GOODS SUBJECT TO SPECIFIC CONTROLS: Agricultural goods, cosmetics, medical equipment, spirits, tobacco, and toxic chemicals.

UNITED KINGDOM

- CONTROLS: European Union common external tariffs are followed, and a VAT tax is imposed on most goods. A few goods require import licenses. Product standards must be met, including labeling requirements.
- GOODS SUBJECT TO SPECIFIC CONTROLS: Textiles, electronic products, firearms, explosives, and controlled drugs.
- PROHIBITED IMPORTS: AM citizen band radios; devices that project toxic, noxious, or harmful substances; counterfeit currency; and certain pornography.

UNITED STATES

- CONTROLS: Imports are restricted if the items could adversely affect the US economy, security, consumer health and well-being, or domestic plant and animal life. Quotas and tariffs are imposed, and a few products require import licenses.
- GOODS SUBJECT TO SPECIFIC CONTROLS: Arms, ammunition, alcoholic beverages, food, dairy products, vehicles, textiles, and toys.

International Payments and Foreign Exchange

In cross-border trading, it is essential to have a working knowledge of the issues surrounding payment of the purchase price. When trading domestically, the buyer and seller will use the same currency, will be subject to the same or at least similar accounting and tax systems, and will be able to seek redress for nonpayment locally by familiar legal means. These advantages are not available in overseas transactions.

To do business successfully, a cross-border trader must know basic international accounting and taxation principles, including accounting for international transactions, translation of income, and consolidation of financial sheets. You must be able to figure currency exchange exposure into your bottom line operating expectations, and you will need to consider specific currency exchange regulations for the importing and exporting countries. Delays in payment and the security of the method of payment must also be taken into account. If all of these terms seem incomprehensible, your best course of action is to find a reliable team of bankers, accountants, and tax experts. See *A Short Course in International Payments*, also by World Trade Press.

Your contract terms on international payment and foreign exchange will vary depending on the countries involved and your history with other traders. The contract should be relatively more complex if you believe that you need complete protection. Less complex clauses may be satisfactory if the contract term is short, the currencies involved are stable, and the other trader has proven to be reliable in making payments. Both buyer and seller should consider the following issues when drafting their contract.

METHOD OF PAYMENT

By what method will payment be made?

Payment should usually be made by a method that is considered secure by the parties. If the buyer has paid regularly in past transactions, an open account may be satisfactorily secure. If not, then the seller should insist on another method. The four basic methods of payment in international transactions are prepayment (including cash on delivery), documentary letter of credit, documentary collection or draft, and open account or other terms.

If you chose to offer terms of payment after delivery is made, you must consider the difficulties inherent in overseas transactions despite what should be the fast-moving world of international banking. Allowing for payment within 15 or 30 days may be common in domestic transactions, but 45, 60, and even 90 days is not uncommon when the transaction stretches across borders. When setting the payment method and terms, be certain to consider whether the buyer will need to obtain government approvals or will be able to obtain at minimal cost the payment instrument from a financial institution in the buyer's country.

CURRENCY

In what currency will payment be made?

International trading is made more complex by the use of different currencies. The relative value of different currencies is constantly changing, and some are more volatile than others. There is a risk that a foreign currency could devalue before a transaction is complete, in which case a seller would receive less money than expected. There is also the chance that the currency could increase in value, giving extra profits. Although a seller often prefers payment in the currency of his or her own country, the seller should also consider which currency is more stable and relatively stronger.

The question of which currency to use for payment is further complicated by foreign exchange and investment controls. National governments often impose these controls to limit, and even to prohibit, the movement of currency in and out of their countries. If possible, you should choose a currency that is relatively free from these controls so that the payment you receive is readily convertible into your country's own currency. Parties often agree to use the currency of the seller's country or of a major trading country—such as US dollars, English pounds, or Swiss francs—which tends to be freely convertible and relatively stable.

If the available currencies are not to your liking, you may consider a more complicated arrangement, such as payment in a unit of account (such as a special drawing right (SDR), which consists of several currencies so that increases in some balance decreases in the others) or use of a factor (such as a factoring house, which buys title to the accounts receivable on a discounted basis). A riskier arrangement would be the use of forward and options contracts in a process known as hedging. None of these alternatives are for the financially weak at heart, and it is wise to seek the counsel of financial advisors for all of them.

IMPOSSIBILITY OF PERFORMANCE

If payment becomes impossible or overly burdensome on one party, what remedies will be allowed?

There is always a risk that a reasonable price will become extremely unfair because of a change in government-imposed restrictions, a significant devaluation of currency, a stock market crash, or other similar circumstances that are beyond the control of the parties. Your contract should anticipate such events, no matter how unlikely. It is common for contracts to provide for termination or renegotiation of the terms.

WARRANTIES

After payment has been made in full, will the seller nevertheless offer further incentives to the buyer? Is the buyer entitled to a refund, replacement, or other warranty of quality and quantity, and if so on what terms?

The issue of returns, refunds, and warranties should be considered in connection with the payment of the purchase price in an international contract. By offering these incentives, the seller may be able to obtain the most secure method of payment—cash in advance or on delivery. In general, if you trust the quality of your goods and services, the trade off for secure payment is worth the cost of customer service and a few returns. Moreover, these incentives tend to build your goodwill and reputation, bring more business and more profits.

PAYMENTS ROUND THE WORLD

STABLE CURRENCIES

The countries with the reputation of having the most stable currencies in the world are Brunei, England, France, Germany, Hong Kong, Japan, Singapore, Switzerland, and the United States.

COUNTRIES WITHOUT FOREIGN EXCHANGE REQUIREMENTS

Countries that do not impose foreign exchange requirements on imports and exports at present include the following: Argentina, Australia, Austria, Bahamas, Bahrain, Belgium, Bermuda, Brazil, Brunei, Bulgaria, Canada, Denmark, Ecuador, Egypt, Estonia, Finland, France, Georgia, Germany, Greece, Guatemala, Honduras, Hong Kong S.A.R., Hungary, Iceland, Ireland, Indonesia, Italy, Jamaica, Japan, Kenya, Kuwait, Latvia, Lebanon, Liechtenstein, Lithuania, Luxembourg, Macau, Malaysia, Malta, Mauritius, Mexico, Morocco, Nepal, The Netherlands, New Zealand, Norway, Oman, Panama, Paraguay, Peru, Philippines, Portugal, Saudi Arabia, Singapore, South Africa, South Korea, Spain, Sweden, Switzerland, Taiwan, Trinidad and Tobago, Tunisia, Turkey, Ukraine, United Arab Emirates, United Kingdom, Uruguay, and Venezuela.

COUNTRIES WITH RESTRICTIONS

- ALGERIA Import payments are made through an Algerian domiciled bank, so take into account possible delays for approvals and red tape.

- BAHAMAS Payments exceeding B$100,000 for imports require approval.

- CHINA Chinese currency cannot be taken out of China and domestic banks may issue foreign exchange to traders only on presentation of valid documents, such as import licenses, contracts, and bids. Be certain documentation and approvals are completed before shipment.

- COLOMBIA Nationals may hold foreign exchange accounts abroad. This arrangement could avoid delays in payment due to domestic foreign exchange restrictions.

- CYPRUS Residents are subject to exchange control restrictions, advance payments for imports must be approved by the Central Bank, and other payments must be made within 200 days of shipment. The custom is to be paid on a collection basis.

- EL SALVADOR Obligations in El Salvador must be paid in national currency, but international obligations payable in or out of the country may be made in currency agreed to by the parties. Residents or nonresidents may maintain local accounts in foreign currencies with authorized banks.

- GABON Payments can be freely made with France, Monaco, former French colonies, and Operations Account countries (nations in Central Africa). If you are outside these zones, exchange controls apply and you should seek a secure payment method.

- INDIA Foreign exchange is freely available for imports of goods or services, but payments for other purposes require approval of the Reserve Bank. Payments for exports must be made within a time and by the manner prescribed by the Reserve Bank. You should plan for lengthy collection terms, and insistence on advance payment could lose you a sale.

- ISRAEL Foreign currency is available for routine trade transactions, but residents must obtain a permit to transfer capital abroad.
- NICARAGUA Customs will not release exports until a guarantee is given for securing payment if it is in a foreign currency.
- RUSSIA (CIS) Rubles are not freely convertible and tend to be unstable, and foreign currencies are not easily available in Russia, therefore, use a secure method of payment and figure the risk of a fluctuating exchange rate into your costs.
- SYRIA Funds must be released by the Commercial Bank of Syria, which has no authority to remit funds if a contract calls for delayed payment or "cash against document" mechanisms. Unless you have an established relationship with the Syrian trader, be certain to sell your goods for cash in advance or a confirmed irrevocable letter of credit; otherwise, if you offer credit, the Syrian trader may be able to avoid the contract because the Bank will not recognize the payment terms, even after you have shipped the goods.
- THAILAND Remittance of payment for imports must be approved by a commercial bank, Bank of Thailand, or Thai Customs, depending on amount of payment.
- VIETNAM Foreign exchange transactions are made through trading floors, and businesses that need foreign exchange for import payments must submit bids to the market seven days in advance of payment. As a nonresident, you might consider establishing a local bank account for the deposit of foreign currencies or convertible Vietnamese dong, which you can freely convert and transfer abroad.

Protection of Industrial and Intellectual Property

Success in business is built on trust. Buyers demand sources that they can trust, and sellers in turn will profit if they prove, and improve, their trustworthiness. As you establish your trustworthiness, your reputation for excellence will spread, customers will seek you out, and the resulting goodwill then becomes one of your company's most valuable assets.

VALUE OF YOUR MARK AND NAME

Trust and goodwill are inevitably connected with the quality and uniqueness of the goods or services you provide. It is therefore immensely important to ensure that your goods or services can be quickly distinguished from those of other traders, which you do by giving your product a "catchy" name, label, or other mark. Buyers often purchase services or goods from "a name they trust." Thus, a name can serve not only to distinguish your goods or services but also to extend the buyer's trust to your entire product or service line.

Unique designs, methods, names, and symbols that distinguish the products or services of one trader from those of another trader constitute industrial and intellectual property. The exclusive rights to such property are valuable—you can stake your reputation on it. A buyer who has been pleased with one of your brand-name products is likely to assume that your other goods or services are of equal quality and well worth the price, and the buyer is also likely to pass your name onto friends and business associates.

CONTRACTUAL PROTECTION

The contractual protection of your exclusive rights to your industrial and intellectual property should be of utmost importance whenever you trade internationally because there is a high risk of infringement. In many countries, the opportunity to make hefty profits by infringing on another trader's high-quality reputation far outweighs the chance that the infringer will face civil or criminal action. In addition to the difficulty and expense of having to discover and fight infringement in a land many thousands of miles away, you are likely to find that remedies for infringement are not enforced or are unavailable. You may even find that the other trader's activities are not considered infringements under the laws of the foreign country.

CONSEQUENCES OF NOT PROTECTING YOUR MARK

If another trader should use your name or copy your design without your consent, that trader will hitch a free ride on the reputation that you have struggled to build. You may lose not only sales but also the value of your reputation because you will have no control over the quality of the services or goods that the other trader provides. You may even lose your exclusive rights to your name, mark, or design—you will no longer be able to claim it as a unique means of distinguishing your products or services from those of all other traders.

SCOPE OF PROTECTION

Whether your contract is for a one-time sale or for an ongoing relationship, both parties should ensure that the industrial and intellectual property rights are clearly set forth—the seller, for protection of the exclusive rights in this property; the buyer, for protection against an infringement action by the seller. Issues to consider in creating your contract include the following.

■ CLARIFYING RIGHTS

Which rights in the Seller's industrial and intellectual property are being granted to the Buyer and which are retained or reserved by the Seller?

In a one-time sale, there is usually no granting of any rights to the industrial and intellectual property except in connection with sale of the specific goods, a fact that the contract should expressly state. If any rights are to be granted to the Buyer, the extent of those rights must be made clear: Is it a license (the Seller retains ownership) or an assignment (the Seller transfers ownership to the Buyer)?

■ ALTERATIONS TO PRODUCTS

Is the Buyer expected or permitted to alter the products or the names, markings, labels, and packaging of the products?

As owner of the industrial and intellectual property, the Seller should be extremely cautious of giving others the right to alter the products, names, markings, labels, or packaging. Such changes will affect the Seller's reputation and goodwill in the market. The Seller should maintain control to ensure that alterations are enhancements, not detriments. The Buyer should be required to disclose expected alterations, and the Seller should consider providing goods that meet the Buyer's specifications. The contract provisions should clearly define the changes, if any, that the Buyer is permitted to make.

■ ADVERTISEMENT

If the Buyer advertises the goods, how will the Seller protect the intellectual property rights?

It is unrealistic to prohibit the Buyer from advertising the goods. The contract should therefore protect the Seller's rights by requiring that all advertising must refer to the source and origin of the goods. The contract should also mandate that a legend must be included to state that the Seller is the sole owner of the names, markings, labels, or other property shown in the advertisement.

■ BUYER'S INFRINGEMENT PROTECTION

When the Buyer sells the goods, what will prevent the Buyer from becoming liable for infringement of industrial and intellectual property rights?

The Buyer could be at risk for claims of infringement from two sources: the Seller, and a third party who claims better title to the industrial and intellectual property rights thought to be owned by the Seller. It is wise to include a contract clause specifying that, provided the Buyer has complied with the provisions of the contract, the Seller agrees that it has no right of action against the Buyer for infringing the Seller's industrial or intellectual property rights. To protect the Buyer against third-party claims, the contract should require the Seller to indemnify the Buyer.

■ SELLER'S PROTECTION AGAINST INFRINGEMENT

How will the Seller's rights in this property be protected against infringement in the Buyer's market?

Never voluntarily allow sales of your goods in a country where you have not applied to register your industrial and/or intellectual property with a government agency. (Note that in the few countries where registration is not available, a cautionary notice is usually published.) First, make the application to register. The application does not need to mature to registration, which often takes several years, for your property to be protected. In many countries, the first person to file the application is given exclusive rights, regardless of whether the Seller is internationally famous and has used the mark for decades elsewhere.

Your contract should specify that you have registered or have a pending registration of the property rights in the Buyer's country, that the Buyer will do nothing to interfere with that registration or application, and that the Buyer acknowledges the Seller's exclusive rights to the property within the Buyer's country. Although such a clause cannot in fact stop the Buyer from infringing, if the language is sufficiently strong, it will act as a preventive measure.

It is also an excellent idea to add an incentive for the Buyer's help in stopping infringement, and even a liquidated damages clause if the Buyer is the cause of infringement or otherwise interferes with registration of the Seller's property. Further, it is essential that the Seller know the Buyer's business background before making the sale. If the Buyer has substantial financial backing, it is wise to visit the Buyer's place of business personally and to establish a strong relationship in the beginning.

After the Buyer has received the goods, the Seller must be certain to follow the progress of the Buyer's sales. It may be a wise idea to agree to buy back goods that have not sold in an untested market. If the Buyer meets with success, the Seller should establish a long-term relationship with the Buyer to try to ensure that the Buyer continues to market on the Seller's behalf. On the other hand, if the Seller intends to limit the contract to a one-time sale, the contract should be very clear on this point. In certain regions, if you do not monitor the sales, the Buyer never places a new order, and the goods are not returned, there is an excellent possibility that unauthorized copies of the goods will soon be on the market there.

Choice of Law, Jurisdiction, and Remedy

Choice of law, jurisdiction, and remedy will generally not arise unless you have a dispute with the other party about the contract terms, but it is always less expensive and less surprising to plan ahead. Even if you have the utmost trust in the other trader, it is best at a minimum to specify which international or national law you would like to have applied in determining the rights and obligations of the parties. This provision allows you to anticipate your future risks by fixing your claims and liabilities in advance. You can further control the risks inherent in the enforcement of your contract by selecting a jurisdiction and remedy for the resolution of a dispute that cannot be soothed by negotiation. All of these advance choices could save you money in the long run. In making your contract, consider the following issues.

CHOICE OF LAW

Which law will be used to determine the meaning of your contract terms?

If a dispute needs to be determined by a third person, such as a judge or arbitrator, that person will first have to decide which law to apply to make the determination. For a domestic contract, there may be several choices: the law of the country, the law of one of the states within the country, or the law of a municipality or other local political division of the state or country. For an international contract, all of the domestic laws could be considered, plus the laws of the foreign trader's country, state, and/or local political division. In addition, one or more international treaties—such as the United Nations Convention on the International Sale of Goods (CISG)—may apply unless you have expressly stated otherwise in your contract.

Keep in mind that your choice of law may be limited by the laws of the importing or exporting country. In some countries, all contracts with their nationals must be subject to their laws. Thus, you may find that your contract clause will not be controlling, and unless you have made an express protective provision, you may even find your entire contract void.

CHOICE OF FORUM

Where will either party be entitled to seek a remedy?

Your choice of law and selection of jurisdiction need not be the same. Thus, you can agree to apply the law of Argentina, where the contract is to be performed, but insist on Miami, Florida, as your forum for the remedy—provided the forum will agree to apply the law that you have selected.

EXERCISE OF JURISDICTION

Will the forum selected have jurisdiction over your transaction, and is it likely to exercise that jurisdiction?

Whether a case is heard in a chosen forum depends on two factors: the forum's right to apply the law, and the forum's willingness to apply the law.

The "right" of a country's courts to take jurisdiction in any particular case is dependent on that country's laws. The laws of some countries take a narrow stance, while others permit extended jurisdiction. It is wise to consult a legal professional who is familiar with the laws of the forum of your choice to determine whether the courts have a legal right to take jurisdiction over the parties or property subject to your contract.

The mere fact that a court has a right to take jurisdiction does not mean that it will agree to hear and decide a case brought before it. In most places, the courts have discretion to refuse jurisdiction over international disputes in favor of another forum that the court believes is more suited to resolve the issues. If both contracting parties have agreed to the choice of forum, the court is likely to consider this preference in exercising its discretion—hopefully in favor of your choice.

ENFORCEMENT

If you are lucky enough to obtain a judgment or award in your favor, where will you need to enforce it?

When selecting a forum, consider whether you will be able to benefit from the resulting judgment or award. If you cannot enforce your judgment or award, there is no point in seeking and obtaining it. Enforcement is a legal process, such as an attachment of property or an order for specific performance, and therefore must be carried out by officials—court officers, police, sheriffs, and so forth—who have authority under law to carry out a court's orders. The bottom line is that the validity of your judgment or award must be recognized by the officials in the place where you seek enforcement. If you obtain your court order in one forum and seek enforcement in another, you may be refused. The recognition of an award or judgment from another country is a matter of discretion. Therefore, think twice about suing in your own country if you will need to seek enforcement elsewhere.

CHOICE OF REMEDIES

What remedies will either party be permitted to seek?

An easy means of limiting your liabilities and costs in the event of a dispute is to choose the remedies ahead of time. The least costly remedy is usually negotiation. But if you need to resort to an objective third party for a decision, arbitration is a good choice, provided it is easily available. Arbitration clauses are common in international commercial contracts because the parties have relatively more control over the proceedings than is the case with lawsuits.

CHAPTER 7

Parties to the Transaction, Part 2

EXPECT THE UNEXPECTED. If you anticipate what might go wrong, you can plan ahead and hopefully avert a catastrophe. The difficulty is to know what might go wrong. When dealing with business, financial, and legal arrangements in cross-border contracts, you should have some idea of what your liabilities might be and what your remedies are. Otherwise, you are unlikely to remain competitive on an international level because the cost of protecting your business will far outweigh the benefits of trading across borders. When you think you have made the best deal, check off all the points discussed below.

Buyer

GET IT IN WRITING

You agree orally to the contract terms. The seller sends you a written contract, but some of the terms are different than your oral agreement, some are missing entirely, and some new ones have been added. If you sign the written agreement, its terms will be binding on you, regardless of your oral understandings. Although oral understandings may sometimes be used to prove intent, the written word is the strongest evidence of your agreement. Be sure it correctly states your understanding of the contract terms. In the absence of mutual agreement, when both parties have the same intent and understanding of the terms, the entire contract could be considered void.

THE MORAL: Be certain the terms are written, that they state what you intended to say, and that your understanding of them is the same as the seller's understanding.

MAKE A DEFINITE AGREEMENT BEFORE YOU ACT ON IT

The seller sends you a written contract, and you modify a few terms, execute it, and send it back. In reliance on the contract, you buy expensive advertising, arrange warehouse space, and hire employees. The goods fail to arrive, and you sue for specific performance and breach of contract. The seller claims that your alterations to the agreement were material and therefore no contract was ever formed. You argue that your changes were minor and that the executed agreement constituted an acceptance when you returned it to the seller. If you cannot amicably resolve the dispute with the seller, you will be at the mercy of a third person's judgment as to whether the alterations were "material"—a standard which is vague, at best.

THE MORAL: Accept the exact terms of an offer or, if you alter any provisions, make formation of the contract contingent on the express acceptance of the other party to the exact terms of your altered offer.

VERIFY THE SELLER'S AUTHORITY TO MAKE THE CONTRACT

You have met the seller for the first time at a trade show. The seller claims to represent the XYZ Company, but her business card is from ABC, Inc. You purchase goods from the seller, exchanging a cash payment for a contract to deliver the goods in fourteen days. In anticipation of the delivery, you contract for the subsequent sale of the goods. The XYZ Company fails to ship the goods and refuses to honor the contract because the seller is not its authorized representative. Your contract with XYZ Company is void because the seller had no authority to make it, and because you had a reasonable clue to the fact that the seller had no authority but you did not check, you cannot enforce the contract based on the seller's apparent authority. Further, you could be in breach of the subsequent contract if you are unable to deliver the goods to that party.

THE MORAL: If you have any reason to suspect that the seller does not have authority to make the contract—whether because the seller is not a representative of the company, is not an adult, or does not appear to be fully cognizant—do not rely on the contract until you have verified the seller's authority and the validity of the agreement.

KNOW WHAT GOODS YOU ARE GETTING

You want to purchase red goods. The contract states that the seller will ship red goods to you, except that if red goods are not available, the seller may substitute other goods of similar type and quality. If you agree to this clause, you will not be able to dispute the receipt of blue goods. If the goods you want must meet certain specifications, be sure those specifications are clear in the contract and that substitute goods are not permitted.

THE MORAL: If you care about the quality, quantity, type, characteristics, and so on of the goods that you order, be certain that your contract specifications are exact and cannot be changed without your prior approval.

LIMIT YOUR RISK FROM FACTORS BEYOND YOUR CONTROL

You agree to make payment in a currency with a reputation for being stable. The political and economical situation in your country is relatively less stable. When the goods arrive and your payment is due, the currency of your own country is devalued and payment of the price becomes impossible. Your contract does not contain an escape clause, such as a clause for renegotiation or force majeure. You may be in breach if you cannot find a way to pay.

THE MORAL: Protect yourself from the vagaries of politics and high finance by insisting that the seller recognize the difficulties you face from your own country's economic and political situation and make accommodations in the contract terms accordingly.

REQUIRE PRECISE TERMS

The seller has provided you with a memorandum or a short contract. You are pleased with how efficient the seller has been at sticking to the basics. The agreement provides that it is governed by the United Nations Convention on International Sales of Goods (CISG) and that there is therefore no need to provide explicitly for every obligation, duty, and liability. A dispute arises, the CISG is applied, and the result is unexpectedly in favor of the seller because the terms implied into your contract under CISG vary from the terms that would have been implied into your contract under your own country's laws.

THE MORAL: Precise terms ensure protection of your rights, even if the terms are more detailed and the contract is a few pages longer. If you want to control the results of a dispute, you must control the intent and interpretation of your contract terms—which is best done by accurate, precise, and complete contractual provisions.

MATCH YOUR ACTIONS TO YOUR WRITTEN WORDS

You have been dealing with one seller for several years, and you have a relatively simple arrangement by which you place an order, the seller immediately ships and you pay net 30 days. This arrangement is not written into any contract. For the next shipment, you fail to pay within the usual time. The seller sues for breach, and you claim that net 90 is a reasonable payment period and should be implied into the contract. The court implies a payment period of net 30 days based on your prior course of conduct, and you are required to pay the full price with interest for the days due past 30.

THE MORAL: It is best to base your course of dealing on a written contract, and if you want to alter your course of dealing, be certain the alteration is in writing.

UNDERSTAND ALL THE TERMS BEFORE YOU SIGN

The contract drafted by the seller states that "CPT New York (Incoterm 1990) and delivery shall be no later than thirty days from the date of the execution of this contract." The seller has many years of business experience. None of the terms are particularly burdensome to you, so you sign the contract. The seller ships the goods within three days of the contract date, but they never arrive in New York. You incur losses, and the seller demands payment. The dispute escalates, and eventually you sue the seller, who countersues you.

The court determines that the contract is ambiguous because, pursuant to the CPT term, the seller's obligation ended when the goods were loaded on the carrier, but the contract also seems to obligate the seller to deliver the goods to New York. The court further presumes that both parties, being merchants, are well-versed in trade and would have followed the usual practices for CPT delivery. As a result, the court decides that the risk passed to the buyer at the time the goods were loaded onto the carrier, and you must pay for the goods and take the loss. Unfortunately, you did not obtain insurance coverage for transit of the goods because you thought the risk was on the seller, so you will have to satisfy the judgment from your own pocket.

THE MORAL: Be careful that you fully understand the contract terms, and if you have any doubt or make an assumptions as to the meaning, be certain to inquire as to the other party's understanding and to obtain your own legal advice prior to agreeing to terms.

MAKE SURE THE REMEDIES ARE MEANT FOR YOU

The contract provides that it will be governed by the law of the seller's country and that either party may seek relief against the other only in a forum located in the seller's country. You believe that the seller is a trustworthy fellow and will perform with precision all of the contract terms. Besides, you would never consider suing any person. You send your advance payment to the seller, but the goods never arrive and the seller does not respond to your demands. You may have to seek redress in the seller's country far from home and at considerable expense (unless the laws of your own country prohibit clauses for choice of law and forum in contracts with nationals).

THE MORAL: Be certain you will be able to use the remedies provided in your contract—just in case the need arises.

Seller

PUT IT IN WRITING

The buyer orally places an order for your goods. The goods are to be shipped cash on delivery. The buyer further specifies that the goods must have a certain label to meet the requirements of consumer laws in the buyer's country. You make and attach the labels, package the goods, and arrange for customs clearance and shipping, and deliver the goods to a carrier within twelve days of the order. One day later and before the buyer receives the goods, the buyer calls and cancels the order. You sue for breach of contract, and the buyer counterclaims that you breached the contract by not delivering the goods within the customary ten days, giving the buyer the right to cancel. The court's decision is likely to be in favor of the customary trade practices because you have no absolute evidence, such as a written contract, modifying the custom. Moreover, as the seller and shipper, it was up to you to ensure that your rights and obligations were clear and definite.

THE MORAL: Be certain your contract is written. For a one-time order, a memorandum of the sale may be sufficient, provided that you have included all of the terms necessary to the transaction.

MAKE A DEFINITE AGREEMENT BEFORE YOU ACT ON IT

You send a contract to the buyer, who returns it with modifications to some of the terms and with a statement that assent to the exact terms is required to form a contract. You review the changes, modify two minor points and send it back to the buyer. Negotiations are going well, and you expect the deal to close at any moment. To meet the tight deadline stated in the contract, you decide to make advance preparations, including printing special labels and retooling your production line for the buyer's specifications. The buyer cancels the order. If you sue for specific performance and breach of contract, you will most likely lose because no definite contract was ever formed—by making two minor changes, you made a counteroffer since the buyer's counteroffer required assent to the exact terms.

THE MORAL: Until you have a contract to which both parties have expressed unconditional acceptance, you have no right to rely on the promises of the other party. If you act in advance, you take the risk that the other party may withdraw.

VERIFY THE BUYER'S AUTHORITY TO MAKE THE CONTRACT

The buyer calls you and claims to represent the LMN Company. You have never dealt with the buyer or the LMN Company before, so you request background information on the buyer and the company. The buyer transmits a brochure for PQR, Inc., with an explanation that it is the parent company of LMN Company. You agree to sell your products to the buyer on terms net thirty days. You ship the goods but never receive payment, and the goods are not returned. The buyer is never heard from again. Neither company heeds your demands for payment or return of the goods, claiming that the buyer was not an authorized representative. Your contract is void because the buyer had no actual or apparent authority to make it, and you will not be able to recover against the companies.

THE MORAL: If you have any reason whatsoever to suspect that the buyer is not authorized to make the contract—whether because the buyer is not a representative of the company, is not an adult, or does not appear to be fully cognizant—be certain to verify the buyer's authority and the validity of the agreement.

LIMIT YOUR RISK FROM FACTORS BEYOND YOUR CONTROL

You agree to ship goods to a country that has a relatively unstable government and economy. The buyer pays for the goods in advance. On the day before the shipment, your own country imposes sanctions against the other country. All transactions between nationals of the two countries come to an abrupt halt. Your contract does not contain an escape clause, such as a clause for renegotiation or force majeure. You may be in breach if you do not deliver the goods, but delivery means that you will be subject to criminal penalties in your own country.

THE MORAL: You are as susceptible to being affected by events beyond your control as the buyer. Both parties should have an escape clause in case performance of the contract becomes overly burdensome or impossible because of events beyond their control.

MAKE YOUR CONTRACT COMPLETE AND PRECISE

Your standard contract provided to all buyers is one page in length. You adamantly prefer a short contract. You include only the basic terms on the goods, price, payment, and delivery. You throw out terms that you consider frills, such as clauses on assignments, trademarks, choice of forum, force majeure, and written modifications. You agree with the foreign buyer that your agreement will be governed by the United Nations Convention on International Sales of Goods (CISG), so if there is no provision related to some obligation, duty, or liability, it may be implied by law pursuant to the CISG. The buyer accepts the goods and fails to place any new orders. Two years later, you attempt to register your trademark in the buyer's country only to discover that the buyer has already registered your trademark in his own country and is selling copies of your goods. The CISG does not cover this situation, your contract has no protective provisions, and you have not registered your trademark. Therefore, you do not have a claim for breach of contract, nor do you have a claim for infringement of a registered trademark. Your options are limited to trying to persuade the buyer—now infringer—to stop infringing and to go legitimate (such as through a license or joint venture with you) or suing the infringer based on judicially recognized wrongful conduct (which also depends on judicial discretion).

THE MORAL: The use of precise, and complete contractual provisions—which can still be simple and straightforward—will minimize the costs and labor needed for resolving disputes or enforcing your contract later, and the results will be more predictable.

MATCH YOUR ACTIONS TO YOUR WRITTEN WORD

You have been supplying goods to the buyer for many years pursuant to a contract by which the goods will be made to the buyer's specifications, provided the buyer gives notice of those specifications forty-five days in advance of shipment. Over the years, you have always shipped the goods to the buyer within fifteen days of receiving the buyer's specifications, and the buyer has come to rely on your fast turnaround. The buyer places an order and gives you specifications for the goods. You manufacture the goods specially for the buyer and ship forty-two days later. The buyer refuses to accept the delivery and sues you for breach of contract for failure to make timely delivery. The court awards damages to the buyer because you have established a course of dealing.

THE MORAL: It is best to base your course of dealing on a written contract. If you alter your course of dealing, be certain the alteration is in writing. If you do not want to change the contract terms despite your course of dealing, be certain your contract contains a no-waiver clause.

MAKE SURE YOU CAN USE THE REMEDIES PROVIDED

The contract provides that it will be governed by the law of your country and that relief must be sought in a forum located in the your country. The buyer accepts the goods but fails to pay for them. You sue the buyer in your own courts and obtain a judgment. The courts of the buyer's country refuse to recognize the judgment. You will not be able to collect your money unless you seek a further remedy, possibly a new trial, in the buyer's country.

THE MORAL: Provide for effective remedies in your contract—just in case you need to use them.

Buyer's Attorney

As the buyer, you may think you have understood and prepared for all of the aspects of your international transaction. You know what might go wrong, and you have protected yourself as best you can. Now comes the difficult question: Have you consulted a legal professional? If you have not, then you should review the following issues. If you are not familiar with them, you should consider consulting an attorney who is versed in international trade practice and law and who will provide the following services.

CHECK OUT THE SELLER

- Review the financial and operational history of the seller, point out conflicting information, and complete several basic background checks.

REVIEW PAYMENT REQUIREMENTS

- Verify that the payment instrument required by the contract is available in your country, determine the cost for obtaining that instrument, and find out the procedure for arranging the payment within time to meet the contract deadline.
- Ensure that, if you make payment in advance, you are protected in the event that the goods never arrive.

REVIEW INSURANCE NEEDS

- Review the contract to determine when title and risk of loss are transferred to the buyer and advise on whether the buyer is sufficiently insured for such risk.

REVIEW IMPORT REQUIREMENTS

- Verify that the imports will not be prohibited by laws restricting the type of import, antidumping regulations, or quotas.
- Verify whether the imports are subject to countervailing duties.
- Verify whether you are responsible for customs clearance and whether you have completed all necessary documentation in the most effective manner for clearance purposes.
- Recommend measures that can be taken to avoid damage to the goods if there is a delay at the border.
- Expedite the release of shipments that have been delayed or seized at the border.
- Advise on electronic customs filings, importation bonds, temporary importation procedures, and bonded warehouses as means of avoiding the border crunch.
- Explain the classification and valuation system used to assess duties, ad valorem taxes, and penalties.
- Verify whether customs is valuing the goods based on a price that has been derived by proper methods or whether the price, and hence the value, is inaccurate.
- Review the classification of the goods and dispute it if necessary.
- Determine whether you are subject to any licenses, permits, taxes, or other liabilities for importing, transporting, using, or selling the goods, and advise on the procedures for compliance.

REVIEW MARKETABILITY REQUIREMENTS

- Advise on consumer, environmental, health, and other regulations that may affect the labeling, marking, transport, storage, use, and sale of the goods, and recommend the most efficient means of compliance.

REVIEW TAX REQUIREMENTS

- Identify tax-free trade zones for imports in your country, explain the qualifications, and assist in getting you into such a zone.

- Verify whether you are keeping proper records for tax or customs authorities.

- REVIEW IMPORT REQUIREMENTS

- Explain drawback, determine whether you qualify, and assist you in collecting it.
- Advise on the advantages of free-trade agreements and preference systems and whether you can take advantage of them.

- REVIEW RISKS INVOLVED

- Review your potential liability for third-party claims for damages from defective goods or infringement of intellectual property rights and advise you on a means of protection, such as insurance, operation of your business through a corporation or other entity, or requesting indemnification from the seller.
- Advise on actions that will constitute infringement of the seller's intellectual property rights and recommend efficient means of protecting the seller's rights so as to avoid infringing on them.

Seller's Attorney

As the seller, you are confident that your contract is airtight. You have used the same contract in one or two foreign countries, and you have never had a problem resolving disputes by negotiation or legal process. You have conquered the international transaction. Why should you bother with legal advice now? Perhaps you have indeed confronted and dealt with all of the following issues. But if not, it's nice to know that an international lawyer is available to answer your questions and to assist you in the following ways.

- REVIEW POLITICAL AND ECONOMIC RISKS

- Recognize and anticipate instability in the economic or political climate of the buyer's country.
- Advise on your own government's restrictions and embargoes affecting whether you can trade with nationals of another country.

- CHECK OUT THE BUYER

- Confirm the buyer's financial and operational history, good standing with banks and government authorities, creditworthiness, and ethical business practices.

- REVIEW PAYMENT OPTIONS

- Advise on the availability and security of various payment instruments.
- Verify that your country's laws do not prohibit or restrict the type of export.

- REVIEW EXPORT IMPORT ISSUES

- Confirm that the laws of the buyer's country do not prohibit the import of the goods, and that the goods are not subject to antidumping regulations or quotas.
- Verify whether you are responsible for customs clearance and whether you have completed all necessary documentation in the most effective manner for clearance purposes.

- Advise on the most desirable time for the transfer of title and the risk of loss to the buyer and on whether you have adequately insured the goods against damage or loss in transit.
- Expedite the release of shipments that have been delayed or seized at the border.
- Advise on electronic customs filings, preshipment customs inspections, and bonded warehouses as means of avoiding the border crunch.
- Explain the classification and valuation system used by your own country and the buyer's country to assess duties, ad valorem taxes, and penalties.
- Review your invoices to ensure that they show the proper valuation of the goods for customs and tax purposes.
- Determine whether you are subject to any licenses, permits, taxes, or other liabilities for exporting, transporting, using, or selling the goods, and advise on the procedures for compliance.
- Advise on consumer, environmental, health, and other regulations that may affect the labeling, marking, transport, storage, use, and sale of the goods, and recommend the most efficient means of compliance.
- Identify tax-free trade zones for exports in your country, explain the qualifications, and assist in getting you into such a zone.
- Confirm whether you qualify for reimbursement of export fees or taxes under any government programs in your own country.
- Advise on the advantages of free-trade agreements and preference systems and whether you can take advantage of them.
- Verify whether you are keeping proper records for tax or customs authorities.

■ REVIEW RISKS INVOLVED

- Review your potential liability for third-party claims for damages from defective goods and advise you on a means of protection, such as insurance or operation of your business through a corporation or other entity.
- Advise on how you can protect your exclusive intellectual property rights against infringement and on the most efficient means of monitoring and fighting against infringement.

CHAPTER 8

Drafting Precise Contract Provisions

AT THE BEGINNING, it is important to recognize that you will not be able to cover every gap and fill all the loopholes in your contract provisions. The reason is simple: you do not know them all. While you can try to plug each one, the one you miss will be the one that is later disputed and renegotiated.

You may not be able to create the perfect contract, but you should nevertheless draft your contract provisions as clearly as you possibly can. The more definitive the terms, the fewer the disputes. Use very precise language. Look for the weak links. Ask: if something will go wrong, where will it go wrong? And remember, when things do go wrong, you should correct your contract provisions to avoid the same mistake in the next transaction.

The following contract clauses and pointers are intended to give you some practice in finding ambiguities and tightening up phrases. These clauses are illustrative, not all-inclusive, because it is impossible to anticipate every turn of a phrase. Your goal should be to review your own contract from the point of view of the other party: what weaknesses in your position might the other party find advantageous? And then, from your side: are the contract requirements for performance and enforcement feasible, sufficient, and efficient?

Specific Contract Clauses

FORMATION OF THE CONTRACT ON SIGNING

- POOR PROVISION:

This contract becomes binding on both parties when it is signed.

ANALYSIS: The intent is to provide the time and means for formation of the contract, but the clause is too indefinite. If the contract is signed by only one party, does it become binding on both, or must both parties sign before it becomes binding? If the parties sign on different dates, which is the effective one? If the last party to sign the contract changes a provision in it before signing, has a contract been formed?

- BETTER PROVISION:

EFFECTIVE DATE: This contract will be binding on both parties as of the date on which it is signed by the [seller/buyer], provided the [seller/buyer] does not alter, delete, or add to the terms of the contract.

FORMATION OF CONTRACT ON ACCEPTANCE OF ORDER

- POOR PROVISION:

This contract will become binding on the parties at the time the seller accepts the order that is detailed in the attached specification.

Stock Contract Forms

You want to make agreements on the spot, to implement uniformity in your business practices, or to save costly legal fees for preparation of contracts. Should you resort to preprinted contract forms? Or at least to a standard form that you can print up whenever needed? While the use of preprinted or standard contract forms is certainly an effective means of doing business, you must at the same time be cautious of the drawbacks and protect yourself from the chance that your contract provisions might be unenforceable in the event that a dispute arises.

KNOW THE DRAWBACKS

- Your preprinted contract may fail to provide for circumstances unique to a particular business transaction.
- It may include complex terms that will not be understood by the national of another country.
- It may be too simple and may, thus, omit terms necessary for the complete protection of your rights in countries where contracts are sacred.
- It may fail to contain provisions that are mandatory under the laws of the other party's country.
- It may contain terms considered unenforceable by the laws of the other party's country, in which event those laws may also invalidate the entire contract.
- Your preprinted contract or any of its terms may violate the public policy of the other party's country, making the contract void.
- It may conflict with the other party's preprinted contract, and if you and the other party agree to use both forms, a dispute may arise as to which of the conflicting clauses should prevail.

PREVENT POTENTIAL ENFORCEMENT PROBLEMS

- Allow for modifications and deletions from your preprinted contract to ensure that the provisions meet public policy and legal requirements.
- Consider using two or more different preprinted forms that will account for differences in cultural approaches to contractual arrangements.
- Seek legal advice from counsel who is familiar with the laws and practices of the country or region to determine whether your preprinted form will be enforceable there.
- Append schedules and addendums to your preprinted form for information that varies with every contract, such as the quantity and description of goods.
- Have all parties to the contract sign or initial each clause or at least each page of your preprinted form to indicate their awareness and comprehension of the terms.
- Vary the size and style of the printed type for the clauses that impose requirements and obligations that are essential to a party's acceptable performance of the contract.

ANALYSIS: This clause does not require acceptance by any particular date—it is entirely open-ended. The general rule is that acceptance must be within a "reasonable time" if there is no designated time, but "reasonableness" is a factual, and hence, discretionary, standard. If the buyer places an order but receives no acceptance within what the buyer considers a reasonable time, the buyer may decide to place the same order with a different seller. Imagine the buyer's surprise when two deliveries arrive from two different sellers.

■ BETTER PROVISION:

EFFECTIVE DATE. This contract will become binding on the parties as of the date the seller signs it, provided the seller does not alter, delete, or add to the terms of this contract and provided the seller signs the contract by [date], transmits a copy of the signed contract by facsimile to the buyer by [date], and sends the original signed contract by post.

DESCRIPTION OF GOODS

■ POOR PROVISION:

The Goods are described as follows: [*give specifications and quantity of all goods covered by the contract*].

ANALYSIS: Although this provision is adequate for purposes of forming the contract, it makes no allowance for the practicalities of trade—particularly international trade where it is difficult to preinspect goods before purchase, expensive to prepare goods for sales overseas, costly to ship them, and prone to delivery after at least some delay. A contract provision that will reflect your cross-border trading practices and still protect your rights will avoid disputes and inconveniences on both sides. The provision should allow for reasonable variations in the buyer's requirements and the seller's performance. Of course, the variations that you provide must fit your situation, and therefore several alternatives are illustrated here to give you ideas for drafting your own.

■ BETTER PROVISION:

ACCEPTABLE QUANTITY/TYPE/COLOR OF GOODS. If the Seller delivers to the Buyer goods that are in quantity more or less than the quantity specified in this Contract, the quantity delivered will be acceptable, provided it varies by no more than [*number*] percent of the quantity specified in this Contract. If the goods delivered differ in type, color, or other characteristics from the description specified in this Contract, the Goods will be accepted provided that [*specify, e.g.*, the only difference is in the color of the trim *or* the difference is the result of a change in production, the goods provided are intended for the same use, the Seller gives the Buyer advance notice of the change before shipment, and the Buyer approves the change in writing.

■ BETTER PROVISION:

ACCEPTABLE COLOR/COMPOSITION OF GOODS. The Seller agrees to sell and the Buyer agrees to purchase goods described as [*specify*] (the "Goods"). The Parties understand that the color or composition of the Goods varies [depending on the raw materials available for manufacture *or* because the Goods

Ten Tips to Tighten Your Clauses

1. Look for vague standards, such as "reasonable," "material," or "substantial." Try to restate these standards more definitively or eliminate them entirely by designating the time that you consider reasonable; identifying the clauses, rights, or obligations that you believe are material; or specifying the amount that you consider substantial.
2. Read the literal meaning of the clause without reading "between the lines" or making any assumptions as to intent. Make sure what it says is what you really mean it to say.
3. Simplify complex provisions by breaking up long sentences, eliminating unnecessary chains of words, and reducing strings of nouns and verbs.
4. Write in "plain English." If you cannot understand your own contract, try to use less legal jargon and fewer bombastic terms.
5. Watch out for missing time limits. If no time for performance is provided, a reasonable time is usually implied, and "reasonable" is one of those vague standards.
6. Use proper grammar. Be certain your clauses relate correctly, your punctuation defines your meaning, your "i"s are dotted and your "t"s are crossed.
7. Search for ambiguities by creating scenarios. Pretend you are your worst enemy. How would you avoid your own contract?
8. Avoid colloquialisms that will have little or no meaning to a party from another country. Say what you mean in straightforward terms.
9. Do not try to be all-inclusive. You will never include it all in a strict listing. Flexible terms will in fact be more inclusive than lists of terms that try to be all-inclusive but end up being exclusive.
10. Look out for words that have several meanings. Try to restate them, or at least to define them. Does "shipped" mean "left the seller's warehouse on the seller's truck" or "transferred to the carrier at the pier"?

are produced by hand]. The color and composition of the Goods is at the discretion of the Seller, provided that the quality of the goods is not affected and provided that if the color is [*specify, e.g.*, any shade of purple] the Seller must give the Buyer written notice [*number*] days in advance of the date of shipment. Within two days of receipt of the notice of change, the Buyer has the option to cancel the contract or to confirm the change, which option can be exercised only by written notice to the Seller. If no written notice of cancellation or confirmation is received, the Seller will ship the available Goods of the preferred color or composition and will make up the difference with goods of at least the same quality.

■ BETTER PROVISION:

DESIGNATED QUANTITY. The Seller agrees to sell and the Buyer agrees to purchase goods described as [*specify*] (the "Goods"). No later than [*date or period, e.g.*, thirty days from the date of this Contract], the Buyer may give the seller written notice of the quantity of the Goods to be purchased, which designated quantity may not be less than [*number*] nor may exceed [*number*]. If the Seller has not received timely notice from the Buyer as to the designated quantity, the quantity of the Goods will be [*number and unit of measurement, e.g.*, 2,000 units *or* 250 cases].

■ BETTER PROVISION:

CHANGE IN QUANTITY/SPECIFICATION. The Seller agrees to sell and the Buyer agrees to purchase goods described as [*specify*] (the "Goods") in the amount of [*number and unit of measurement, e.g.*, 2,000 units *or* 250 cases]. No later than [*number*] of days in advance of the date of delivery, either party may notify the other party in writing of a change in the quantity or specification of the Goods, provided that any requested change in quantity will not be more than [*number*] nor less than [*number*], and the reason for any requested change in specification must be given in the written notice. Within two days of receipt of the notice of change, the notified party has the option to cancel the contract or to agree to the change, which option can be exercised only by written notice to the other party.

■ BETTER PROVISION:

ENTIRE OUTPUT. The Seller agrees to sell and the Buyer agrees to purchase from the Seller, all [*describe goods*] that the Seller manufacturers at its factory located at [*address*] ("the Goods") from [*date*] to [*date*]. The parties agree that the quantity of Goods will be approximately [*number*]. The purchase price of the Goods will be [*currency and amount*] per [*quantity*], which shall include [*costs included*].

■ BETTER PROVISION:

ALL REQUIREMENTS. The Seller agrees to sell to the Buyer the quantities of [*describe goods*] ("the Goods") that the Buyer requires from [*date*] to [*date*], and the Buyer agrees to purchase the Goods at the price of [*currency and amount per quantity*], which shall include [*costs included*]. The parties agree that the Seller will sell and the Buyer will purchase at least [*number*] of the Goods, but the Seller will not be required to supply more than [*number*] of the Goods.

QUALITY OF THE GOODS

■ POOR PROVISION:

FITNESS OF GOODS. The Goods must be of merchantable quality.

ANALYSIS: The phrase "merchantable quality" merely means that the goods are fit for any ordinary purpose to which they might reasonably be put, which could include a use not intended but within reason. This standard of performance is vague and of little meaning to either buyer or seller. For example, a chair is meant for sitting, but when a footstool is not immediately at hand, a chair is often a convenient substitute. Therefore, when a manufacturer sells a chair of merchantable quality, the manufacturer should keep in mind that somebody may stand on it. A buyer who purchases the chair cannot be certain of whether the chair can be used for purposes other than the obvious one of sitting. Even if the chair is used for sitting only, "merchantable quality" does not identify the maximum weight that than can safely be put on the chair without collapsing it. A specific standard of performance will protect both parties from harm caused when the goods are used for an unintended, although reasonable, purpose.

■ BETTER PROVISION:

FITNESS OF GOODS WITH NO SPECIFICATION BY BUYER. The Goods [*state standard of performance, e.g.*, are in compliance with the technical standards required by the (*name of law*) of (*country*), *or* meet the industry standards for household usage *or* will support a maximum of (*standard*)]. The Goods are for use as [*specify use*], and for no other use. The Buyer has not informed the Seller of any particular purpose for which the goods are needed, and the Seller has made no representations to the Buyer that the Goods can be used for any other purpose, other than that which is stated in this Paragraph.

■ BETTER PROVISION:

FITNESS OF GOODS WITH SPECIFICATION BY BUYER. The Goods [*state standard of performance, e.g.*, are in compliance with the technical standards required by the (*name of law*) of (*country*) *or* meet the industry standards for household usage *or* will support a maximum of (*standard*)]. The Goods have been modified to meet the Buyer's specifications without altering the standard stated here. The Goods are for use as [*specify use*], and for no other use. The Seller makes no representations that the Goods as modified will fit the Buyer's intended purpose.

PURCHASE PRICE FIXED

■ POOR PROVISION:

PURCHASE PRICE. The Buyer agrees to purchase the Goods for [*currency and amount*] per [*unit of measure, e.g.*, case of 250 units].

ANALYSIS: In an international context, estimation of the manufacturing and packaging costs is often more difficult than in a domestic transaction because of the need to prepare the goods to meet the legal and cultural requirements for sale in a foreign country. It is also more than likely that different packaging will be required for the lengthy voyage and for transfer between more than one carrier. On the buyer's side of the ocean, the market could change before the goods even reach the buyer, particularly in an economy with high inflation or other instability. To reflect these difficulties and to encourage the parties to avoid breaching a burdensome contract, a contract for international trade may allow for adjustments in the purchase price.

■ BETTER PROVISION:

PURCHASE PRICE. The Buyer agrees to purchase the Goods for [*currency and amount*] per [*unit of measure, e.g.*, case of 250 units] ("Purchase Price"). The Purchase Price for the Goods may be adjusted on the following terms:

1. If for any reason before the Goods are delivered, the Seller's manufacturing and production costs increase so much that the Seller will incur extreme hardship by selling the Goods at the Purchase Price, the parties agree that they will endeavor to renegotiate a fair and reasonable price. To request renegotiation, at least [*number*] days before the Delivery Date, the Seller must notify the Buyer in writing of the need to renegotiate the Purchase Price. If the parties fail to agree to a new purchase price, this Agreement will terminate without liability to either party.

2. If for any reason before the Goods are delivered, the market price of the Goods in [*country*] decreases so much that the Buyer will incur extreme hardship by purchasing them at the Purchase Price, the Buyer will have the same right as the Seller to seek renegotiation. To request renegotiation, at least [*number*] days before the Delivery Date, the Buyer must notify the Seller in writing of the need to renegotiate the purchase price. If the parties fail to agree to a new purchase price, this agreement will terminate without liability to either party.

PURCHASE PRICE WITH COSTS

■ POOR PROVISION:

PURCHASE PRICE. The Purchase Price is inclusive of packaging, handling, shipping, freight, and customs fees and costs.

ANALYSIS: You cannot possibly anticipate the amounts charged and expended for the costs associated with moving the goods from the seller's locale to the buyer's location. If the estimate is too low, the seller's profits could be substantially cut or even eliminated. If the estimate is too high, the products are likely to appear at first glance—which is often the glance that counts the most—to be noncompetitive. Moreover, the buyer is likely to object that the costs are too high or are not applicable to the particular shipment. The better provision is an itemization of the costs and the parties responsible for payment, and also the amounts should remain flexible to allow for changes in fees and charges.

■ BETTER PROVISION:

PURCHASE PRICE. The purchase price includes the following: [*specify, e.g.*, the cost of packaging and handling before shipment]. The purchase price does not include the following, for which the Seller will charge the Buyer separately: [*specify, e.g.*, taxes or other charges imposed by any government authority on the production, sale, shipment, import, or export of the Goods and all freight, transport, and shipping costs]. Payment for the separate charges will be made C.O.D.

DELIVERY TIME AND SHIPPING TERMS

■ POOR PROVISION:

DELIVERY. The Goods will be delivered FOB New York on or before [*date*].

ANALYSIS: Abbreviated delivery terms, including the Incoterm shown here, should never be used alone unless the parties are willing to accept implied terms from their course of dealing or the practice of the industry. The abbreviated terms fail to define all requirements for shipping and delivery. Moreover, the meaning of such terms often varies from country to country, creating a potential for ambiguity in your contract. It is wise to add a few brief but explicit details to your delivery and shipping term to cover your precise circumstances. For example, if the goods are suspended by a crane, have crossed the ship's rail, but have not yet been stowed, does FOB mean that delivery has been made? The meaning of FOB can vary depending on the custom of the port. Further, if the buyer has a preferred carrier, the transport arrangements should not be left solely to the discretion of the seller. Also, it is always wise to provide for the effect of a delay in delivery.

■ BETTER PROVISION:

DELIVERY. The Goods will be delivered FOB, stowed on ship, New York, on or before [*date*] ("Delivery Date"). The mode of transport to the point of delivery is at the Seller's discretion. If delivery is delayed, the Seller will immediately notify the Buyer of the expected time for delivery and the reason for the delay. Provided the delay is no more than [*number*] days after the Delivery Date, the delay will not constitute a breach of this Agreement. If the delay is longer, the Buyer will have the option of terminating this Agreement.

DELIVERY PLACE AND SHIPPING TERMS

■ POOR PROVISION:

DELIVERY. The Goods will be delivered FOB, to the cargo terminal at the pier for the vessel of transport, New York.

ANALYSIS: The parties have used an incorrect trade term for identifying delivery and transfer of risk of loss. The term FOB does not reflect the apparent arrangement being made for transport first to a pier and then again on board the vessel. The trade terms FAS, FOB, CFR, and CIF are for use when the goods are delivered to the buyer after they have been handed over the ship's side. Use of the incorrect trade term can result in an unforeseen risk and an unwanted surprise. In this case, the seller would continue to bear the risk of loss until the goods had moved over the ship's rail. It is essential that you consider each step of the transport in light of which party will have the risk of loss at the various stages. You should then make certain that your intent with respect to which party should bear the risk during transport is reflected in the shipping and delivery trade terms.

■ BETTER PROVISION:

DELIVERY. The Goods will be delivered FCA, New York.

INSURANCE

■ POOR PROVISION:

INSURANCE. The [Buyer/Seller] must insure the Goods while in transit for [*currency and amount*]. A copy of the policy or other statement provided by the insurer must be provided to the [Seller/Buyer] before the Goods are shipped. Failure to insure the Goods is grounds for cancellation of this Agreement. Each party is responsible for obtaining on its own account any other insurance coverage for the Goods that it may desire.

ANALYSIS: This clause may be reasonable in a domestic transaction where the parties are familiar with available insurance policies, but it is too strict for an international transaction. Unless the parties are certain that the coverage is available in the amount designated, the failure of a party to obtain insurance coverage should not be grounds for cancellation of the contract.

■ BETTER PROVISION:

INSURANCE. The [Buyer/Seller] is responsible for obtaining and maintaining insurance on the Goods while in transit. The insurance coverage must be for the invoiced value of the goods, and the [Seller/Buyer] must be named as a loss payee. A copy of the policy or other statement provided by the insurer must be provided to the [Seller/Buyer] before the Goods are shipped. If the [Buyer/Seller] fails to obtain such insurance, the [Seller/Buyer] has a right to purchase insurance coverage and to charge the cost of premiums to the [Buyer/Seller]. Each party is responsible for obtaining on its own account any other insurance coverage for the Goods that it may desire.

TRANSFER OF TITLE TIME

■ POOR PROVISION:

TITLE TO GOODS. Title to the Goods will pass to the Buyer when the Goods are shipped.

ANALYSIS: When title passes, so does the risk of loss. Therefore, this critical provision should be clear and definite. However, the term "shipped" has many meanings. It could simply mean that the goods have left the seller's warehouse but not the seller's possession. Another alternative is that the seller has transferred the goods to a land carrier, such as a railway or trucking company. Or it could mean that the goods are shipped when placed on board a vessel, even if first carted over land by another carrier.

■ BETTER PROVISION:

TITLE TO GOODS. Title to the Goods will pass to the Buyer at the time the Seller delivers the Goods to the Buyer. The Goods will be deemed delivered at the time they are stowed on board the vessel.

TRANSFER OF TITLE: SIMULTANEOUS WITH RISK

■ POOR PROVISION:

TITLE TO GOODS. Title to the Goods will remain with the Seller until the Goods are accepted by the Buyer at the Buyer's place of business. The risk of loss for the Goods will pass to the buyer at the time the Buyer accepts this offer.

ANALYSIS: This is an extreme version illustrating the problems that can arise when title and risk of loss are transferred at different times. When the buyer accepts the offer, the goods are sitting in the seller's warehouse. The warehouse burns down. The buyer incurs the loss, even though the buyer had no title. Unfortunately, without title to goods, it is also more difficult to obtain insurance coverage.

■ BETTER PROVISION:

TITLE TO GOODS. The title to the Goods and the risk of loss for the Goods will transfer to the Buyer at the time the Goods are stowed on board the vessel for transport.

RETURN OF GOODS

■ POOR PROVISION:

RETURN OF GOODS. After the initial shipment, the Buyer is entitled to return to the Seller any Goods that it has not been able to sell after a period of [*number*] days despite reasonable and diligent marketing efforts.

ANALYSIS: The intent of this clause is ambiguous because the term *after* connotes time. In a literal reading of this clause, the buyer is entitled to return goods regardless of whether they were part of the initial shipment or a later shipment. However, by this interpretation, the phrase "after the initial shipment" is extraneous. Most likely, the parties intended to except the goods in the initial shipment from the return policy. Unfortunately, the literal meaning of *after* does not include "except for."

■ BETTER PROVISION:

RETURN OF GOODS. With the exception of Goods delivered in the initial shipment, the Buyer is entitled to return to the Seller any Goods that it has not been able to sell after a period of [*number*] days despite reasonable and diligent marketing efforts. The Buyer's right to return Goods does not extend to any Goods that were part of the first shipment delivered to the Buyer.

CLEARANCE OF CUSTOMS

■ POOR PROVISION:

CUSTOMS CLEARANCE. The Seller will be responsible for clearing the Goods through customs. When clearance is completed, the Seller will promptly notify the Buyer that the Goods are available for delivery.

ANALYSIS: This clause does not specify whether the seller must clear the goods through customs in the exporting country, the importing country, or both. Further, it could place the seller in breach if the goods cannot be cleared through no fault of the seller. Assuming the goods do clear, the seller will apparently have to store them until notice can be given to the buyer and the buyer is able to arrange for acceptance of the delivery.

■ BETTER PROVISION:

CUSTOMS CLEARANCE. The Seller will be responsible for obtaining, completing, and presenting all documentation and fees required for clearance of customs in both the exporting and importing countries in time sufficient to deliver the Goods to the Buyer's place of business no later than [*date*]. The Buyer will cooperate fully in supplying documentation and information required by the Seller to clear customs. If a delay in clearance is caused by the Buyer's failure to provide documentation or information, the Seller will not be deemed in breach of this Agreement for failure to deliver on the designated dated. The Seller is entitled to charge the Buyer for all costs of storage or preservation of the Goods incurred because the Buyer is not prepared to accept the Goods at the time of delivery, provided delivery is no earlier than [*date*].

INSPECTION RIGHTS

■ POOR PROVISION:

INSPECTION RIGHTS. Before accepting the Goods, the Buyer has a right to inspect them at the time and place where they are delivered.

ANALYSIS: If the time and place of delivery is convenient for the buyer, this clause will suffice. However, the buyer's inspection rights are useless if the buyer is unable to exercise them. Thus, if delivery is made Ex Works (meaning at the seller's warehouse), a foreign buyer is unlikely to be able to inspect the goods before having to accept them. At a minimum, inspection rights should be granted to the buyer or an authorized representative and the buyer should have a reasonable time within which to complete the inspection.

■ BETTER PROVISION:

INSPECTION RIGHTS. Before accepting the Goods, the Buyer has a right to inspect them after they reach the Buyer's [*designate place, e.g.,* store]. Acceptance or rejection must be made within [*number*] of working days from the date the Goods reach that destination. The Buyer's failure to inspect the Goods will be deemed a waiver of the right of inspection.

CHAPTER 9

Parties to the Transaction, Part 3

IN THE CENTER OF YOUR DESK, on top of all your lists of possible contract terms, your notes from negotiation, several memoranda, and lots of letters, there rests THE CONTRACT. You have not signed it. You have not even read it all the way through from beginning to end. Maybe you have peeked inside at a few provisions, in particular the payment clauses. Does it state your intentions? Does it cover all of the basics? Does it cover all of the extras? And the most important question looms on the horizon: should you sign it?

It is wise to read the contract several times, keeping in mind different concerns each time to be certain that your contract states your entire agreement. You should first read it to become familiar with the organization of the provisions. The next review should include a comparison to the terms that you have already negotiated and to which you have orally agreed. On the third review, you should consider whether the contract defines every aspect of the relationship that you intended in terms of the practices in your industry and in your own particular business. Finally, you should always be certain that you have covered the legal and business issues common to all international contracts, and in this regard you should consider whether the contract answers the points listed here.

Buyer

Although the seller or the seller's attorney often drafts the sales contract, as the buyer you had better review and understand every term before signing. Further, it is wise to have your own attorney's advice on the terms. To protect your interests and to work with your attorney to your best advantage, keep in mind the following issues related to the contract terms.

COMMITMENT TO RELATIONSHIP

Is the contract for a one-time transaction, or does it create an ongoing relationship?

Contract terms tend to differ depending on whether the parties intend to establish a long-term relationship. The basic distinction is in the flexibility permitted to the contracting parties to negotiate details as their relationship continues. In a one-time transaction, the terms of the sale are established and in the absence of a major problem, the parties rarely renegotiate. If the parties intend to work together for a long time, they may still set up a contract for a single transaction, but generally the contract will allow the parties to alter terms as necessary to make the performance of the contract profitable for both. Alternatively, the parties may enter into an agreement that establishes the basic parameters of all transactions that will subsequently occur between them. Such an agreement will not deal with the particulars of any one sale, but will be in effect for all sales. It usually allows the parties to agree to the details by giving notices to each other as needed to effect a certain transaction. You should consider whether your contract terms provide for the following:

- Does your contract state your intent to create a long-term relationship or to make a one-time purchase?
- Does your contract allow for renegotiation of the essential terms for delivery, identification of the goods, and even compensation, in the event that performance becomes overly burdensome or impossible?
- If your contract provides for more than one transaction, have you provided for reasonable means of modifying the terms of the contract over time?
- Are the provisions of your contract easily modifiable by addendums or changes in schedules so that you do not need to execute waivers or written modifications every time a small detail is altered?

AUTHORITY TO CONTRACT

Does the seller or the seller's representative have authority or appear to have authority to make the contract?

A party's authority to contract only becomes significant if you need to enforce the contract or if you want to dispute the contract. If a party has no authority to contract but does so anyway, the contract may be fully performed, all parties may be happy, and authority to contract never becomes an issue. That is an ideal world, however, and therefore you would be wise to obtain written evidence of the other party's authority to contract. Written evidence simply means that your contract should include a clause that covers authority to contract. In reviewing this clause, you should consider the following points:

- Is the seller an individual or a business entity?
- If the seller is a business entity, has the seller's representative provided you with proof of authority to act for the seller?
- Has the seller or the seller's representative given you any reason to doubt the seller's authority?
- Does it appear that the seller or the seller's representative is older than age twenty-one and in full control of his or her faculties?

ESSENTIAL TERMS

Have you included the essential terms?

If your contract does not provide the terms that are necessary to complete the transaction, in some jurisdictions the contract will not be enforceable. In others, the courts will imply terms into your contract that you may or may not have intended. Therefore, always review your contract to see if it answers all of the following questions:

- Does the contract contain a clear and definite description of the type, quality, and quantity of all the goods that you intend to purchase?
- Is the price specified, and is it given in total or per unit of measurement (such as weight, item, and so forth)?
- Is the delivery date specified, or is there a method for determining the date?
- Are the terms of payment clear? Will you be able to comply with the method of payment specified?
- Is the currency designated likely to decrease in value as against the currency of the seller's country?

- Do you anticipate a currency fluctuation because of economic instability, resulting in a substantial change in the value of the currency?
- Does the contract specify an exchange rate?
- Does the contract allow for renegotiation or other alteration of the price in the event of a currency devaluation?
- What provisions might be implied into your contract?
- Is your contract subject to the United Nations Convention on International Sale of Goods (CISG)?

INSPECTION OF GOODS

What are your inspection rights?

If you have agreed to take the goods without warranties, you should insist on adequate inspection rights, meaning you have the time, labor, and facilities available to conduct a meaningful inspection. Even if warranties are provided, inspection rights are important. Exercising a warranty is less convenient than simply returning goods that are not in satisfactory condition on arrival. Review your inspection rights in the contract with the following points in mind:

- Will you be able to exercise your inspection rights, or will it be impossible within the time or place allowed?
- Do you have to pay for the goods before you inspect them?
- Will you need to arrange inspection by a third party because you will not be able to personally inspect the goods?

DELIVERY TERMS

What are the delivery terms of the contract?

The delivery terms will determine when you take title to the goods and when you assume risk of loss or damage. These two events can be separate, so be careful. Avoid assuming the risk if you do not yet have title to the goods. Also remember that international shipping can be fraught with delays, and inflexible delivery terms could result in failure of performance. The following points should be covered by your agreement:

- Does it provide for a specific shipment date or a means of determining the shipment date?
- Is it clear when title and risk of loss are transferred to you from the seller?
- Are title and risk of loss transferred at the same time?
- Has the seller retained title to the goods even after you have paid for them and assumed the risk of loss during transport?
- Does the contract encourage renegotiation of terms in the event a party defaults in performance?
- Is there an allowance of time for delays in complying with government requirements for import, export, licensing, inspection, and so forth?

SPECIFICATION OF GOODS

If you have a choice in the design, manufacture, quality, or characteristics of the goods, does the contract give you adequate control over these factors?

If you are permitted to give the seller specifications for the goods, you will expect to receive goods that are in compliance with your requests. Unfortunately, this will not always be the case. You will need to consider whether variations are permissible. If the seller makes a supreme effort to comply but requires more time than expected, you will may need to make some allowances. By considering the following issues when you first make your contract, you can set up procedures for dealing with problems, thereby avoiding surprises later:

- Is the seller permitted to request an extension of time to prepare the goods for shipment?
- Is there a clause allowing performance to be delayed during a crisis beyond the control of the parties?
- Is there an allowance for variations in the type or amount of goods shipped? Are the variations limited and subject to your rejection? Is the seller required to notify you of the variations?
- Does the contract require absolute compliance with your specifications?
- Does the seller warrant compliance?
- Do your specifications include all labeling, marking, packaging, and other requirements imposed by your own country for sale or use of the goods?

CUSTOMS CLEARANCE

What are your obligations with regard to customs clearance?

The complexities of clearing customs can be simplified if the provisions of your contract clearly allocate the responsibilities between you and the seller. To answer many of these questions, it would be best if you knew the export and import requirements for the particular country, although you can, of course, write generic terms to cover the issues regardless of whether they in fact exist. Review the following points to consider whether you know the customs procedures and requirements for the particular countries involved in your transaction and whether your contract covers all possibilities:

- Are you required to pay export or import duties, taxes, and charges?
- Will you be subject to port or freight charges?
- Are you required to provide clearance documentation?
- Do you need to obtain any licenses or permits for importing the goods?

TRANSPORT TERMS AND INSURANCE

Does the contract require you to make transport arrangements for the goods?

Delivery and transport responsibilities are highly dependent on the type of goods and the industry involved. For small consumer goods, the seller may well make all delivery and transport arrangements right to your very door. In other situations, you may be required to take over the transportation of the goods at some point along the way. Consider whether your contract states your intentions for the following points:

- Where will you take delivery of the goods?
- Is the contract clear as to whether the seller will load the goods onto your designated carrier, or is loading your responsibility?
- Will you have to insure the goods against loss or damage during transit?

- Is the seller providing any insurance coverage for you?
- Do you have a copy of the seller's insurance policy?
- What is the cost of insuring the goods on your own account?
- Will you have to store the goods during transit?

WARRANTIES AND RETURNS

What warranties and servicing are offered with the goods?

If the seller is in competition for your business, you are likely to be offered various warranty and servicing incentives for the sale. If competition is minimal, you may need to insist on and negotiate for the incentives that you want. Incentives will vary depending on the practices common in the industry and countries involved. For example, if you are buying consumer goods for retail in your own country, the seller may offer a return policy and a warranty. If the goods are extremely expensive, high-tech, immovable once installed, or otherwise difficult to return, the seller will probably offer a maintenance or repair service. Another important incentive to look for is a warranty or indemnity against third-party claims. In reviewing the incentives provided in your contract, check the following issues:

- Can you pass the warranties on to the next buyer?
- Is the seller required to replace defective goods?
- Is there a return policy?
- Are you indemnified against damages that arise solely because of negligent or wrongful actions of the seller—such as defective design or manufacturing of the goods?
- Is the seller obligated to maintain the goods after you have accepted them?
- Do the warranty and service obligations continue after delivery, even if the contract terminates effective as of the delivery?
- Has the seller indemnified you against third-party claims arising from defects in the goods or infringement of intellectual property rights?
- Are you allowed to return the goods for any reason?
- Is there a reasonable period of time allowed for returns?
- Is the return period applicable to all shipments of the goods?
- Does the seller pay for the return shipment?

ASSIGNMENTS

Does the contract provide for assignments?

If the contract will be performed within a short time, the assignment rights are probably not significant. Nevertheless, many things can happen within a short time, including bankruptcy or an unresolvable conflict. Assignment rights should be mutual, which means both parties should have the same rights to assign the contract, and the courts will often imply mutuality of assignment if the contract provisions are otherwise. The most common practice is to allow for assignment, provided the other party consents. A complete prohibition against all assignments is rarely made, and in many countries it is unenforceable. For these reasons, you should review your contract for the following provisions:

- May you transfer all of your interest in the contract to another person?
- May you delegate part of your rights or obligations to another person?

- Does the seller have the same right? Is the seller's right limited by a requirement that you must give prior consent?

TERMINATION RIGHTS

What are the termination rights in the contract?

Similar to the right to assign, the right to cancel or terminate a contract may often not be exercised but will be important if the occasion arises. Express cancellation rights should be provided in every sales contract, whether domestic or international, even if the parties do not anticipate the need. In international contracts, the termination clause takes on added significance because the parties are dealing with more factors that are beyond their control than in domestic contracts, including long distance transport, customs clearance, different markets and customs, and distinct economic and political forces. If termination is not expressly covered by the contract, courts are likely to imply that the parties intended termination based on a reasonable justification only. Termination for no cause is not favored. If you intend to permit termination without cause, you should be certain that your contract states this intent clearly. Your should review the termination clause for the following points:

- Do you have a right to cancel the contract? Does the seller have the same right?
- Does a reason have to be given for cancellation?
- By what procedure may you exercise the cancellation right?

REMEDIES ON DEFAULT

What remedies do you have for the seller's breach?

You will probably not need to resort to the remedies provided in your contract, but there is always at least a remote possibility that the seller will default in performance. The best means to control the risk of a default and the attendant costs is to provide for your remedies. If you fail to provide for remedies that you believe will be satisfactory compensation on breach, you will have to resort to the relief allowed by law, which may be less than satisfactory. Consider the following issues:

- Does the contract encourage negotiation or mediation of all disputes?
- Does it provide for liquidated damages?
- Does the contract provide for arbitration? Is the arbitration binding or nonbinding? Which arbitration organization has been selected?
- Does the contract allow for an award of legal fees and costs to the prevailing party in any arbitration or litigation?
- Is the designated forum convenient to you for purposes of commencing action against the seller?
- Will you be able to enforce a judgment against the seller if you obtain it in the forum identified?
- Have you specified the law that is to govern interpretation of your contract?

INDEPENDENT COUNSEL

Have you been given the opportunity to consult independent counsel?

The opportunity to consult independent counsel should be stated in the contract to avoid any later questions about whether the parties understood the terms to the contract and formed a mutual intent. Lack of mutual intent can be grounds for avoiding the contract. An independent counsel clause may be useful in establishing that the parties have entered the contract voluntarily and with comprehension of the meaning and effect of the terms. In drafting and reviewing this clause, you should note the following issues:

- In addition to giving the right to consult independent counsel, does your clause establish that the parties had this opportunity before they executed the contract?
- Does the contract provide that counsel must be independent for each party?
- Does the contract indicate that the parties have had a chance to modify the contract in accordance with the independent advice of counsel?

Seller

As the seller, you will probably draft, or have your attorney draft, the sales contract. If you draft the contract, it is wise to have your attorney review it. To ensure that you have protected all of your interests and to work with your attorney to your best advantage, be careful to consider the following clauses and issues.

COMMITMENT TO RELATIONSHIP

Is the contract for a one-time transaction, or does it create an ongoing relationship?

The terms of a contract for sale will differ depending on whether the parties intend to make a one-time sale or to establish a long-term relationship. The basic distinction is in the flexibility granted to the parties to negotiate details as their relationship continues. In a one-time transaction, the terms are usually fixed and, in the absence of a major problem, the parties rarely renegotiate. Parties who intend to work together for a long time may still set up a contract for a single transaction, but generally the contract will allow the parties to alter terms as necessary to keep performance of the contract profitable for both. Alternatively, the parties may enter into an agreement that establishes the basic parameters of all transactions that will subsequently occur between them. Such an agreement will not deal with the particulars of any one sale, but will be in effect for all sales. It usually allows the parties to agree to the details by giving notices to each other as needed to effect a certain transaction. You should consider whether your contract terms provide for the following:

- Does your contract state your intent to create a long-term relationship or to make a one-time sale?
- If your contract provides for more than one transaction, have you provided for reasonable means of modifying the terms of the contract over time?
- Are the provisions of your contract easily modifiable by addendums or changes in schedules so that you do not need to execute waivers or written modifications every time a small detail is altered?
- Does the contract encourage renegotiation of terms in the event a party defaults?
- Is there an allowance of time for delays in complying with government

requirements for import, export, licensing, inspection, and so forth?
- Are you permitted to request an extension of time to prepare the goods for shipment?
- Is there a clause allowing performance to be delayed during a crisis beyond the control of the parties?
- Is there an allowance for variations in the type or amount of goods shipped?

AUTHORITY TO CONTRACT

Does the buyer or the buyer's representative have authority or appear to have authority to make the contract?

A party's authority to contract only becomes significant if you need to enforce the contract or if you want to dispute it. If a party has no authority to contract but does so anyway, the contract may be fully performed, all parties may be happy, and authority to contract never becomes an issue. That is an ideal world, however, and therefore you would be wise to obtain written evidence of the other party's authority to contract. Written evidence simply means that your contract should include a clause that covers authority to contract. In reviewing this clause, you should consider the following points:

- Is the buyer an individual or a business entity?
- If the buyer is a business entity, has the buyer's representative provided you with proof of authority to act for the buyer?
- Has the buyer or the buyer's representative given you any reason to doubt the buyer's authority?
- Does it appear that the buyer or the buyer's representative is older than age twenty-one and in full control of his or her faculties?

ESSENTIAL TERMS

Have you included the essential terms?

If your contract does not provide the terms that are necessary to complete the transaction, in some jurisdictions the contract will not be enforceable. In others, the courts will imply terms into your contract, terms that you may or may not have intended. Therefore, always review your contract to see if it answers all of the following questions:

- Does the contract contain a clear and definite description of the type, quality, and quantity of all the goods that you intend to sell?
- Is the price specified, and is it given in total or per unit of measurement (such as weight, item, and so forth)?
- Is it clear whether other costs, such as taxes and duties, will be charged separately from the price?
- Are you allowed to request adjustment of the price if circumstances beyond your control result in an overly burdensome increase in your production costs?
- Is the delivery date specified, or is there a method for determining the date?
- Are the terms of payment clear? Is the method of payment as secure as possible? Will payment be made in advance of shipment? If not, how will you verify that payment has been made before delivery of the goods to the buyer?
- Is the currency designated likely to increase in value as against the currency of the buyer's country?

- Do you anticipate a currency fluctuation because of economic instability, resulting in a substantial change in the value of the currency?
- Does the contract specify an exchange rate?
- Is your contract subject to the United Nations Convention on International Sale of Goods (CISG)?

DELIVERY TERMS

What are the delivery terms of the contract?

You should pay close attention to the terms of delivery included in your sales contract. As seller, you are responsible for sending or handing over the goods to the buyer. Until delivery is made, you remain liable for loss or damage to the goods. To ensure that you can perform the contract timely, you should be certain that your production, packaging, and transport arrangements can all be completed within the deadline set for delivery. Remember that the additional factors involved in international shipping can slow the process, and extra time should be provided accordingly. Consider the delivery terms in light of the following issues:

- Does it provide for a specific shipment date or a means of determining the shipment date?
- Is the delivery date sufficient to allow for delays inherent in international transport and customs clearance?
- Have you used the proper delivery terms for the mode of transport?
- Will you need to provide for multimodal transport?
- What is the destination of the delivery?
- Is it clear when title and risk of loss are transferred from you to the buyer?
- Are title and risk of loss transferred at the same time?
- Have you transferred title before verification of payment of the price?

CUSTOMS CLEARANCE

What are your obligations with regard to customs clearance?

The complexities of clearing customs can be simplified if the provisions of your contract clearly allocate the responsibilities between you and the buyer. To answer many of these questions, it would be best if you knew the export and import requirements for the particular countries, although you can, of course, write generic terms to cover the issues regardless of whether they in fact exist. Review the following points to consider whether you know the customs procedures and requirements for the particular countries involved in your transaction and whether your contract covers all possibilities:

- Are you required to pay export or import duties, taxes, and charges?
- Will you be subject to port or freight charges?
- Are you required to provide clearance documentation?
- Do you need to obtain any licenses or permits for exporting the goods?

SPECIFICATIONS OF GOODS

Has the buyer provided specifications to you?

If the buyer is permitted to give specifications for the goods, you will be expected to comply. To ensure that you have the ability to comply, the contract should require that specifications be made in accordance with the parameters that you define. It should also allow for reasonable substitutions in the event that you are unable to comply despite your best efforts. By considering the following issues when you first make your contract, you can set up procedures for dealing with problems, thereby avoiding surprises later:

- Are you required to warrant compliance with the specifications?
- Do the specifications include labeling, marking, packaging, and other requirements imposed by your own country for sale or use of the goods?
- Will you be able to comply with the specifications within sufficient time to ensure that the goods will be delivered on time?

TRANSPORT AND INSURANCE TERMS

What arrangements will you be required to make during transport of the goods?

Delivery and transport responsibilities are highly dependent on the type of goods and the industry involved. For small consumer goods, you may well make all delivery and transport arrangements right to the buyer's door. In other situations, the buyer may take over the transportation of the goods at some point along the way. Consider whether your contract states your intentions for the following points:

- Is the buyer providing any insurance coverage during transport?
- Do you have a copy of the buyer's insurance policy?
- What is the cost of insuring the goods on your own account?
- Will you have to store the goods during transit?

WARRANTIES AND SERVICE PROVISIONS

What warranties and servicing have you offered with the goods?

To win a sale away from your competitors, you might consider offering various warranty and servicing incentives to the buyer. Incentives will vary depending on the practices common in the industry and countries involved. For example, if you are selling consumer goods, you might offer a return policy and a warranty. If the goods are extremely expensive, high-tech, immovable once installed, or otherwise difficult to return, you might offer a maintenance or repair service. Another important incentive is a warranty or indemnity against third-party claims. In reviewing the incentives provided in your contract, check the following issues:

- Are you selling the goods in "as is" condition, such that no express or implied warranties are being extended?
- Have you limited your warranties to the buyer, or are you allowing them to pass through to the next buyer?
- Have you limited any warranties to goods that are unaltered by the buyer?
- Are you obligated to maintain the goods after delivery to the buyer?
- Have you granted the buyer the right to return goods?
- Is the right limited to certain reasons?
- Is the return made at the expense of the buyer?

INTELLECTUAL PROPERTY RIGHTS

Have you protected your rights in your intellectual property?

The value of your intellectual property rights—whether in trademarks, service marks, trade names, brand names, patents, designs, or otherwise—should never be underestimated. People who infringe on your intellectual property rights know the value of those rights, as their sales will be based on your good will and reputation. By failing to protect your rights when dealing with overseas parties, you are leaving yourself open to infringement and dilution of those rights. Your contract should therefore deal with the following issues:

- Is the buyer prohibited from altering the labels, packaging, brochures, manuals, and other materials associated with the goods?
- Have you established rules and policies to control the content of advertising, which will reflect on your reputation and goodwill even if you do not directly sell your products to the consuming public?
- Is the buyer required to acknowledge your exclusive rights in all advertising, marketing promotions, and so forth?
- Have you covered your company name and trade secrets?

ASSIGNMENTS

Does the contract provide for assignments?

If the contract will be performed within a short time, the assignment rights are probably not significant. Nevertheless, many things can happen within a short time, including bankruptcy or an unresolvable conflict. Assignment rights should be mutual, which means both parties should have the same rights to assign the contract, and the courts will often imply mutuality of assignment if the contract provisions are otherwise. The most common practice is to allow for assignment, provided the other party consents. A complete prohibition against all assignments is rarely made, and in many countries it is unenforceable. For these reasons, you should review your contract for the following provisions:

- May you transfer all of your interest in the contract to another person?
- May you delegate part of your rights or obligations to another person?
- Does the buyer have the same right? Is the buyer's right limited by a requirement that you must give prior consent?

TERMINATION RIGHTS

What are the termination rights in the contract?

Similar to the right to assign, the right to cancel or terminate a contract may often not be exercised but will be important if the occasion arises. Express cancellation rights should be provided in every sales contract, whether domestic or international, even if the parties do not anticipate the need. In international contracts, the termination clause takes on added significance because the parties are dealing with more factors that are beyond their control than in domestic contracts, including long distance transport, customs clearance, different markets and customs, and distinct economic and political forces. If termination is not expressly covered by the contract, courts are likely to imply that the parties intended termination based on a reasonable justification only. Termination for no cause is not favored. If you intend to permit termination without cause, you should be certain that your contract states this intent clearly. Your should review the termination clause for the following points:

- Do you have a right to cancel the contract? Does the buyer have the same right?
- Does a reason have to be given for cancellation?
- By what procedure may you exercise the cancellation right?

REMEDIES ON DEFAULT

What remedies do you have for the buyer's breach?

You will probably not need to resort to the remedies provided in your contract, but there is always at least a remote possibility that the buyer will default in performance. The best means to control the risk of a default and the attendant costs is to provide for your remedies. If you fail to provide for remedies that you believe will be satisfactory compensation on breach, you will have to resort to the relief allowed by law, which may be less than satisfactory. Consider the following issues:

- Does the contract encourage negotiation or mediation of all disputes?
- Does it provide for liquidated damages?
- Does the contract provide for arbitration? Is the arbitration binding or nonbinding? Which arbitration organization has been selected?
- Does the contract allow for an award of legal fees and costs to the prevailing party in any arbitration or litigation?
- Is the designated forum convenient to you for purposes of commencing action against the buyer?
- Will you be able to enforce a judgment against the buyer if you obtain it in the forum identified?
- Have you specified the law that is to govern interpretation of your contract?

INDEPENDENT COUNSEL

Have you been given the opportunity to consult independent counsel?

The opportunity to consult independent counsel should be stated in the contract to avoid any later questions about whether the parties understood the terms to the contract and formed a mutual intent. Lack of mutual intent can be grounds for avoiding the contract. An independent counsel clause may be useful in establishing that the parties have entered the contract voluntarily and with comprehension of the meaning and effect of the terms. In drafting and reviewing this clause, you should note the following issues:

- In addition to giving the right to consult independent counsel, does the clause establish that the parties had this opportunity before they executed the contract?
- Does the contract provide that counsel must be independent for each party?
- Does the contract indicate that the parties have had a chance to modify the contract in accordance with the independent advice of counsel?

Attorney for Buyer

Once you have a contract for the sale of goods—regardless of whether you drafted it, the seller prepared it, or it resulted from a combination effort—you should have it reviewed by your favorite international lawyer. The lawyer will be able to point out the strengths and weaknesses of the agreement and may suggest clauses that you should renegotiate before you sign. You should not consult the same lawyer as the seller, as the seller is effectively an adverse party with conflicting interests. To ensure that you learn all you can about your legal rights and obligations under the agreement, be certain to ask your lawyer about the following issues.

VOID OR VOIDABLE PROVISIONS

- Is there any prohibition against the parties' right to choose a forum or the law to be applied in interpreting the agreement?
- Is the intent of the parties to arbitrate likely to be upheld?
- Are liquidated damages clauses permissible?
- If a contract provision is determined to be invalid, will it render the entire agreement void?

FORMALITIES OF THE CONTRACT

- What evidence is needed of the seller's authority to make the contract?
- Are any formalities, other than the mere signing and dating the agreement, required for it to become effective? Should it be notarized? Should it be witnessed?

PAYMENT AND DELIVERY TERMS

- What problems could arise if the payment method is unavailable?
- What is the United Nations Convention on International Sale of Goods (CISG)? Is it applicable, and if so how will it affect your contract? Can you limit its application?
- Should you obtain insurance in addition to the coverage to be furnished by the seller?
- If there is a delay in the shipment and you incur costs for warehouse rental and labor charges, do you have any remedies against the seller?
- Do the delivery terms match the modes of transport and the destination?

EXPORT AND IMPORT PROVISIONS

- What licenses or permits do you need to obtain to comply with the contract?
- What are the requirements for clearing customs?
- What documentation will be required for import of the goods?
- Will an inspection of the goods be required, and where can it be made?
- What labeling, marking, packaging, and other requirements are imposed by your own country for sale or use of the goods?

WARRANTIES AND REMEDIES

- What warranties are usually implied into a contract for the sale of goods? Should you demand other warranties from the seller?

- How effective are the remedies for the seller's breach?
- Will you be able to take advantage of the remedies provided?
- What does each remedy involve in terms of procedure, cost, and time?
- What are the advantages and disadvantages of the various remedies?
- Are there any remedies available other than the ones provided in the contract? Are you limited to the ones provided in the contract?
- Is the governing law designated in the contract favorable to you?

Attorney for Seller

Before you sign a contract with the buyer for a sale of goods, be certain to have it reviewed by your favorite international lawyer. The lawyer will be able to point out the strengths and weaknesses of the agreement and may suggest clauses that you should renegotiate before you sign. You should not consult the same lawyer as the buyer, as the buyer is effectively an adverse party with conflicting interests. To ensure that you know your legal rights and obligations under the agreement, be certain to ask you lawyer about the following issues.

VOID OR VOIDABLE PROVISIONS

- Is there any prohibition against the parties' right to choose a forum or the law to be applied in interpreting the agreement?
- Is the intent of the parties to arbitrate likely to be upheld?
- Are liquidated damages clauses permissible?
- If a contract provision is determined to be invalid, will it render the entire agreement void?

FORMALITIES OF THE CONTRACT

- What evidence is needed of the buyer's authority to make the contract?
- Are any formalities, other than the mere signing and dating the agreement, required for it to become effective? Should it be notarized? Should it be witnessed?

PAYMENT AND DELIVERY TERMS

- How secure is the method of payment?
- Is the United Nations Convention on International Sale of Goods (CISG) applicable, and if so how will it affect your contract? Can you limit its application?
- Should you obtain insurance in addition to the coverage furnished by the buyer?
- If the buyer is delayed in arranging for the delivery of the goods, can you obtain reimbursement for storage, labor, and other such charges?
- Do the delivery terms match the modes of transport and the destination?

EXPORT AND IMPORT PROVISIONS

- What licenses or permits do you need to obtain to comply with the contract?
- What are the requirements for clearing customs?
- What documentation will be required for export of the goods?
- Will an inspection of the goods be required, and where can the inspection be made?

WARRANTIES AND REMEDIES

- Do you have to offer any warranties? What warranties would usually be implied?
- How effective are the remedies for the buyer's breach?
- Will you be able to take advantage of the remedies provided?
- What does each remedy involve in terms of procedure, cost, and time?
- What are the advantages and disadvantages of the various remedies?
- Are there any remedies available other than the ones provided in the contract? Are you limited to the ones provided in the contract?
- Is the governing law designated in the contract favorable to you?

CHAPTER 10

Validity of Contracts Locally

Culture and Custom

After seeing an advertisement in a trade journal, you send a brief yet comprehensive inquiry for the sale of goods to a foreign trader. It is a mere five pages in length. Two days later, and you still have not received a reply. You had thought that the trader would have jumped at the opportunity to transact business with you, but since there is no response you move ahead and forget the trader. Six months later, the trader sends a short note asking whether you are still interested in the transaction. You immediately send a notice confirming your acceptance of the deal, the foreign trader backs off, and you are ready to sue for breach of contract. You have now made so many errors in business etiquette that you'll be lucky to succeed at all.

If you intend to establish contracts in foreign countries, you must proceed with an understanding of the cultural norms and business practices of those countries. Arrogance will not gain clients. Whether you seek trading partners in Asia, Europe, Africa, Latin America, North America, or the Pacific Rim you must learn that the key to forming long-lasting relationships—and maybe any relationships at all—is in respecting the other party. Courtesy in the initial contact, development of business relationships over a period of time, and enjoyment of the bargaining process are concepts often alien in a fast-paced world. But in many locales, these are the concepts that you must come to understand if you intend to succeed in business there. In some countries, detailed contracts are essential, while in others less so. If you do your homework before you make your initial contact, you will make fewer faux pas.

THE CONTRACT

Before you send a written inquiry or contract, learn about the trader who is the intended recipient. Research the general business customs for that country and determine whether contracts are the foundation of relationships or relationships the basis of contracts. If you are uncertain about whether to send a full-fledged contract, send a short inquiry note that explains the background of your own firm and requests some information about the other trader. This is a courteous introduction and invites a response.

In many countries, written contracts are insignificant relative to personal relationships. Thus, the transmission of a detailed inquiry or contract may be disregarded because you have neglected to establish the relationship first. What counts is your personal commitment to your business associates. You, your son, and your son's son could operate in accordance with custom for generations. By your relationship, you create your contractual obligations.

In societies where relationships are more valued than contracts, parties tend to follow the spirit of a contract. A contract represents a loose commitment between the parties, often consisting merely of a short statement of principle. Details are worked out as the relationship develops, and amendments are common. Many transactions can fall under a single contract because the contract defines a relationship, not a specific sale. Assignment of the contract may not be possible because the personal relationship is so significant.

In other countries where contracts have a high significance, parties lean toward adherence to the letter of the contract. Contracts are the basis of relationships; without the contract, there would be no relationship. Every facet must be covered, and length is no object. If any alterations in the relationship need to be made, the parties make them in a writing that amends the original writing. For the most part, a single contract covers a single transaction. An ongoing relationship is not contemplated—it must be renewed by the parties at regular intervals to remain in effect.

THE PACE

Relationships take a long time to grow, and so if you are courting the business of a trader whose culture treasures relationships, be patient. A business transaction does not have to be completed today, tomorrow, or even next week. The foreign trader is likely to be thinking about the relationship in the long term, maybe even a decade or two from now. With that kind of foresight, the foreign trader will be able to pass a successfully established business to his children. This traditional view remains prevalent in many countries today. If you are too aggressive, you will probably continue to do transactions one at a time because the foreign trader will not want to move at break-neck speed.

In contrast, business deals in many countries are made quickly. Time is of the essence not only in the contract, but also at the negotiating table. Be aware of the other party's signals that indicate you should speed up the process. Is the foreign trader peeking at a clock? Tapping a shoe? Somewhat impatient? You should address the business at hand.

THE BARGAIN

An essential ingredient of doing business, bargaining for the best terms is a part of human nature. If you do not know how to haggle, you will need to learn. International transactions are rarely made based on the first offer presented. An inquiry is not intended to be accepted. If you tender an acceptance when one is not requested, the foreign trader may dislike your aggressive stance. You must learn the difference between an inquiry and an offer.

As simple as it sounds, bargaining is in fact very complex on a global level because of variations among different cultures. In some countries, negotiating can be intense. The issues may be set down and discussed at length until an agreement is finally reached. Other traders may sit silently watching you and simply punctuate your comments with a nod or an "ahem." Tactics may include use of competitor's quotes, leaving the table, and delaying negotiations until just before you must depart. Provided you have done your research, you should be able to turn many of the strategies to your own use.

Part of the trick to successful bargaining is to be well-prepared, and the other part is to recognize that the other party is probably just as prepared as you are, if not more so. First, you may want to adopt some of the other trader's cultural style and to learn the trader's body language. Next, you must know your own issues thoroughly. What is your bottom line? What result would you desire most? Where are you willing to compromise? Keep your incentives in reserve for strategic intervals. Finally, you need to practice your persuasive and charismatic qualities. Timing and sincerity are important. A little humor can break the ice or create a glacier. Sincere flattery is appreciated in some cultures, but a superficial polished manner may negate your efforts.

THE NETWORK

In many cultures, it is who you know that makes the deal. In one sense, this aspect of the culture is related to the importance of relationships over contracts. However, you will also find networks operating in countries where contracts are more significant. Use of a network to extend your business is extremely important. You should make every effort to seek out contacts who are willing to make you a part of their circle of business associates. Even if you commit a faux pas in the early stages of a relationship, if you know someone who knows someone who knows the trader, you are likely to get back on track in a hurry.

Contract Dispute Resolution

Parties who enter into a contract are in effect putting aside their adverse interests and joining in a transaction for their mutual benefit. If that benefit is reduced or eliminated for either or both parties, dispute is inevitable. Although the majority of contracts are completed without any, or at most minor, disagreements, advance planning for dispute resolution is essential because the parties are most unlikely to come to an agreement on this issue after they have fallen into discord.

In an international contract, the methods of dispute resolution selected will depend on what is most familiar to and preferred by the nationals of the country where the transaction takes place. In addition, parties must consider the costs involved in cross-border contract enforcement, the delay inherent in obtaining certain types of relief, and the extent to which available mechanisms have developed into efficient means of dispute resolution. Americans are quick to resort to court actions, while Chinese and Japanese nationals are loath to do so. Binding arbitration is favored in some countries, while others prefer informal negotiation and conciliation. You must know the options and their usefulness in the country where you do business.

COMMUNICATION, WAIVER, MODIFICATION AND NEGOTIATION

Communication between you and your foreign business partner is essential to keeping the relationship smooth. For minor discrepancies, or even major calamities, your business relationships and reputation will benefit if you approach the problem with understanding and a view toward resolving it such that everyone will be satisfied. A good rule to remember: create a working relationship with your foreign business parties, not an adversarial one.

Negotiation, followed by written confirmation of any waiver or modified contract term, is the most effective means of resolution in terms of cost and time. It is generally an informal, unstructured process, subject only to the limitations imposed by the parties themselves. Its success depends on the desire of both parties to participate and to settle their differences.

The very characteristics that make negotiation advantageous—lack of structure, formality, and neutral assistance—can also contribute to its failure if parties are unable to communicate without formal procedures. If a dispute continues despite your informal attempts to resolve it, you should take steps to protect your rights. Your most imminent concern will probably be to recover your own property quickly or to find an immediate replacement supplier so that you can honor your commitments to third parties.

Ten Tips To Completing Your Contract

1. Avoid approaching the other party with overt suspicion; do not assume that the other party is entirely at fault for what appears to be a breach of contract.
2. Do not rashly threaten dire consequences and penalties; you are supposed to be working out your differences, not increasing them.
3. Attempt to incorporate local business culture into your own style, and respect the customs of the other party.
4. Take a slow pace. Allow ideas to germinate. Do not fill every second with chatter. Give the other party a chance to mull over what you have said.
5. Accomplish a bit at a time. Don't expect the entire problem to be resolved at the first meeting. It may take several meetings. You may need to implement some stopgap measures to allow for the time required to resolve the dispute.
6. Do not get stuck on one point. Move to a concern that can be more easily resolved, become more comfortable in working together, and then tackle the tough questions.
7. Be willing to compromise, provided you believe that in the long term the benefits of keeping the contract will come back to you.
8. Offer the other party a way to "save face" without embarrassment or obligation to you.
9. Do not become overly emotional or agitated.
10. Before each meeting create a positive vision of the result that you intend to achieve.

Mediation

The process of mediation is in essence a negotiation that is facilitated by an objective third person. The parties remain the decision makers in the process, and the mediator assists in keeping the channels of communication open, guiding the parties in the process of identifying and resolving each issue separately, and preparing a final agreement. Although for many years the use of mediation has been a common means of resolving noncommercial disputes, it is increasingly being used in the business and international arenas.

ADVANTAGES AND DISADVANTAGES

The focus of mediation is on the future relationship of the parties. The process is intended to allow the parties to repair and then build a more durable relationship that will hopefully continue to their mutual benefit. Often, mediation results in a compromise by both parties, and they both come out winners.

This process is informal, relatively easy and fast, and less costly than arbitration or trial. It is also nonbinding and voluntary, so that the parties can be less concerned about fighting for their rights and more constructive in protecting their interests. Another advantage of mediation is that it is confidential; information revealed during the process and any agreement made will not be on the public record.

PROCEDURES

The parties typically choose a mediator or are referred to mediation by a court before litigation is pursued. A mediator may meet with the parties separately to identify and clarify the issues and hold joint sessions to assist them in arriving at an agreement. Sessions will be devoted to improving communication between the parties and guiding them toward their own solution. A mediator may develop solutions and recommend them to the parties but will not impose a settlement on the parties. If no agreement is reached, the mediator will not decide in favor of one party. Rather, the mediation will simply be unsuccessful.

Arbitration

The parties to a commercial transaction may provide in their contract that any disputes about interpretation or performance of the agreement will be resolved through arbitration. Arbitration is an adjudicatory process that is held before an objective third party who renders a decision based on the adversarial presentations of the disputing parties. Arbitration is fairly popular in business circles because of its formality and decisiveness.

ADVANTAGES TO ARBITRATION

Arbitration may be appealing for a number of reasons. First, it is less expensive and faster than a court trial. Second, the parties tend to have more control over the choice of the decision makers, since the parties usually select arbitrators but have no influence over the judge appointed to hear their case. Third, many of the rules governing procedures and admission of evidence are relaxed in arbitration proceedings, at least in comparison to the trial setting.

DISADVANTAGES TO ARBITRATION

Approach arbitration in an international setting with caution. In many countries, arbitration is unavailable or is just being developed. Moreover,

Arbitration Tips

Arbitration is an effective remedy if you adhere to the following tips.

1. Choose a well-recognized set of rules to govern the proceedings.
2. Appoint an arbitrator who understands the process, is familiar with the matters in dispute, has technical expertise in your particular industry, is knowledgeable in the law governing your contract, and actively manages the process.
3. Hire legal counsel who is familiar with the arbitration process and international trade practices.
4. Adhere to the time limits that the arbitrator imposes before and during the hearing.
5. Limit your requests for procedural and evidentiary decisions to those that are truly necessary.
6. Cooperate in making documentary evidence and witnesses available.
7. Avoid emotional overtones and focus on the issues.
8. Present an organized, strong argument (whether through counsel or on your own).
9. Listen carefully to the other party and be certain your statements are precisely to the point. Do not overstate your case.

although less adversarial than a court trial, arbitration is still viewed in many cultures with suspicion, if not abhorrence. A request for arbitration may be viewed as a personal insult to your foreign counterpart, and instead of being a means of dispute resolution, it may destroy the potential for settlement through private negotiation.

The relatively low cost of arbitration when compared with trial proceedings does not mean that arbitration is cheap. You will still need to obtain legal advice and representation, to compile evidence, to pay the costs of the arbitrators and arbitration, to pay witnesses, and to pay an award if arbitration is not in your favor.

The arbitration process tends to focus on the facts of the case and the rights of the parties, rather than on their future needs and goals. The arbitration will resolve past differences but often will not build a continuing relationship. Inherent in the adversarial nature of the proceeding is the fact that the decision will result in one party being a winner and the other a loser. This result can tend to overshadow the future dealings of the parties.

Arbitration is perhaps best saved for disputes that cannot be resolved by less formal means. The parties can still avoid the cost of a trial, while gaining the neutrality of a third-party decision maker.

PROCEDURES

The process of arbitration is controlled by laws, rules, and regulations specific to the forum chosen for the arbitration. Thus, the procedures will vary depending on the forum selected by the parties. In cross-border transactions, parties often designate that their disputes will be resolved through an internationally recognized arbitration organization. These include the American Arbitration Association (AAA), the International Chamber of Commerce (ICC) in Paris, the London Court of Arbitration, the Japan Commercial Arbitration Association, the United Nations Commission on International Trade Law (UNCITRAL), the United Nations Economic Commission for Europe, the United Nations Economic and Social Commission for Asia and the Pacific (ACAPE), and the Inter-American Arbitration Commission.

The arbitration process is somewhat like a trial. Parties generally select the arbitrator or request that one be appointed to their case. In some arbitrations, a panel of arbitrators—usually consisting of three—is appointed. The arbitrator controls the proceedings and even has power to subpoena witnesses (issue an order requiring them to appear in the proceedings). A short time is allowed for the parties to conduct discovery and prepare their evidence. During the arbitration hearing, each party will be given a chance to present his or her case. The arbitrator will decide procedural, evidentiary, and substantive matters; determine the claim; and make an award. The arbitrator's award may include damages, costs of the proceedings, and attorney's fees. This decision may be enforced by a court.

Litigation

At best, litigation is costly, time consuming, and even if ultimately resolved in your favor still does not address a primary concern: collection of money owed or specific performance of the contract terms. In reality, undertaking litigation proceedings in foreign courts does not often result in a favorable outcome—even after all the time and expense. The courts of many countries are biased in favor of their own nationals, and foreigners rarely, if ever, obtain satisfaction. The best advice is to avoid litigation altogether. If you do become embroiled in a legal battle abroad, obtain the best local counsel available as soon as possible.

ADVANTAGES AND DISADVANTAGES

The decision in a court case will set legal precedent in many jurisdictions. A case decision involving an international transaction may even be persuasive or recognized across country borders. If you want to set legal precedent, you should sue.

In many countries, the court systems are well-developed and effective, even more so than the other alternative means of dispute resolution. You may just get a quick and fair trial. You may even be awarded costs and attorney's fees as the winning party, and you may find that enforcement is fairly easy because it is strictly administered by court officers.

The first disadvantage you will encounter in filing a lawsuit in your selection of the jurisdiction and forum. You will have to find a court that not only can but will agree to exercise its authority over you and the other party. Assuming you get as far as a judgment, you will then find out how difficult it can be to enforce the award, collect the moneys owed, or force return of your property. If the other party has no assets in the jurisdiction where you received the judgment, you will have the onerous task of having to seek recognition of the judgment by the courts or authorities of the country where the other party does have some assets.

PROCEDURES

Court procedures differ from country to country and, within countries, from state to state and municipality to municipality. The major characteristic that they all share is their complexity. In general, lawsuits are commenced by the filing of lots of papers and documents, many of which must be furnished to the person being sued through a procedure often known as "service of process." What follows is a lengthy period of trading back and forth between the parties, who may file responses, counterclaims, counterresponses, and so forth.

Some courts have pretrial sessions and hearings with the parties to handle their motions, discovery problems, potential settlements, and so forth. Discovery tends to be a long process of hide and seek, and parties may have to go to court to gain the cooperation of their adversaries. When the dust settles, the parties will present their arguments before the judge, panel of judges, or jury in a very regimented framework, replete with procedural and evidentiary requirements. Their fate will then be left to the decision maker's interpretation of the facts, laws, prior court decisions, and even the demeanor of the parties and witnesses. Of course, there is usually an appeal process, and if the parties try hard enough, they can continue to litigate through many levels and many years.

CHAPTER 11

Contract Fundamentals in International Legal Systems

BEFORE YOU ENTER into a contract with a person in a foreign country, you should become familiar with that country's legal system and its laws that will affect your contractual arrangement. You should also gain an understanding of the distinctions between your own country's legal system and the legal system of the other party's country. This knowledge can be as important as running a background check on your supplier for two reasons. First, the laws in both countries will determine certain aspects of your contractual relationship. Second, the laws of one country (and not necessarily your own country) may be more favorable to you than those of the other country.

Legal Systems Worldwide

There are four major types of legal systems in the world that provide for commercial law: common law, civil law, Islamic (*Shari'ah*) law, and communist (socialist) law. Many countries have adopted a combination of these legal systems and in addition have retained some influences from various cultures throughout their histories. For example, Japan looked to Germany when developing its modern laws, and therefore it follows the civil law system although its commercial code shows US influence. Malaysian law is a combination of common law, Islamic law, and Malay principles. The civil law system adopted in Egypt combines Islamic principles with French civil law and some common law rules reflecting a lingering British influence. In Asia, Africa, and South America, the legal system of each country is usually that of its former colonial master—Brazil applies civil law reflecting its Portuguese history, while Singapore applies common law on account of its English heritage.

Common Law

The common law system developed as a court system in England before any statutes were adopted for the country. By the time statutes were drafted, the courts were well-entrenched and a tremendous body of law, common law, had already been established. The statutes served to confirm, codify, limit, and supplement the common law of the courts. As a result, its distinguishing feature is its reliance on precedents established by judges in earlier cases. In other words, the courts in common law countries apply and interpret statutes by following the principles developed in earlier decisions or by extrapolating new principles from the old ones to apply in new factual situations.

The Influence of Local Laws

In most countries, parties are allowed substantial freedom in making contracts, including choice of the law to be applied. However, local laws will apply to restrict your choices and to supplement the agreement with implied contractual terms to the extent that you fail to provide for your rights and obligations. These laws will influence your choices from initial negotiation through enforcement of the contract. For example, you need to know the following details.

- Which terms of the agreement are controlled by law and which are left to negotiation—you will waste your time and give away your negotiating edge if you negotiate a point already fixed by law, and your negotiated term will be enforceable only to the extent allowed by law.
- Whether the agreement you have in mind will be valid—if void, it will be unenforceable.
- Which law would be more favorable to your position—your choice of law should be an informed one.
- To what extent the law will protect your interests beyond the terms of the contract—if the law is inadequate or silent, you should insist on protective contract terms.
- What liabilities—civil lawsuits, government-imposed fines, or other penalties—you might incur on account of the other party's actions or omissions so that you can negotiate protective terms such as for indemnity, proof of authority, proof of quality control, or proof of compliance.
- What procedures are available to enforce the contract and to recover for losses in the event of breach and to what extent those procedures will be effective remedies.
- What your liabilities will be if you do not perform the contract.

Therefore, before negotiating a contract, you should be aware of how local laws could affect your contractual arrangement. Otherwise, you may be caught by surprise when you find that performance and enforcement of the terms are not what you expected.

To get a brief overview of the law of a particular country, you might consult the *Digest of Commercial Laws of the World* (Oceana Publications) or the *International Law Digest* (Martindale-Hubbell). These sources are available in the reference section of most large public and law libraries.

Countries that apply common law to commercial transactions include the United Kingdom, the United States, Canada, Australia, Singapore, the Hong Kong S.A.R., Israel, India, Egypt, Malaysia, and South Africa. In these countries, trials are typically before one judge, and the parties may request a jury. To ensure a fair trial, complex rules and procedures have been developed, and an appeal process is available.

ARBITRATION

Arbitration systems are generally well-developed and effective and serve as a means of alleviating litigation delays in the court. Contracts that require the parties to resolve disputes through arbitration will be upheld.

CONTRACTS

Contracts for the sale of goods are typically regulated by uniform laws that are similar to the United Nations Convention on International Sales Contracts (CISG). The parties have freedom to agree to any terms desired, provided the terms neither violate public policy nor require the performance of an illegal act. If contract terms are missing, reasonable rights and obligations will be implied from the law or business practices of the parties or industry. Damages are commonly measured by the rule of "lost benefit of the bargain." This rule allows a party to claim an amount damages based on the benefit that the party can prove it would have received if the other party had not breached the contract. In most jurisdictions, a party will also be awarded damages for losses that arise from the breach, known as consequential damages.

Civil Law

Most countries that do not apply common law have civil law systems. Civil law is characterized by comprehensive and systematic compilations of statutes, known as codes of law, that govern most aspects of human endeavor. These countries have developed their codes first and then their courts. Therefore, judicial decisions are based on the legal principles set forth in the codes.

Civil law systems use nonjury trials, except in criminal cases, and the courts are typically composed of a panel of judges. In comparison to common law systems, there are few well-defined rules of evidence, and minimal oral testimony or argument is permitted before the court. Most evidence and arguments are presented to the court in writing.

Legal decisions are generally based on one-time interpretations of the codified laws without reference to preceding cases, although in some countries prior case decisions are recognized after the same decision has been made a certain number of times. As a result, the decision in any particular lawsuit is less predictable than it would be in a common law court, which will rely on the preceding case law.

ARBITRATION

Many civil law countries have procedures for the recognition of arbitration awards. Efficient arbitration systems are also available in many of them, although there is often a limit on the types of disputes that may be decided by arbitration. In general, commercial disputes can be arbitrated.

CONTRACTS

Commercial contracts (between merchants) usually do not need to be written. In transactions for the sales of goods, the terms of the contract are often specified by a country's civil law, although the law allows the parties to agree expressly to different terms. Good faith and fair dealing are usually implied into commercial contracts. The enforcement of oral contracts is difficult in practice because many civil law courts accept written evidence instead of oral testimony. Negotiation is the preferred method of dealing with disputes or minor alterations in contract terms.

In many civil law codes, rules for calculating damages for breach of contract did not exist. This standard is still not clearly defined in a number of civil law countries. However, courts in these countries tend to be more willing than their common law counterparts to award specific performance in contract actions. This award requires a party to perform a specific action mandated by the court, such as the return of property or remittance of payment. Many of the civil law court systems have well-developed enforcement and monitoring mechanisms to make this effective.

Islamic (Shari'ah) Law

In criminal, family, and personal injury matters, Moslem or Islamic countries apply the Law of Islam, originally derived from the Koran and the Sunna. The Koran is believed by its adherents to contain the revelations of Allah to the Prophet Mohammed, and the Sunna is a recording of the Prophet's later teachings and actions. These sacred volumes do not contain detailed codes, but rather principles and precepts of the Muslim religion. The Muslims do not modify these laws because of their belief that after the Prophet's death the direct revelations of God ceased and the words of God are immutable.

With some exceptions, most Muslim countries no longer adhere to the strict traditional form of *Shari'ah* law. Today, its application tends to be limited to family and estate succession law. Even these laws have been codified, so reference to the traditional texts is rarely made except when existing statutes and codes fail to cover a specific situation. To accommodate changes in modern societies and international business practices, most Muslim countries have adopted modified codes based on European legal models, particularly French or Napoleonic Code. A separate division of commercial courts or administrative tribunals usually handles commercial disputes in accordance with civil law concepts. Case decisions are based on the law; case precedents are not binding on later cases.

ARBITRATION

Private commercial disputes can be resolved through arbitration in many of the Muslim countries. The arbitration agreement and award will have to be approved by the courts of the country where enforcement is sought.

CONTRACTS

Parties are free to contract, provided the terms do not alter any standard legal precepts and practices of the religious tradition of *Shari'ah* law. Some written evidence of a contract is often required for enforcement purposes, although an oral contract may be proved by a witness. A clause for the application of a governing law other than *Shari'ah* law will not be recognized. Transactions involving interest may be considered usurious and, therefore, prohibited. The courts will award only actual damages; lost profits and opportunity are considered too speculative. Many contractual terms are limited or unenforceable, including those for repossession of goods on default, retention of title by the seller, remedies, disclaimers, and limitations on liability. Warranties usually follow *Shari'ah* precepts.

Communist Law

The communist law system is used in the People's Republic of China, Cubá, the Democratic People's Republic of Korea, and Vietnam. It originated from the Communist Manifesto of Karl Marx and Friedrich Engels. The Manifesto is a philosophical mandate under which individual rights were subsumed for the good of all society on the assumption that the rights of each citizen inhere in the goals of the state. A code of laws was gradually developed from the Manifesto for the purpose of transforming society into a socialist and then a communist order, at which time the laws were supposed to cease because the new society would function smoothly without the need for rules and regulations.

In the communist system, commercial and foreign trade is primarily operated by the state. Commercial relationships with state-owned entities are heavily affected by whatever government policy is currently in effect, and a modification of contract terms can be required by a sudden shift in state ideology for purposes of implementing a planned economy. To the extent that you are able to trade with private individuals, you will find that individual rights to contract vary depending on state policies as well because the right of society as a whole prevails over individuals.

Private individuals rarely resort to the communist court system for resolution of commercial disputes. The laws applied tend to have a strong ideological content that is unsuitable for interpreting commercial relations. Communist court proceedings are open, direct, and heavily reliant on oral testimony and examination. The rules of evidence are minimal, and prior case decisions carry little weight. The court will consider all evidence presented, decide the relative value and importance of the facts, and make a determination based on general legal principles and communist ideology.

CONTRACTS

More and more private individuals are making contracts for the sale of goods in communist countries, but commercial contracts are still primarily made with government agencies. Imports and exports of commodities must be channeled through licensed trading companies. The difficulty of negotiating terms with government agencies tends to limit the freedom to contract. Communist countries that have been heavily trading internationally have developed some private contract law. For example, in China no particular form is mandated for an agreement for the sale of goods, but preprinted forms are in common use for international sales.

The law in communist nations is rapidly changing. Most of these nations are in the process of modernizing their economies and have found that they need to conform their commercial practices to today's international business world. With regard to contracts for the sale of goods, their legal systems are a bit of mixture of civil and common law. When doing business with traders of these nations, it is important to recognize that the unpredictable state of the government bureaucracies makes contractual arrangements inherently unreliable. You should seek to establish relationships with foreign traders of these countries in an effort to stabilize your agreements regardless of the political and economic situation.

CHAPTER 12

Offer to Sell Goods

WHEN A SELLER receives an inquiry from a buyer, one option is to return an offer to sell the goods in an informal format, such as a letter. The letter usually is brief, containing only the essential terms of the offer. If the buyer places an order, the letter offer and the order will be sufficient evidence of your contract for enforcement purposes, but it is best used for one-time, smaller transactions when the parties are not establishing a continuing relationship. If you use such a letter, it is wise to append additional contract provisions that are more detailed. You might print them on the reverse side of the letter.

Sample Contract: Offer to Sell Goods (front side)

[*seller's letterhead*]

[*date*]

[*buyer's company name*]

[*buyer's address*]

COMMENT: Your contract is binding against the parties who sign it. These parties should be identified by their legal names, company names, and addresses. A party who later needs to give notice to the other should use the address specified in the contract.

Re: Sale of [*identification of goods*]

Dear [Sir/Madam]:

We thank you for your inquiry of [*date*] regarding the purchase of [*identify goods*]. We are pleased to offer you our most competitive price of [*currency and amount, e.g.*, US$50 per case of twenty-five]. The minimum order is [*amount and unit, e.g.*, twenty cases].

COMMENT: This clause covers the essential terms of the agreement, with the exception of delivery. The identification of the goods should be a specific description, which may include a model number. Consider attaching the description to the letter to ensure that the specifications are clear.

Please note that our acceptance of your order will be subject to the conditions printed on the reverse of this letter. Also, your order will not create a binding contract between us. After we have received your order, we will confirm in writing our acceptance, at which time we will then have a binding contract with you.

COMMENT: To avoid disputes over whether the buyer's order constitutes an acceptance and creates a binding contract, you should make your intent clear. If you do not want to take the extra step of confirming the order, you may modify this provision to allow for formation of a contract on receipt of the order instead.

Special shipping terms for this order are as follows: [*specify*].

COMMENT: The preprinted, standard clauses on the reverse side of the letter will not usually be modified for the particular circumstances. If there are any special shipping requirements, be sure to include them in the letter.

We will deliver the goods ordered to your address as stated above, unless you specify a different address in your order. The delivery will be within [*number*] days of our receipt of your order, unless we otherwise inform you. The terms of delivery are as follows: [*specify*].

COMMENT: Until you receive the buyer's order, you will not be able to designate a delivery date. Your offer should nevertheless provide a means of determining that date. Another option is for the seller to notify the buyer of the delivery date at the time the order is confirmed.

If we do not receive an order from you by [*date*], this offer is withdrawn. We look forward to hearing from you.

Sincerely yours,

[*signature of seller*]

Sample Contract: Offer to Sell Goods (reverse side)

CONDITIONS OF SALE

1. AMENDMENTS TO CONDITIONS. No alteration, deletion, or addition to these conditions will have any effect unless the seller accepts the change in writing.

2. DESIGNATED DELIVERY TIMES. Any delivery time or date designated by the seller is an estimate only. The seller will notify the buyer of any delay and of a new estimated delivery date. If delivery is delayed more than thirty days after the date originally designated, the buyer has a right to cancel the contract by giving written notice to the seller at least five days in advance of the estimated delivery date then current. However, if the delay in delivery results because of the seller's efforts to comply with particular specifications supplied by the buyer, the buyer will not have a right to cancel. In this event, the seller will notify the buyer of the delay and the parties will renegotiate another delivery date. The seller's inability to meet the delivery date designated because the buyer has furnished particular specifications will not be a breach of contract.

3. FIRM PRICE. If the buyer places an order within the time designated in this offer, the price for the goods will remain firm notwithstanding any variation in the costs of producing the goods.

4. NO WARRANTIES. No express or implied condition or warranty is made regarding the life or wear of the goods supplied. Nor does the seller warrant the suitability of the goods for any purpose or use under any specific conditions, regardless of whether the seller may know or may have been informed of any purpose or use intended for the goods.

5. DEFECTIVE GOODS. If the buyer believes that any goods delivered are defective, the buyer's only remedy will be to return the goods to the seller. The buyer will not have any claim for loss, damage, or expense arising directly or indirectly from the defects. If the goods are returned to the seller and are accepted as defective, the seller will replace the goods as originally ordered, provided the buyer requests replacement and provided that replacement goods can still be provided.

6. NOTICE OF DAMAGE, SHORTAGE, OR LOSS. The buyer must present any claims for damage in transit, shortage of delivery, or loss of goods to the seller within [number] of days after the buyer receives the goods. The seller will not consider any claim for damage, shortage, or loss unless the buyer presents a separate written notice and claim to the carrier concerned.

7. LICENSES AND RAW MATERIALS. The seller's acceptance of any order is subject to the seller's receipt of all licenses required for purchase and manufacture and to the seller's ability to acquire the raw materials. If the seller cannot complete an order because licenses or raw materials are unavailable, the seller has the right to cancel the contract.

8. STOPPAGE, DELAY, OR INTERRUPTION OF WORK. The seller has a right to suspend all deliveries and to add the time of that suspension to the period originally designated in the contract in the event that work in the seller's business is stopped, delayed, or interrupted because of strikes, lockouts, trade disputes, breakdown, accident, or any cause whatsoever beyond the seller's control.

9. FORCE MAJEURE. If the seller is unable to deliver the goods because of the occurrence of an event beyond the seller's control—whether hostilities arise between nations, war is declared, a national emergency arises, the seller's property or products are taken by the government, a natural catastrophe strikes, or otherwise—the seller will be entitled to notify the buyer that only partial deliveries will be made or that the contract is terminated.

10. INDEMNIFICATION FOR SPECIFICATIONS. If the buyer supplies particular specifications for the goods to the seller, the buyer will indemnify the seller against all damages, penalties, costs, and expense that result because the specifications infringe on any patents, designs, trademarks, or other intellectual property rights of any third parties.

11. INTELLECTUAL PROPERTY RIGHTS. All intellectual property rights associated with the goods—including but not limited to company names, trade names, trademarks, service marks, trade dress, patents, designs, and copyrights—remain the property of the seller, provided that any such rights associated with particular specifications supplied by the buyer are not the seller's property. The buyer will not modify the goods or the design, packaging, or labeling of the goods in any way, and all advertising must specify that the seller owns the intellectual property rights.

12. ARBITRATION. The parties agree to submit any dispute under the contract to an arbitrator or arbitrators to be appointed by the parties. The parties will accept the arbitrator's decision as binding. The arbitration will be conducted in accordance with the [*name of arbitration rules*].

13. GOVERNING LAW. These conditions, and the contract, will be subject to and construed in accordance with the law of [*country*].

CHAPTER 13

Memorandum of Sale

FOR MANY SALES OF GOODS, a short memorandum of the agreement may be more than satisfactory. It may be a sufficient record for an order placed by telephone or facsimile for a one-time sale and immediate delivery of goods—a transaction that is completed before the parties would even have time to consider and negotiate a full sales agreement. It may also be adapted for use as a record of each purchase made pursuant to an underlying agreement between the parties establishing a long-term relationship. A memorandum can be drafted quickly and the goods can be sent immediately. Most parties use a letter or invoice format for the memorandum.

Use of Form

If you decide to use a memorandum of sale, be certain to cover all essential points of the sale: goods, delivery, price, and payment terms. It is also important that you recognize that the memorandum is merely a sketch of your relationship with the other party and that it does not define that relationship fully. For example, the memorandum does not provide mechanisms for the resolution of disputes that might arise, nor does it state any specific warranties, governing law, rights of inspection, or obligations to mitigate damages. Therefore, before using a memorandum of sale, you should consider whether the following apply.

- You already have an ongoing relationship with the other party in which such factors are already established and a satisfactory level of trust has been reached.
- You have sufficient reasons to trust the other party because you have made a background check or have received a solid referral.
- Your transaction is small and your risk of loss is minimal.
- You are willing and able to take the risk of loss, perhaps because there will be long-term benefits if you can establish the relationship.
- You are willing to negotiate or modify the memorandum rather than seek enforcement through legal action.
- You are making the memorandum to make a quick sales transaction at minimal cost.
- You are not concerned with which laws will govern and whether the memorandum will be enforceable because you will not seek legal remedies in connection with the agreement.

Sample Contract: Memorandum of Sale

[*seller's letterhead*]
[*date*]

COMMENT: Both parties should date the memorandum when they sign it. The latest date will be the effective date of the agreement. The effective date may be important if any terms of the agreement require a calculation from that date. For example, the parties may agree to delivery within thirty days of its effective date.

[*buyer's company name*]
[*buyer's address*]

COMMENT: Your contract is binding against the parties identified in it. Be certain that they are designated by their legal names, company names, and addresses. A party who needs to give notice to the other should use the address specified in the contract.

We confirm your order received on [*date*] for the following goods:

COMMENT: It is wise to confirm in writing any order received. This confirmation will indicate that you have already come to terms. The confirmation is in effect an acceptance and creates a binding contract.

[*List the goods, including quantity, type, model numbers, color, and other identifying characteristics. If the types of goods differ in price, include the price per item and the price for the total quantity ordered.*]

COMMENT: The clause that describes the type, quantity, and quality of the goods is essential to the agreement. Without this clause, your agreement will usually be unenforceable because the quantity and type of goods cannot be implied—the goods must be chosen by the contracting parties.

The terms of this order are as follows:

Date of delivery: On or before [*date*]
Price: Total [*currency and amount, e.g.*, US$12,000.00] [*specify trade terms e.g.*, F.O.B.]
Special packing arrangements: [*specify*]
Payment: Deposit paid at time of order [*currency and amount, e.g.*, US$6,000.00]
Net on receipt of [*goods/invoice*] [*currency and amount, e.g.*, US$6,000.00]

Return policy: If the goods are not to your satisfaction, you may return them to us within 10 working days of receiving them for a full refund of deposit.

Your signature below will create a binding contract between us.
Sincerely yours,

[*Name of Seller's Company*]
by: [*signature*]
[*name and title of person signing*]
[*Company Address*]

Accepted:
[*Name of Buyer's Company*]
by: [*signature*]
[*name and title of person signing*]
Dated: [*date*]

CHAPTER 14

Purchase Order

ONCE THE BUYER knows the goods being offered for sale, the price, and the sale conditions, the buyer may submit an order—commonly known as a purchase order, or P.O.—to the seller. In effect, a purchase order is an offer to buy. No contract is formed until the order has been accepted by the seller. Standard clauses are often printed on the reverse side of the purchase order. The parties should be careful that the standard clauses attached to the purchase order are not in conflict with any conditions that the seller has placed on the sale. Conflicting clauses should be renegotiated and changed before the parties sign the contract.

Sample Contract: Purchase Order (front side)

[*buyer's letterhead*]

Purchase Order No: [*number*]

Dated: [*date*]

Issued to: [*name and address of seller*]

We are pleased to place the following order, subject to the conditions appearing on the reverse of this purchase order:

Model Number	Description	Quantity	Price/Item	Total Price
[*list*]	[*list*]	[*list*]	[*list*]	[*list*]

Subtotal
Tax
Shipping
Total Price

Terms of Shipping and Delivery: [*specify, including import and export costs and documentation, destinations, delivery times, and insurance requirements*].

[*signature of buyer*]

Sample Contract: Purchase Terms (reverse side)

CONDITIONS OF PURCHASE ORDER

The Purchase Order on the reverse side is conditioned on the following terms.

1. ACCEPTANCE. The Seller is deemed to have accepted the Offer made in this Purchase Order by confirming to the Buyer in writing the Order and the Delivery Date.

2. DELIVERY. The Buyer has set its own production schedule in reliance on the delivery period specified in this Purchase Order. If delivery is delayed, the Buyer will incur substantial losses. By initializing this clause, the Seller expressly acknowledges that the delivery period is material to this contract and that any delay will be considered a breach of the contract. If delivery is delayed, the Buyer has a right to cancel this Purchase Order, to purchase replacement Goods from another source, and to hold the Seller accountable for resulting losses. ______(initials)

COMMENT: The seller will usually request a more flexible delivery period so that any delays will not be a breach of contract. In contrast, the buyer usually has plans to use the goods, and therefore will want a fairly accurate estimate, if not an exact date and time. These two positions are in conflict, and the parties will have to negotiate a compromise. The delivery clause provided here is strictly against the seller, and it should be modified to reflect the negotiated agreement of the parties.

3. PRICE AND PAYMENT TERMS. The price for the Goods must not be higher than the price last quoted or charged to the Buyer, unless the Buyer otherwise consents in writing. Payment will be net 30 days. The Buyer will be allowed a discount of [*number*] percent for transmitting payment within 30 days of the billing date.

COMMENT: If the seller has not allowed an incentive for early payment, the buyer may request one. Again, this clause will have to be negotiated between the parties. It should not conflict with payment terms offered by the seller.

4. QUANTITIES. If the Seller is unable to ship the quantity of Goods ordered, the Seller must notify the Buyer before shipment. The Buyer then has a right to cancel the entire contract, accept substitute goods, or accept the reduced quantity. The price will be adjusted to reflect the Goods actually received.

5. INSURANCE. The Seller will insure all Goods shipped.

COMMENT: If shipping terms are included in the purchase order, it would be wise to detail there the responsibilities of the parties regarding insurance on the goods. This clause could then be eliminated. In any event, the parties should agree to the amount of insurance, the point at which the risk of loss will transfer to the buyer, and the extent to which either party will be a beneficiary of the other's insurance.

6. SHIPMENT DOCUMENTATION. As evidence that the Goods have been shipped, the Seller will transmit to the Buyer the invoice for the Goods and the carrier's signed express receipt or bill of lading. The Seller will further prepare complete customs documentation required for exporting and importing the Goods.

7. TITLE TO DRAWINGS AND SPECIFICATIONS. If the Buyer has supplied drawings and/or specifications to the Seller, the Buyer, retains at all times, title to them. The Seller undertakes to use them in connection with this Purchase Order only and to hold them in confidence. No disclosure of them will be made to any person or entity other than the Seller's employees, subcontractors, or government inspectors. When this Purchase Order is complete, or at any time the Buyer requests, the Seller will promptly return all drawings and specifications to the Buyer.

COMMENT: Always remember to protect your intellectual property. Disclosure of designs, trademarks, plans, trade secrets, and similar properties could result in loss of your exclusive rights. You should include a nondisclosure clause and an express statement of title to your intellectual property.

8. SELLER'S WARRANTIES. The Seller warrants that the Goods delivered are free from defects in material or workmanship and conform strictly to the Buyer's specifications, drawings, or samples, if provided. This warranty remains in force after all inspections, deliveries, acceptances, and payments have been made for the Goods.

9. INSPECTIONS. The Buyer is entitled to inspect the Goods on the Buyer's premises. The Buyer is entitled to reject any Goods that do not conform to this Purchase Order and to return them to the Seller at the Seller's expense. At the Buyer's request, the Seller will replace the Goods returned.

COMMENT: When goods are shipped long distances, it is often wise to inspect them for conformance before shipping and for damage and loss after shipping. If the buyer cannot personally inspect the goods before shipping, there are companies that will provide an objective inspection. Be certain that you receive written certification of the results if a third party conducts the inspection.

10. ASSIGNMENT. No assignments or delegations are allowed under this Purchase Order by either party without the prior written consent of the other party. Any attempted assignment or delegation without prior consent will be void.

COMMENT: If the parties prohibit all assignments or delegations of rights, they will not be able to enforce such a clause. The law implies a right to assign or delegate. However, the parties may limit these rights, such as by requiring prior consent.

11. CREATION OF CONTRACT. If the Seller accepts this Purchase Order without alteration, deletion, or addition to any provisions, the parties will have a contract that binds both of them. Alterations, deletions, or additions to any provisions will be considered a counteroffer, and the Buyer's acceptance will be required to form a binding contract.

COMMENT: It is wise to control the creation of your contract by a clause similar to the one shown here. When the parties are merchants, the alteration of a provision that is immaterial to the contract does not necessarily constitute a counteroffer. It can be an acceptance, resulting in a binding contract. If you are unhappy with the alteration, you are then stuck with arguing whether the alteration affects a material provision, which is an imprecise standard and will vary depending on the interpreter.

12. GOVERNING LAW AND FORUM. This Purchase Order is to be interpreted in accordance with the law of [*country*]. Any disputes between the parties must be resolved in a forum located in [*country*].

COMMENT: Both parties may prefer their own law and forum for the resolution of disputes, and this clause will therefore need to be negotiated. Be certain to come to an agreement; if this clause conflicts with the seller's clause, the forum is likely to ignore both of the provisions. Remember, there are also good reasons for choosing the law and forum of the other party's country. That law may be more developed or more favorable to you. There may be an expedited procedure, and enforcement will be easier if you can avoid the process of presenting a foreign judgment for recognition.

CHAPTER 15

Conditional Contract of Sale

IF GOODS ARE OF HIGH VALUE, a buyer may want to have the use of the goods immediately and pay for them over time. The following contract is for a sale of this type—known as a conditional sale. This contract should be used only if the payment period is relatively short, such as six months. If payments will extend for one year or more, a more detailed lease or credit agreement should be made instead.

Sample: Conditional Contract of Sale

On [*date*], this Agreement is made between [*name*], [a/an] [*description and nationality*] of [*address*] (the Seller) and [*name*], [a/an] [*description and nationality*] of [*address*] (the Buyer). The parties agree as follows:

COMMENT: The agreement is binding on the parties who sign it, and these should be the parties identified in this clause. Give the full name of each party, and if a party is an entity, describe the type of entity (partnership, corporation, limited liability company, nonprofit corporation, and so forth). The business address of each party may be given here or at the end of the agreement immediately following their signatures. In international contracts, the description of each party includes the party's nationality. Examples of descriptions: "a Société Anonyme organized and existing under the laws of France," "a partnership organized and existing under the laws of the State of California in the United States of America," or "an individual who is a citizen of Singapore."

1. SALE OF GOODS. The Seller agrees to sell and the Buyer agrees to purchase the following goods (the "Goods"): [*list*].

COMMENT: The description of the goods should be specific, including as appropriate model numbers, colors, quantities, and so forth. If specifications are furnished by the Buyer, it is wise to include them as a separate attachment with a reference here incorporating them into the agreement.

2. PURCHASE PRICE. The Buyer agrees to pay [*currency and amount, e.g.*, US$18,000] for the Goods (the "Purchase Price") in accordance with the following schedule: [*specify, e.g.*, US$6,000 in cash at the time this Agreement is signed by both parties; and the balance of US$12,000 in 6 equal monthly installments of US$2,000 each, to be paid on the tenth day of each month beginning on (*date*) and ending on (*date*).

COMMENT: Although the period of payment is short, the parties may modify this clause to add interest to the payments. Interest should be made payable at the same time as each monthly payment to which the interest applies. As an incentive for early payment, the seller might waive interest "penalties" for pre-payment.

3. TITLE. The Seller will retain title to the Goods until the Buyer has paid the Purchase Price in full as provided in this Agreement, notwithstanding that the Goods are delivered to the Buyer before full payment is made.

4. USE OF GOODS. Until the Buyer has paid the Purchase Price in full, the Buyer must keep and use the Goods at the following location(s) only: [*list*]. The Buyer may not mortgage, sell, pledge, or otherwise encumber, lend, or dispose of the Goods while title to the Goods is held by the Seller.

COMMENT: This clause is probably broad enough to cover the various uses of the goods that would be prohibited. However, the seller should check the laws of the buyer's country to determine whether other possibilities exist that should be expressly stated. The seller should remember that the goods while in the possession of the buyer may still be subject to involuntary liens or attachments, such as by tax authorities or bankruptcy courts. The effect of involuntary liens is a point for negotiation between the parties: Is the contract breached by imposition of such a lien? How will the seller be compensated for the balance of the payments or ensured that the goods will be returned?

5. INSURANCE. Until the Buyer has paid the Purchase Price in full, the Buyer must obtain and maintain insurance coverage in the amount of [*currency and amount*] for loss, damage, or destruction of the Goods. The policy must name the Seller as loss payee. The policy must be issued by a reputable and solvent insurance company, and the Buyer must deliver a copy of the policy to the Seller. If the Buyer is unable or otherwise fails to obtain or maintain this insurance, the Seller has the option to obtain the insurance and to charge the premiums to the Buyer. If the Goods are lost, damaged, or destroyed before the Purchase Price is paid in full, the Seller will be entitled to the insurance proceeds paid to the Buyer up to the amount of the outstanding balance on the Purchase Price.

COMMENT: It is important to provide that the seller may obtain insurance for the goods in the event that the buyer is unable to cover them. Adequate insurance coverage may or may not be available in the buyer's country.

6. INTELLECTUAL PROPERTY RIGHTS. No intellectual property rights are being transferred, licensed, or otherwise given to the Buyer by this Agreement. These rights are the exclusive property of the Seller, and Buyer has no rights in the intellectual property rights connected with the Goods. The Buyer covenants not to infringe on the Seller's intellectual property rights.

7. DEFAULT AND ACCELERATION. If the Buyer defaults on the payment of two or more installments of the Purchase Price or on any covenant of this Agreement, the Seller will have the right to demand full payment of the outstanding balance of the Purchase Price. If the Buyer fails to comply with the Seller's demand, the parties will make diligent efforts to renegotiate the payment terms. If the parties fail to resolve the dispute, the Buyer will either return the Goods to the Seller or will give the Seller access to the Buyer's premises during reasonable business hours to retake the Goods. The Seller may resell the Goods for the Buyer's account or may repurchase the Goods at current market value. If the Goods are resold, the price obtained for them will be first applied to payment of expenses incurred in retaking and reselling them and next to payment of the outstanding balance of the Purchase Price. Any excess will be paid to the Buyer, but if there is a deficiency, the Buyer will pay the amount of that deficiency to the Seller.

COMMENT: This clause provides for renegotiation of the payment terms in the event of a default. Although renegotiation is not necessary, it is highly recommended. Otherwise, the seller will end up with used equipment of minimal value instead of full payment for the equipment, and neither party is likely to recoup all of the costs spent in shipping, installing, and so forth. Parties to overseas transactions should remember to remain flexible in consideration of the inherent variations in economies and markets, at least to the point where profit is still being made.

[*signatures of both parties*]

CHAPTER 16

Consulting Contract

THE PRIMARY FOCUS of this book is on contracts for the sales of goods. A contract for the sale of services has its own special problems, some of which are noted here. In the process of selling or buying goods, it is quite possible that you will need to establish service contracts. You may need a survey of the markets, a public relations promotion, or undercover investigation on infringement. The following contract is for a one-time consultation. If the need for services is ongoing, you may consider entering a retainer contract, by which the service provider agrees to furnish services for a monthly or annual fee. However, you must be extremely careful when making long-term service contracts overseas. In some countries, labor laws may require substantial payments for the termination of a consultant hired under a retainer agreement.

Sample: Consulting Contract

This Agreement is made as of [*date*], between [*name*], [a/an] [*description and nationality*] of [*address*] (the "Company") and [*name*] of [*address*], [a/an] [*description and nationality*] (the "Consultant"), on the terms following:

COMMENT: The parties identified in this clause should be the ones signing the agreement. Give the full name of each party and their business address. If a party is an entity, describe the type of entity (partnership, corporation, limited liability company, nonprofit corporation, and so forth). In international contracts, the description of each party includes the party's nationality. Examples of descriptions: "a Société Anonyme organized and existing under the laws of France," "a partnership organized and existing under the laws of the State of California in the United States of America," or "an individual who is a citizen of Singapore."

1. ENGAGEMENT. The Company engages the Consultant and the Consultant agrees to provide independent consulting services for purposes of [*specify, e.g.*, surveying the consumer market in (*country*) for the sale of the Company's Goods].

2. TERM. This Agreement will begin on [*date*] and will continue until the Consultant renders a final market survey report to the Company. The parties agree that the market survey report will be submitted to the Company no later than [*date*].

3. EFFORTS OF CONSULTANT. The Consultant will furnish the consulting services to the best of the Consultant's ability. The Consultant will devote reasonable and conscientious effort to the consulting services. The parties acknowledge that the Consultant's services are provided on a nonexclusive basis and will be performed at the locations and times that are convenient to the Consultant. Further, the Consultant will ensure that the services are in compliance with all applicable laws. The Company takes no responsibility for the manner in which the Consultant performs the consulting services.

COMMENT: This contract assumes that the consultant is an independent contractor, which means that the consultant is not an employee of the company. The distinction between independent contractor and employee is made for purposes of labor and tax laws. The laws of some countries may not recognize this distinction, in which case it is not important to keep the distance between the company and the consultant, as all persons hired will be considered employees.

4. COMPENSATION. The Company will pay the Consultant [*currency and amount*] as compensation for all consulting services rendered pursuant to this Agreement. The Company will pay the Consultant within [*number*] days after the Consultant completes the consulting services. No deductions will be made for any taxes, labor charges, licenses, or medical, or other purposes.

COMMENT: Again, the assumption is that the consultant is an independent contractor. If that is the situation, the consultant should not be paid through the same payroll methods as the company's employees, and employment deductions should not be made from the compensation.

5. INDEPENDENT CONTRACTOR STATUS. In making and performing this Agreement, the Consultant is acting at all times as an independent contractor. Neither party may make any commitment nor incur any charges or expenses on the other's behalf. The Consultant is not an employee of the Company and is not entitled to participate in any pension plan, unemployment insurance, bonus, worker's compensation insurance, stock, or similar benefits that the Company provides for its employees. The Consultant is responsible for performing the work under this Agreement in a skillful manner and will be liable for the consequences of his or her own acts and/or omissions, if any. The Consultant will be responsible for all payments of taxes, penalties, and/or other similar contributions that have arisen or may arise out of the Consultant's services under this Agreement. The Consultant may engage assistants at his or her own expense, which assistants are also not employed by the Company. The Consultant will furnish all materials, tools, and equipment required to perform the consulting services.

COMMENT: The legal presumption is that a person who is engaged by another party is an employee. If you want to engage an independent contractor, it is important to expressly negate this legal presumption. You should attempt to plug all the holes that would otherwise create an employment relationship.

6. CONSULTING REPORT. The Consultant will prepare and submit a report to the Company on the Consultant's findings. The report must include the following information: [*specify*]. The Consultant will retain a duplicate copy of the report for at least six months after the termination of this Agreement.

COMMENT: The company may specify the desired results of the consulting services without jeopardizing the independent contractor status of the consultant. Depending on the extent of the requirements, you may consider attaching a separate checklist as an addendum to this agreement.

7. CONFLICTS OF INTEREST. The Consultant warrants that he or she has no potential financial or other conflicts of interest in performing the consulting services, except those already disclosed to the Company.

COMMENT: It is important that the consultant not have any conflicts of interest that will affect the objectivity of the consulting services. If the company later learns that there is a conflict of interest, the consultant will be in breach of this contract.

8. CONFIDENTIALITY. All information provided by the Company relating to the manufacture and sale of its products is provided in confidence, and the Consultant agrees not to disclose such information without the Company's authorization.

9. INTELLECTUAL PROPERTY RIGHTS. The Company holds exclusive rights in the intellectual property connected with its goods and services. No transfer of these rights is being made to the Consultant. The Consultant covenants to protect the Company's exclusive rights and to avoid infringing them.

10. TERMINATION. Either party may terminate this Agreement by giving written notice to the other party effective as of the date of mailing or the date stated in the notice, whichever is later. If the Consultant has partially performed the consulting services at the date of termination, the Consultant may submit to the Company the materials compiled up to that time with a statement of fees based on an hourly charge. For purposes of termination only, the parties agree that a reasonable hourly charge for the consulting services is [*currency and amount*].

COMMENT: Termination at will is common in service contracts with independent contractors because of the difficulty in forcing someone to perform services when they are unhappy. The right to terminate the contract should be mutual (both parties should have the same right). Thus, if the company is unhappy with the consultant, termination of employment may be made without justification.

11. ASSIGNMENTS. This Agreement is for the personal services of the Consultant, and therefore neither party may assign or delegate the rights and obligations without the prior written consent of the other.

COMMENT: Generally, parties cannot completely prohibit assignments or delegations of the contract because such provisions are void at law. However, they may limit these rights by requiring advance consent to the assignment or delegation. In a contract for services, this limitation is particularly significant because of the personal nature of the agreement—that is, both parties have agreed to work with each other because they like and respect each other's abilities, philosophies, personalities, work ethic, and so forth.

12. NOTICE. If either party gives a notice to the other under the terms of this Agreement, the notice will be effective only if it is in writing and delivered by certified or registered mail. Notices must be sent to a party at the address specified in this Agreement, unless the party has notified the other of a change of address.

13. GOVERNING LAW. This Agreement shall be considered as entered into and governed by the laws of [*country*].

CHAPTER 17

Sales Representative Contract

ANOTHER COMMON CONTRACT associated with the sale of goods is a contract by which the company hires a local representative to sell its products. When operating overseas, a company should treat the hiring of a sales representative as carefully as if it were a marriage. The representative should be met personally, the relationship should be established over a period of time, and it should be monitored constantly. The hiring of a sales representative is a step up in commitment to selling in a foreign market—be certain you are ready to take this step.

Sample: Contract for Services of Sales Representative

This Agreement is made on [*date*] between [*name*], [a/an] [*individual or type of entity and nationality or place of formation*] of [*address*] (the "Manufacturer"), and [*name*], [a/an] [*individual or type of entity and nationality or place of formation*] of [*address*] ("Sales Representative").

COMMENT: This clause should identify the parties signing the agreement. To ensure that there is no misunderstanding, the full name of each party and the party's business address should be given. If a party is an entity, partnership, corporation, limited company, or otherwise, the type of entity should be disclosed here. In international contracts, the description of each party includes the party's nationality. Examples of descriptions: "a Société Anonyme organized and existing under the laws of France," "a partnership organized and existing under the laws of the State of California in the United States of America," or "an individual who is a citizen of Singapore."

The parties acknowledge that the Manufacturer produces and sells [describe goods *or* the goods listed in Exhibit A attached to this Agreement] (the "Goods") and seeks to engage the Sales Representative to offer and sell the Goods for the Manufacturer in [*country*]. Therefore, the parties agree as follows:

COMMENT: Commonly called the *recitals*, this paragraph sets out the intent of the parties and sometimes the definitions, such as of the goods, of terms used in the contract. By tradition, the recitals are not numbered, but parties need not stick to tradition if numbers are more convenient for reference.

APPOINTMENT. The Manufacturer engages the sales representative to sell the Goods for resale in accordance with the terms and conditions of this Agreement to persons and companies that are doing business in [*country*].

COMMENT: This clause assumes that sales are being made for purposes of resale. If the goods are to be sold to consumers at the retail level, additional clauses must be added to this agreement to cover obligations related to consumer sales. This clause should also be amended if the manufacturer is granting exclusive sales rights to the sales representative. For exclusive rights, the contract should provide that the manufacturer agrees not to sell and not to authorize any others to sell or otherwise distribute its products in the country. Exclusivity of sales benefits the sales representative and is most often granted when a market is relatively small. For larger markets, companies may consider granting exclusive rights within certain territories, which allows for sufficient market penetration while at the same time prevents competition among different representatives selling the same products. If exclusive rights are granted, the manufacturer should not reserve any selling rights for itself, because such sales will cut into the representative's sales. It is in the manufacturer's best interest if the local sales representative succeeds; direct sales are likely to be less profitable because of the extra overhead costs inherent in selling overseas.

OBLIGATIONS OF SALES REPRESENTATIVE. The Sales Representative agrees to sell and market the Goods aggressively within [*country*] on behalf of the Manufacturer. The Sales Representative will forward all customer orders to the Manufacturer in a timely manner, and in no event more than [*number*] days from receipt of the order. The Sales Representative will not promote, advertise, offer for sale, or sell any goods that are identical to, confusingly or deceptively similar to, or otherwise competitive with the Goods. The Sales Representative will comply with the Manufacturer's guidelines on prices, charges, terms, and conditions for the sale of the Goods, which guidelines are subject to change from time to time. For purposes of achieving maximum sales within [*country*], the Manufacturer will formulate these guidelines in consultation with the Sales Representative, although the Manufacturer will make the final decision. The Manufacturer will give the Sales Representative written notice of changes in the guidelines at least [*number*] days in advance of implementation.

COMMENT: In many form contracts, a clause is included that prohibits the sale of competing products unless the company consents to such sales. It is recommended that the noncompetition clause be an absolute prohibition, unless the company really does have a good reason for authorizing competing sales, which is probably unlikely. With regard to company guidelines, the local representative is probably in the best position to know the market. Therefore, company guidelines should be formulated with the representative's advice. As an international trader, you may tend toward imposing uniform guidelines worldwide, but a successful trader must recognize that each market is distinctively unique. It is therefore important to keep international uniform guidelines flexible, and hence no longer uniform. At a minimum, adjustments may be required for price, warranties, and promotional services to ensure a share of a foreign market against competing domestic goods or to introduce a new product—and often a new concept—to another culture.

TERM. The term of this Agreement is [*number*] days from [*date*] through [*date*], and it will then continue in effect for successive periods of [*number*] days unless either party terminates it by giving to the other party written notice of the intention not to renew. This notice must be delivered by registered mail at least [*number*] days before the end of the term of the Agreement then current.

COMMENT: A short term, such as 180 days, with options to renew or cancel is recommended for several reasons. First, when the relationship between the parties is new or the market is untested, it is unwise for either party to commit to the other for a long period. An even more important reason is that the laws of some countries form a protective cushion around employees and other persons who are hired or engaged to work in any capacity for some time. These laws impose burdens on the employers to provide substantial benefits, justify termination, and compensate the employee for losses on dismissal. In an attempt to clarify the intent of the parties not to form an employment relationship, the term of the contract should be limited to a relatively short time. For this same reason, the term *agent* should be avoided—this contract uses *representative*—in an attempt to show that the local representative is operating on his or her own with minimal guidance from the manufacturer and is not empowered to obligate the manufacturer.

OBLIGATIONS OF MANUFACTURER. The Manufacturer agrees to manufacture and to maintain a quantity of Goods sufficient to deliver timely all Goods that the Sales Representative may sell. The Manufacturer will invoice or otherwise acknowledge the orders of the customers and will ship the goods to them in accordance with the Manufacturer's guidelines. If the Manufacturer modifies or ceases the production of any of the Goods, the Manufacturer will inform the Sales Representative immediately and will offer replacement goods. If the Sales Representative refuses to sell the replacement Goods, this Agreement will terminate and the parties will have no further claims or liabilities as to each other.

COMMENT: This clause allows some flexibility in the manufacturer's obligations in an attempt to prevent a breach of the contract in the event that the manufacturer no longer has a particular product available. In practical terms, most products are rarely available for a lengthy time—there is always a new and improved version not far in the future. The contract should allow for common practice; otherwise the parties will be constantly amending their agreement or making new contracts to replace the outdated ones.

COMMISSIONS. For the services performed under this Agreement, the Manufacturer will pay to the Sales Representative a commission at the rate of [*number*] percent on the wholesale list price of the Goods sold. The commissions payable will be remitted to the Sales Representative once a month, during the next month following the month in which the Goods are sent to the customer, and all amounts will be paid in [*currency*].

COMMENT: It is common practice for companies to pay different commission rates for various types of sales. For example, the commission may be reduced or eliminated if goods are sold through special promotions. The commission clause should specify whether the representative is entitled to a commission on sales made by another person within the same country. Similarly, this clause should indicate whether any deductions are allowed against the commissions. The currency of payment—preferably a stable one—should be given, as this is an international contract.

INDEPENDENT CONTRACTOR RELATIONSHIP. The Sales Representative acknowledges and agrees that the relationship intended by this Agreement is that of independent contractor and not that of employee. This Agreement is not to be construed as creating a partnership, joint venture, fiduciary, or other similar relationship, neither party is liable for the debts or obligations of the other, and neither has authority to bind the other to any contracts at all. The Sales Representative is free to employ staff or independent contractors, and the Manufacturer has no power to limit, fire, or hire such persons. It is the Sales Representative's responsibility to ensure that all local law requirements for doing business in [*country*] have been met. The Sales Representative is further responsible for the payment of all taxes and fees arising from sales of the Goods in [*country*]. The Manufacturer will neither indemnify nor insure the Sales Representative against losses, claims, or other liabilities that arise in connection with sales of the Goods. The Sales Representative will assist in the delivery of Goods to the customers on the reasonable request of the Manufacturer.

COMMENT: A company may try to establish an independent contractor relationship with a local sales representative, but the company should be wary. Not every country will recognize this type of relationship, in which event the representative will be treated as an employee and the company will become subject to laws intended to protect employees—such as substantial notice and payment on termination. Even where recognized, independent contractor status must be strictly maintained because it is against the usual presumption. The representative should be given as much freedom as possible in determining how, where, and when to sell the goods. The more guidelines and systems imposed by the manufacturer, the more likely the representative will be deemed an employee—with adverse tax and labor consequences to the manufacturer.

INTELLECTUAL PROPERTY RIGHTS. The Sales Representative understands and agrees that the Manufacturer owns valuable property rights in all of the marks, names, designs, patents, and trade secrets (the "Intellectual Property") connected with the Goods. None of these rights are being granted to the Sales Representative. The Sales Representative must not represent that he/she owns any rights in the Manufacturer's Intellectual Property. All advertisements must state that the Manufacturer owns the Intellectual Property appearing in the advertisements, and all advertisements must be submitted for review and approval of the Manufacturer prior to issuance or publication. Violation of this clause will result in immediate termination of this Agreement.

COMMENT: The value of intellectual property rights should never be underestimated. The manufacturer's goodwill and reputation are connected to its name and product markings, and the uniqueness of its goods are preserved through patent and design registrations. Foreign traders know the value of these property rights—which is why infringement is big business. Your reputation sells products, whether the products are legitimately your own or illegitimately copied. If you do not protect your intellectual property, you may lose not only sales but also the exclusive rights to that property.

ASSIGNMENT. Neither party may assign this Agreement without the written consent of the other. An assignment will not have the effect of delegating the duties of the assigning party, and that party will continue to be obligated under this Agreement.

COMMENT: The parties to a personal services contract are making the agreement based on characteristics that are unique to the parties. One party's assignment of the obligations under this contract would leave the other with an unknown partner. A prohibition against all assignments is usually not enforceable, but parties can protect themselves by demanding prior authorization of any assignment.

REMEDIES FOR VIOLATIONS. The parties acknowledge that they intend to establish a mutually beneficial relationship and that, to this end, they will strive to resolve any disagreements between them through amicable negotiations. Nevertheless, if a dispute does arise that they are unable to resolve otherwise, the parties will submit it to binding arbitration before the [*name of arbitration association*]. This clause will not limit the rights of the Manufacturer to pursue against the Sales Representative any remedy available for infringement of its exclusive rights in its Intellectual Property.

COMMENT: If arbitration is available within the local representative's country, it may be chosen as a means of resolving disputes. You should be cautious, however, in providing for arbitration because not all countries have such systems easily available. Moreover, arbitration is adversarial and usually involves more cost and delay than negotiation and compromise, although generally less than litigation. In some cultures, arbitration has the same stigma as court proceedings, both of which are viewed with suspicion and as personal insults.

MODIFICATION. This Agreement is modifiable only by a writing signed by both parties.

COMMENT: Always insist on written modifications to avoid any subsequent question of what was agreed. Proof of oral modifications may not be allowed in court to alter the terms of a contract that is otherwise definite and clear.

NOTICES. All notices that may be given under this Agreement must be delivered in writing to the other party at the address specified in this Agreement. A party must notify the other party of a change of address within [*number*] days after it becomes effective. Notices are deemed to be delivered on the date of receipt.

COMMENT: A notice clause is usually a wise provision to ensure that the parties understand the procedure for giving notice. This clause can prevent disputes over what constitutes notice.

INTENTION OF PARTIES. The Manufacturer and the Sales Representative have executed this Agreement to demonstrate their intent to be bound by its terms. The parties declare that this Agreement constitutes their entire agreement and replaces all of their prior negotiations, understandings, and representations. Each party has been encouraged and has had the opportunity to obtain the advice of independent professionals, including attorneys and accountants, and each has made an independent decision to undertake the obligations set forth.

COMMENT: These standard clauses are important and should rarely be eliminated from your contracts. They serve to establish the basic contractual notions of mutual understanding and intent. In international contracts, these clauses have added significance because each party's understanding of the contract terms could indeed be very different from that of the other party, given such invisible barriers as language, culture, environment, and inexperience.

[*Name of Company*]

by [*signature*]

Sales Representative

[*Name of Company*]

Manufacturer

By [*signature*]

[*name and title of person signing*]

CHAPTER 18

Franchise Agreement

THE FOLLOWING AGREEMENT is a short franchise contract, which is provided for illustrative purposes only. Franchising is a complex business arrangement and should only be undertaken with legal advice. This contract should suggest to you what would be involved in franchising your business overseas. A franchise is a means by which an independent business enterprise may distribute goods or services in connection with a network of other independent owners. Each owner of a franchise will benefit from the support of the central organization, while at the same time have the advantage of being a sole proprietor.

Sample Contract: Franchise Agreement

This Agreement is made on [*date*] between [*name*], [a/an] [*specify e.g.*, individual or type of entity and nationality *or* place of formation] of [*address*] (the "Franchisor"), and [*name*], [a/an] [*specify e.g.*, individual or type of entity and nationality *or* place of formation] of [*address*] ("Franchisee").

COMMENT: This clause should identify the parties signing the agreement. To ensure that there is no misunderstanding, the full name of each party and the party's business address should be given. If a party is an entity, partnership, corporation, limited company, or otherwise, the type of entity should be disclosed here. In international contracts, the description of each party includes the party's nationality. Examples of descriptions: "a Société Anonyme organized and existing under the laws of France," "a partnership organized and existing under the laws of the State of California in the United States of America," or "an individual who is a citizen of Singapore."

RECITALS

A. The Franchisor possesses rights under various registered trademarks, service marks, trade names, and styles (including distinctive logos and copyrighted materials in which those items are used), including the name [*name of trademark*] ("the Intellectual Property"). Further, the Franchisor has promoted the use of and acceptance of the Intellectual Property through its own operations and the operations of its licensees and has developed an international [*type of business*] system (the System), which is identified with its Intellectual Property and which has public acceptance and good will; and

B. The Franchisee desires to become a part of the System and to establish and operate a [*type of business*] using the Franchisor's Intellectual Property and good will.

Therefore, the Franchisor and the Franchisee agree as follows:

AGREEMENT

1. LICENSE. The Franchisor grants to the Franchisee a license, within the following territory (the "Territory"), to operate a [*type of business*] under the Intellectual Property during the term of the Agreement and any renewal of this Agreement. The Franchisee agrees to use the Intellectual Property in connection with, and exclusively for, the promotion and conduct of [*type of business*], as provided in this Agreement. To protect and enhance the value and good will of the Intellectual Property and to ensure that the public may rely on this Intellectual Property as identifying the quality, type, and standard of the [*type of business*], the Franchisee's license is subject to the Franchisee's continued adherence to the standards, terms, and conditions of this Agreement and of the Franchisor's Business Manual. The Franchisor agrees to operate its [*type of business*] in accordance with the rules and procedures as prescribed by the Franchisor from time to time. The Franchisee acknowledges that the Franchisor is the exclusive owner of the Intellectual Property and agrees not to register or attempt to register the Intellectual Property in the name of any person or entity. The Franchisee will further not use the Intellectual Property or any part of it as any part of the Franchisee's corporate name. Immediately on expiration or termination of this Agreement or any renewal, the Franchisee agrees to cease using the marks and to return to the Franchisor or to destroy effectively all documents, instructions, display items, and the like that bear any of the Franchisor's Intellectual Property.

2. INITIAL FEE. In consideration of the opportunity to establish and maintain a [*type of business*], the Franchisee will pay the Franchisor as an initial fee [*currency and amount*]. This initial fee is based on the market potential of the Territory. The Franchisee acknowledges that this fee is reasonable. It is expressly understood that the fee will not be refunded to the Franchisee on expiration or termination of this Agreement for any reason.

3. FRANCHISEE'S OBLIGATION. The Franchisee will purchase [*products*] from the Franchisor for sale in the [*type of business*]. The terms of payment will be cash on receipt of invoice.

4. FRANCHISOR'S OBLIGATIONS. During the term of this Agreement, or any renewal of it, the Franchisor will do all of the following:

a. Maintain and promote the System identified with the Intellectual Property within the Territory;

b. Maintain a national advertising program;

c. Supply at no charge initial quantities of business advertising and promotional materials and provide additional material at reasonable prices;

d. Provide signs, business forms, stationery, uniforms, and other standardized items at reasonable prices;

e. Make available to the Franchisee on request the Franchisor's management consultant facilities, know-how, and trade secrets in establishing, operating, and promoting a [*type of business*] regarding the selection of the premises, establishment of the outlets, institution and maintenance of office management systems and business operation procedures, institution and maintenance of advertising and marketing programs and promotional campaigns, and selection, acquisition, and disposition of [*products*];

f. Assist the Franchisee, on request, to obtain its [*product*] shipments by arranging for delivery to the Franchisee.

5. FRANCHISEE'S OBLIGATIONS REGARDING OPERATIONS. The Franchisee has the following obligations:

a. The Franchisee will commence operations within 90 days from the date of this Agreement from at least one location within the Territory.

b. The Franchisee will devote its primary and best efforts toward the development of the Territory, establishment and maintenance of an adequate number of outlets to serve the available market.

c. The Franchisee's locations will be suitable for the operation of a [*type of business*] with the public. All locations will be kept in a clean and presentable condition at all times and adequately staffed by competent personnel.

d. The Franchisee will provide and maintain telephone advertisements in the directories published for telephone service within the Territory. These advertisements must comply with the standard specification furnished by the Franchisor from time to time.

e. The Franchisee will prominently display at each outlet the Franchisor's then current Intellectual Property, as specified from time to time by the Franchisor to promote the public's uniform recognition of the Franchisor's Intellectual Property.

f. The Franchisee will require its personnel to wear uniforms and other standardized insignia and will comply with programs of standardization as promulgated by the Franchisor from time to time to promote the acceptance of good will of the System and the Intellectual Property.

g. The Franchisee will render prompt and courteous service and will conduct its [*type of business*] in such a fashion as to reflect favorably at all times on the System and on the good name, good will, and reputation of the Franchisor. The Franchisee will further avoid all deceptive, misleading, and unethical practices. The Franchisee will not use or cause to be used any mark in any advertising or promotion without the Franchisor's prior written approval.

h. The Franchisee will prepare and maintain true and accurate records, reports, accounts, books, and data that will accurately reflect all particulars relating to the Franchisee's procedures and specification and that are or may be prescribed from time to time by the Franchisor for record keeping and reporting. The Franchisee will permit the Franchisor and its representatives to examine and audit such records, reports, accounts, books, and data at any reasonable time. The Franchisee will utilize in the [*type of business*] only forms that are in compliance with the Franchisor's standard specifications and that have been approved by the Franchisor. The Franchisee will furnish such information and make such standard reports as the Franchisor may request for the proper administration of the System within a reasonable period of time after such a request. The Franchisee acknowledges that it has been furnished copies of the Franchisor's forms and has been advised of the franchisor's standard procedures and specifications referred to in this paragraph.

i. The Franchisee will support and promote in its Territory all national promotions that the Franchisor may from time to time create for the System's benefit. Such promotions may entail the issuance of certificates redeemable at any authorized Franchisee's place of business to be applied as a credit against purchase of the [*products*]. The Franchisee will accept all certificates valued at 50 percent of the face value against any obligation it may have for payments to the Franchisor. When this limit is exceeded, all such certificates will be redeemed by the Franchisor at full face value.

j. The dealer will operate the [*type of business*] in accordance with the standard procedures and methods established and modified from time to time by the Franchisor and set forth in its procedure and sales manual. The Franchisor acknowledges that it has been furnished and has examined a copy of this manual. The manual will remain at all times at the property of the Franchisee. The Franchisee will not disclose or cause to be disclosed the contents of the manual to anyone without the express written consent of the Franchisor. On termination or expiration of this agreement, the Franchisee will return the manual to the Franchisor.

6. INDEMNIFICATION. The Franchisee agrees to indemnify and hold the Franchisor, its parent corporation, and their respective subsidiaries, officers, agents, and employees harmless for and against all loss, damage, liability and expenses incurred as a result of a violation of this Agreement and from all claims, damages, cause of action, or suits of any persons, firms or corporations arising from the Franchisee's operation of the [*type of business*].

7. INSURANCE. The Franchisee will procure and maintain in full force and effect insurance with companies approved by the Franchisor and with such limits as the Franchisor may specify from time to time to cover all insurable risks of the [*type of business*]. This shall include worker's compensation, fire, burglary, and other insurance as may be deemed by the Franchisee and the Franchisor to be necessary or advisable for the proper protection in the name of the Franchisor and the Franchisee as their interest may appear. The Franchisee will furnish the Franchisor with evidence that the policy is in force.

8. NONCOMPETITION. During the term of this agreement and for [*number*] years after its expiration or termination, or any renewal, neither the Franchisee nor the Franchisee's principals or associates, may engage in any operation of any [*type of business*] either within the Territory or in any event within a radius of [*number*] miles of any outlet operated pursuant to this Agreement.

9. DEFAULT. No failure to perform in accordance with any of the terms or conditions of this or any collateral agreement or other fault or defect shall be deemed to exist or occur unless such failure cannot be cured, or if curable shall continue for thirty days following the mailing or wiring to the party to be put into default of written notification of such failure.

10. TERM. This Agreement will be in effect from the date of acceptance by the Franchisor and continue for [*number*] years unless terminated sooner. This Agreement may be renewed at the option of the Franchisee for a term of [*number*] years. The Franchisee must notify the Franchisor of the election to exercise such option to renew in writing 90 days before expiration of this Agreement or any renewal.

11. TERMINATION. Provided the Franchisee is in good standing, the Franchisee may terminate this Agreement at any time by giving 90 days written notice to the Franchisor, except that such termination shall not relieve the Franchisee of any obligation to the Franchisor that shall have matured under or survived this Agreement or any collateral written Agreement of the parties.

12. FRANCHISOR'S RIGHTS ON TERMINATION. On termination of this Agreement, the Franchisor will be entitled to recover from the Franchisee all funds due under this Agreement, together with all costs and expenses, including reasonably attorney's fees and disbursements, incurred or accrued by the Franchisor in enforcing its rights under this Agreement. The Franchisee will return to the Franchisor or destroy all literature, signs, advertising material, promotional matter, and other materials identifying the Franchisee with the Franchisor and will immediately cease to refer to or identity itself with the Franchisor or to use Intellectual Property or any simulation of it. The Franchisee will thereafter take no action detrimental to the Franchisor or the System.

13. COMPLIANCE WITH LAWS. The Franchisee is solely reasonable for compliance with all laws, statutes, ordinances, or codes of any public or governmental authority pertaining to the Franchisee for payment of all taxes, permits, licenses, registration fees, and other charges or assessments arising out of the establishment and operation of the business.

14. INDEPENDENT CONTRACTORS. The parties are not and shall not be considered joint venturers, partners, agents, servants, employees, or fiduciaries of each other, and neither shall have the power to bind or obligate the other except as set forth in this Agreement. There is no liability on the part of the Franchisor to any person for any debts incurred by the Franchisee unless the Franchisor agrees in writing to pay such debts.

15. WAIVER. The failure of either party to enforce at any time any of the provisions of this agreement or to exercise any option or remedy provided, shall in no way be construed to be a waiver of such provision or in any way to affect the validity of this Agreement.

16. NO ORAL REPRESENTATIONS. This Agreement, when accepted by an authorized officer of the Franchisor, together with any collateral written Agreement, signed by an authorized officer of the Franchisor, constitutes the entire Agreement between the parties. No other representation, provision, or agreement is of any force or effect.

Date:

[*signature*]

Franchisee

[*Name of Company*]

Franchisor

By [*signature*]

[*name and title of person signing*]

CHAPTER 19

Distribution Agreement

A DISTRIBUTOR not only possesses, but owns title to the goods being sold, unlike a sales representative, who may possess the goods temporarily (or who may simply take orders that are filled directly by the manufacturer) but does not own them. A distributor is usually not considered an agent of the manufacturer. The distributor is acting on his or her own behalf, typically by purchasing the goods from the manufacturer, adding a profit margin, and reselling the goods. In comparison to a franchise, a distributorship is less controlled by the manufacturer. A distributor is supplied with products, while a franchisee is supplied with an entire marketing package, business operation training, and the product line. The following agreement is purely illustrative. Your final contract should be reviewed by an attorney familiar with the laws of countries of both the manufacturer and the distributor because of the complexity of this relationship.

Sample Contract: Distribution Agreement

This Agreement is made on [*date*] between [*name*], [a/an] [*specify e.g.*, individual or type of entity and nationality *or* place of formation] of [*address*] (the "Manufacturer"), and [*name*], [a/an] [*individual or type of entity and nationality or place of formation*] of [*address*] ("Distributor").

COMMENT: The agreement binds the parties who sign it, and these should be identified here. To ensure that there is no misunderstanding, the full name and business address of each party should be given. If a party is an entity, partnership, corporation, limited company, or otherwise, the type of entity should be disclosed here. In international contracts, the description of each party includes the party's nationality. Examples of descriptions: "a Société Anonyme organized and existing under the laws of France," "a partnership organized and existing under the laws of the State of California in the United States of America," or "an individual who is a citizen of Singapore."

RECITALS

A. The parties acknowledge that the Manufacturer produces and sells [*describe goods or* the goods listed in the Current Product List attached to this Agreement] and may develop and manufacture additional [*type of goods*] for similar purposes in the future (the "Goods").

B. The Manufacturer desires to appoint the Distributor as its sole and exclusive distributor in [*state and/or country*] ("Territory").

C. The Distributor desires to act as the exclusive distributor for the Manufacturer's Goods in the Territory.

COMMENT: The recitals are preliminary provisions that set out the intent of the parties, and sometimes definitions—such as of the goods—of terms used in the contract.

Therefore, the parties agree as follows:

AGREEMENT

1. APPOINTMENT. The Manufacturer appoints the Distributor as its sole and exclusive distributor for the resale, lease, or rent of the Goods in the Territory. The Distributor accepts this appointment.

COMMENT: Exclusivity benefits the distributor, and it is most often granted when a market is relatively small. For larger markets, companies may consider granting nonexclusive rights or exclusive rights within certain smaller regions, which allow for sufficient market penetration while at the same time prevents competition among different distributors selling the same products. If exclusive rights are granted, the manufacturer should not reserve any selling rights for itself, because such sales will cut into the distributor's sales. It is in the manufacturer's best interest if the local distributor succeeds; direct sales are likely to be less profitable because of the extra overhead costs inherent in selling overseas.

2. TERM OF AGREEMENT. The term of this Agreement begins on the date the last party signs it and expires after [*number*] years, unless it is terminated earlier as provided in this Agreement. At the expiration of this Agreement, the parties may negotiate a renewal or extension of the term, provided that the Distributor is in full compliance with this Agreement at that time.

COMMENT: A distributorship is more of a commitment than appointment of a sales representative. For this reason, the term provided should be reasonably long to allow the distributor to grow a profitable business. This type of arrangement should not be set up until the market has been pretested; a "test" distributorship for a few months is not recommended. You may agree to an indefinite term, with termination at will by either party on advance notice, but you should be cautious in agreeing to an indefinite term. In some countries, a distributorship with an indefinite term may be considered as creating an agency relationship. The result would be to subject the manufacturer to agency laws, such as statutes that strictly regulate termination of agency relationships only for certain reasons and only on payment of significant separation packages.

3. RELATIONSHIP OF THE PARTIES. The parties acknowledge and agree that the Distributor is separate and independent of the Manufacturer. This Agreement is not to be construed as creating an employment, partnership, joint venture, fiduciary, or other similar relationship. Neither party is liable for the debts or obligations of the other, and neither has authority to bind the other to any contracts at all. The Distributor is free to employ or engage any staff or independent contractors, and the Manufacturer has no power to limit, fire, or hire such persons. It is the Distributor's responsibility to ensure that all local law requirements for doing business in [*country*] have been met. The Distributor is further responsible for the payment of all taxes and fees arising from sales of the Goods in [*country*]. The Manufacturer will neither indemnify nor insure the Distributor against losses, claims, or other liabilities that arise in connection with the Distributor's actions with regard to resales, leases, or rentals of the Goods.

COMMENT: The status of the distributor as separate from the manufacturer should be made very clear. Nevertheless, some jurisdictions may treat distributors in a similar fashion as employees and sales representatives. There is a potential that the manufacturer will have to comply with labor laws regulating benefits and termination regardless of the attempt to include protective provisions.

4. OBLIGATIONS OF DISTRIBUTOR. The Distributor will do the following:

a. The Distributor will aggressively promote, sell, lease, rent, and service the Products that it purchases from the Manufacturer to customers in the Territory.

b. The Distributor will utilize, at its discretion, various selling strategies, including catalog, mail order, telephone, and electronic sales within the Territory.

c. The Distributor will open at least one retail shop in the Territory at a location of its choosing for the sale, lease, or rental of the Goods. This retail shop must be opened within [*days*] after the effective date of this Agreement. The opening of additional retail shops in the Territory will be at the Distributor's sole discretion.

d. The Distributor will not sell, lease, or rent any other goods, items, or parts that are not made by the Manufacturer and that serve the same, or a confusingly or deceptively similar function, as the Manufacturer's Goods.

e. The Distributor will not sell, lease, or rent the Manufacturer's Goods to any other companies that are predominantly engaged in the sale, lease, or rental of the same or confusingly or deceptively similar goods.

f. The Distributor will be responsible for all costs of the business operation, including all taxes, labor costs, and penalties related to such operation.

g. The Distributor will be responsible for procuring and maintaining all import licenses, transport permits, business licenses, and other similar permits required for the import, transport, storage, and sale of the Goods in the Distributor's country. The Distributor will also be responsible for providing to the Manufacturer all documentation required for the import and transport of the Goods to the Distributor's destination. If the Distributor fails to provide this documentation to the Manufacturer within time for the Manufacturer to meet a delivery deadline, any delay in delivery caused by the Distributor will not be deemed a breach of this Agreement.

COMMENT: In many form contracts, a clause is included that prohibits the sale of competing products unless the company consents to such sales. It is recommended that the noncompetition clause be an absolute prohibition, unless the company really does have a good reason for authorizing competing sales—which is probably unlikely. The noncompetition clause must be limited to sales of competing goods, as opposed to sales of all goods. Most jurisdictions will not enforce contracts that prohibit an independent operator from selling products that are not in competition with each other. Moreover, in some countries, you might find that the noncompetition clause should be eliminated because there are only a few entities (often government operated) that import and distribute all products or there are distributors that specialize in certain types of products, such as cosmetic product lines or building supplies. If you want your product to gain a fast foothold on retail shelves, the distributor who specializes may be your answer.

5. OBLIGATIONS OF MANUFACTURER.

a. The Manufacturer will deliver within [*number*] days to the Distributor all Goods for which the Distributor places orders, except when delivery is delayed because of the Distributor's fault or because it becomes impossible as provided in this Agreement.

b. The Manufacturer will deliver the ordered Goods by shipment to the locations designated by the Distributor within the Territory, provided the Distributor has complied with its obligations with respect to importing. The Manufacturer is responsible for procuring all export licenses and inspections and for completing all export requirements within time to deliver the Goods.

c. If the Manufacturer discontinues the production of any Goods for any reason, the Manufacturer will immediately notify the Distributor and will continue for a reasonable time after discontinuance to furnish replacement parts and to offer service for the discontinued Goods already sold to the Distributor.

d. The Manufacturer will not sell any Goods to any person or entity, other than the Distributor, that sells, resells, leases, or rents products identical or confusingly or deceptively similar to the Manufacturer's Goods within the Territory.

e. The Manufacturer will not sell any Goods to any person or entity, other than the Distributor, for direct use if delivery is to be made within the Territory.

f. The Manufacturer will immediately refer to the Distributor all leads, prospects, and similar information that it obtains or receives regarding potential customers of the Goods within the Territory.

g. The Manufacturer will provide a list of suggested retail sale, lease, and rental prices for the Goods, but these prices will not be binding on the Distributor.

h. The Manufacturer will offer training and technical assistance to the Distributor and its personnel with regard to the use, operation, maintenance, and repair of the Goods.

i. The Manufacturer will maintain an advertising program to develop a quality image and goodwill in the industry and among the public.

j. The Manufacturer will supply sales materials and technical specifications for its Goods to the Distributor as needed.

COMMENT: This clause allows some flexibility in the manufacturer's obligations in an attempt to prevent a breach of the contract in the event that the manufacturer no longer has a particular product available. In practical terms, most products are rarely available for a lengthy time—there is always a new and improved version not far in the future. The contract should allow for common practice; otherwise the parties will be constantly amending their agreement or making new contracts to replace the outdated ones. Caution must be exercised when providing a "suggested retail price list" because of the potential for violating antitrust laws. It should be made very clear that the list is merely a suggested guideline (avoid using the word *recommended*, which implies a stronger directive than a suggestion).

6. ORDERS OF GOODS. The parties agree that the Distributor will order the Goods as follows:

a. Initial Order. Within [*number*] days of the effective date of this Agreement, the Distributor will place an initial order of the Goods for a total purchase price of no less than [*currency and amount*]. The Manufacturer will deliver the Goods and the

Distributor will pay for them as provided in this Agreement. The prices for the initial purchase of Goods will be [*specify currency and amount per unit or* as stated on the Current Product List attached to this Agreement].

b. Subsequent Minimum Orders. To maintain the exclusive right to distribute in the Territory, the Distributor must continue after the initial order to place orders for Goods at least as often and at least in the amounts following:

   i. Within the first [*number*] months after the effective date of this Agreement, one or more orders totaling at least [*currency and amount*].

   ii. Within the second [*number*]-month period after the effective date of this Agreement, at least one order totaling at least [*currency and amount*] every [*number months*] until this Agreement is terminated.

   iii. Within the third [*number*]-month period after the effective date of this Agreement, at least one order totaling at least [*currency and amount*] every [*number months*] until this Agreement is terminated.

   iv. Within the fourth [*number*]-month period after the effective date of this Agreement, at least one order totaling at least [*currency and amount*] every [*number months*] until this Agreement is terminated.

   v. Within each subsequent [*number*]-month period after the effective date of this Agreement, at least one order totaling at least [*currency and amount*] until this Agreement is terminated.

c. Force Majeure. If market demand for the Goods declines in the Territory for any reason beyond the Distributor's control to such an extent that the Distributor's orders of Goods at the amounts stated in this Agreement are no longer commercially feasible, the minimum order requirements will not apply for so long as the condition continues.

COMMENT: It is wise to provide for minimum orders when an exclusive arrangement is made. If the distributor fails to place orders in compliance with the minimum requirements, the manufacturer may assign distribution rights to another person within the same territory. However, the distributor should not be penalized merely because of events beyond his or her control, and therefore minimum order requirements should be lifted if they are commercially infeasible.

7. PRICES AND PAYMENT TERMS. The Manufacturer will charge the Distributor the prices on the Current Product List for all Goods listed on it until the Manufacturer determines to change any of the prices. The Manufacturer reserves the right to change any of the prices for its Goods, in which event the Manufacturer will immediately furnish the Distributor with a new price list. The prices for the Goods do not include transportation costs, insurance costs, or importing duty charges, all of which will be charged separately to the Distributor. The Manufacturer will be responsible for exporting license fees and charges. If an order from the Distributor is postmarked before the Manufacturer has notified the Distributor of a price change, the Manufacturer will honor the order at the prices in effect just prior to the change. Payment of the price for all Goods delivered to the Distributor will be cash, net [*number*] days. The Distributor is entitled to a discount of [*number*] percent for payments made within [*number*] days from the date of the invoice for the Goods.

COMMENT: Presumably, by agreeing to the hardier relationship of an exclusive distributorship, you have come to trust the other party. Therefore, a less secure method of payment may be agreed. However, this is not always the case, and you may want to require payment C.O.D. or at least partial payment at the time the order is made. It is always wise to include a discount as an incentive for early payment.

8. PAYMENT METHOD FOR BLOCKED EXCHANGE. If the country of either party restricts the remittance of funds to the other party's country, the Manufacturer may instruct the Distributor to deposit sums due into an account in the Distributor's country but in the Manufacturer's name. This account must be held at a bank selected by the Manufacturer. When the Distributor presents the Manufacturer with documents that show the making of such a deposit, the Manufacturer will provide the Distributor with a receipt.

COMMENT: If there is any potential for disharmony between the countries of the parties, it is wise to provide a means for payment in the event that the governments restrict financial dealings after goods have been transferred but before payment has been received. This clause suggests one method for assuring payment—at least once the restrictions are lifted and assuming the account is still intact.

9. WARRANTIES. The Manufacturer will give the Distributor the same limited warranty for each of the Goods sold as the Manufacturer provides for its own customers. The Distributor must furnish the Manufacturer's warranty to every person that purchases any Goods from it. The Distributor is prohibited from altering any terms of the Manufacturer's warranty. The Manufacturer will promptly repair or replace any Goods that malfunction, fail to operate, or are otherwise defective and that are covered under the warranty, regardless of whether the Distributor or the Distributor's customer own the goods at the time.

COMMENT: Manufacturers commonly extend warranties, particularly in overseas markets. Customer service and seller responsiveness are extremely important marketing features. Local products are often preferred if the buying public believes that customer service will be personal and fast. To gain market share, imports have to be offered better service than the local suppliers. Warranties are one method by which this can be done. The manufacturer may agree to offer extended or limited warranties, or no warranties at all, as to fitness or quality of the goods. The exact terms of the warranties should be given in the contract. In some countries, the law will imply warranties unless the seller expressly disclaims them. Implied warranties also arise under the United Nations Convention on International Sale of Goods.

10. INDEMNITIES. The parties agree to the following mutual indemnities:

a. The Distributor will indemnify, hold harmless, and defend the Manufacturer as against all claims and damages for injury to, or death of, one or more persons and for damage to, or loss of, property arising from or attributed to the conduct, operations, or performance of the Distributor.

b. The Manufacturer will indemnify, hold harmless, and defend the Distributor against all claims and damages arising out of any defects, failures, or malfunctions of any of the Goods, except those caused by the Distributor or otherwise arising out of or attributed to the Distributor's conduct, operations, or performance. At all times during the term of this Agreement, the Manufacturer will maintain product liability insurance covering all Goods sold to the Distributor in aggregate limits of at least [*currency and amount*] per occurrence, which polices will name the Distributor as an additional insured.

COMMENT: An indemnification clause is optional. In international contracts, the manufacturer will sometimes agree to hold the distributor harmless from damages that arise from specific causes, such as a design flaw or manufacturing defect, in order to encourage the distributor to debut the products in a new market. Product liability insurance is not available in all jurisdictions. The manufacturer should be certain to request advice on this type of insurance. Extension of it to the distributor is a voluntary gesture—after all, the defect or design flaw is the responsibility of the manufacturer, not the person selling the manufactured goods. Often, distributors in less-developed countries will be unable to obtain product liability insurance.

11. INTELLECTUAL PROPERTY RIGHTS. The parties agree as follows:

a. The Manufacturer owns valuable property rights in all of the marks, names, designs, patents, and trade secrets (the "Intellectual Property") connected with the Goods. None of these rights are being granted to the Distributor. The Distributor must not represent that he or she owns any rights in the Manufacturer's Intellectual Property, nor is the Distributor permitted to use the Manufacturer's name as any part of its own name. The rights to the Intellectual Property remain vested in the Manufacturer.

b. The Distributor is granted a right to use the Intellectual Property of the Manufacturer in connection with operating the distributorship and reselling, leasing, and renting the Goods. The Distributor has no right to use the Intellectual Property for any other purpose.

c. All advertisements, promotional materials, quotations, invoices, labels, containers, and other materials used in conjunction with the Goods must include a notice stating that the Manufacturer owns the Intellectual Property associated with the Goods. Such materials must also state that the Distributor is an authorized dealer or distributor of the Goods.

d. The Distributor is prohibited from altering in any way the Manufacturer's Intellectual Property used in connection with the Goods. All details, colors, and designs must be exactly as provided by the Manufacturer.

e. The Distributor may resell, lease, or rent Goods only if the Manufacturer's Intellectual Property is used in connection with the Goods. The Distributor is prohibited from using the Manufacturer's Intellectual Property in connection with any products that are not furnished by the Manufacturer.

f. The Distributor will not duplicate or attempt to duplicate any of the Goods, will not make the Goods available to another person for purposes of duplication, and will not make or sell any products that are confusingly or deceptively similar to the Goods.

g. The Distributor undertakes not to do any act that would or might invalidate or dilute the Manufacturer's registrations of, or title to, the Intellectual Property. The Distributor will not attempt to vary or cancel any registrations of the Intellectual Property. The Distributor will not assist any other person in any of these actions.

h. Violation of this entire Paragraph will result in immediate termination of this Agreement. Further, both parties agree that violation of this Paragraph will result in the dilution or destruction of the Manufacturer's valuable rights in its reputation, goodwill, and intellectual property, resulting in substantial damages. These damages will be impractical or impossible to measure because of the difficulty in measuring intangible rights. Therefore, the parties agree that if the Distributor violates this Paragraph, the Manufacturer has a right to assess liquidated damages against the Distributor in an amount equal to [*number*] percent of the price listed on the Manufacturer's Current Product List for each of the Goods that is subject of the violation.

COMMENT: The value of intellectual property rights should never be underestimated. The manufacturer's goodwill and reputation are connected to its name and product markings, and the uniqueness of its goods are preserved through patent and design registrations. Foreign traders know the value of these property rights—which is why infringement is big business. Your reputation sells products, whether the products are legitimately your own or illegitimately copied. If you do not protect your intellectual property, you may lose not only sales, but also the exclusive rights to that property. This clause will not on its own be effective. You should be certain that your trademarks, service marks, patents, and other intellectual property have been registered in the distributor's country, and you need to establish a system to monitor use of the mark in that country.

12. ASSIGNMENT. Neither party may assign this Agreement without the prior written consent of the other. Neither party may withhold consent unreasonably. The Manufacturer may withhold consent on any of the following grounds: the Distributor is in default of an obligation of this Agreement when consent is requested, the proposed assignee cannot financially perform the Distributor's obligations remaining under this Agreement, the proposed assignee refuses to assume all of the Distributor's remaining obligations under this Agreement, or the proposed assignee fails to meet the Manufacturer's standards for new distributors in effect at the time consent is requested.

COMMENT: The parties to a services contract are making the agreement based on characteristics that are unique to the parties. One party's assignment of the obligations under this contract would leave the other with an unknown partner. A prohibition against all assignments is usually not enforceable, but parties can protect themselves by demanding prior consent to any assignment.

13. TERMINATION OF EXCLUSIVE DISTRIBUTION RIGHTS. If the Distributor fails to make and pay for the minimum orders as required by this Agreement, and if the Distributor's failure cannot be excused or justified by a force beyond the Distributor's control as allowed in this Agreement, the Manufacturer's only remedy will be to terminate the Distributor's right to exclusive distribution within the Territory. The Manufacturer may terminate the exclusivity right only after giving the Distributor [*number*] days' advance written notice of the failure to perform and of the intent to terminate the exclusivity right. If the Distributor cures the failure within the notice period, the Distributor's exclusivity will not terminate. Termination of exclusivity rights will not automatically terminate this Agreement. Regardless of whether the Distributor has exclusive distribution rights, so long as the Distributor is otherwise not in default of any other provision of this Agreement, this Agreement will remain in full effect with only the following modification: the Distributor does not have exclusive distribution rights within the Territory, and the Manufacturer has no obligation to refrain from selling or engaging others to sell the Goods within the Territory or to refer prospective customers to the Distributor.

14. TERMINATION OF AGREEMENT BY MANUFACTURER. The Manufacturer may terminate this Agreement, without affecting any other remedy that the Manufacturer may seek by law, as follows:

a. Immediately by notice to the Distributor if

   i. The Distributor is adjudicated bankrupt voluntarily or involuntarily

   ii. The Distributor allows any money judgment against it to remain unsatisfied for [*number*] days or more

   iii. The Distributor becomes insolvent or a receiver is appointed for the Distributor's assets

   iv. The Distributor assigns its rights or property for the benefit of creditors

   v. The Distributor commences any proceeding, or any proceeding is commenced against the Distributor, for reorganization or rearrangement of its financial and business affairs

b. After [*number*] days, having given advance written notice and a demand to cure to the Distributor, if the Distributor defaults in performing this Agreement, with the exception of the minimum order requirements, provided that if the Distributor cures the default within the notice period, the notice will not take effect.

COMMENT: A common practice in business contracts is to allow for termination in several different ways, depending on the circumstances. For some events, immediate termination may be warranted, while for others, the party in default may be allowed to cure the default. It is not necessary to list every possible reason for termination by notice—you are bound to miss a few and therefore limit yourself to the ones you have listed. In deciding which events will give a right to terminate the contract, it is important to research the law of both the manufacturer's and the distributor's countries. Your termination rights could be subject to limitation by protective laws. Also, you should avoid using terms such as default of a "material" obligation because such terms are unclear. The parties may state certain defaults that are not grounds for termination, such as a delay in payment of only five days.

15. TERMINATION OF AGREEMENT BY DISTRIBUTOR. The Distributor may terminate this Agreement, without affecting any other remedies that it may seek by law, as follows:

a. Immediately by notice to the Manufacturer if:

   i. The Manufacturer is adjudicated bankrupt voluntarily or involuntarily

   ii. The Manufacturer becomes insolvent or a receiver is appointed for the Manufacturer's assets

   iii. The Manufacturer assigns its rights or property for the benefit of creditors

   iv. The Manufacturer commences any proceeding, or any proceeding is commenced against the Manufacturer, for reorganization or rearrangement of its financial and business affairs

b. After [*number*] days, having given advance written notice and a demand to cure to the Manufacturer, if the Manufacturer defaults in performing this Agreement, with the exception of the minimum order requirements, provided that if the Manufacturer cures the default within the notice period, the notice will not take effect.

COMMENTS: It is generally best to provide for termination rights that are the same or similar for both parties. The courts will usually allow mutual rights—if one party has the right, the same right may be implied for the other party. To make clear that both parties have rights of termination, two separate clauses are often included in the contract, one for each party.

16. REPURCHASE OF PRODUCTS ON TERMINATION. If this Agreement is terminated for any reason at all, the Manufacturer may, but need not, repurchase the Goods that the Distributor has not yet resold. Provided the Goods are in new and resalable condition, the Manufacturer will repurchase the Goods at the Distributor's cost, not including any shipping, freight, customs, or storage charges. If the Goods are not repurchased by the Manufacturer, the Distributor is solely responsible for their disposal, and the Distributor undertakes to dispose of the Goods in such a manner as will not infringe on the Manufacturer's Intellectual Property or interfere with the Manufacturer's goodwill. The Distributor will return or destroy all materials that the Distributor possesses and on which the Manufacturer's Intellectual Property appears.

COMMENT: The provision allows the manufacturer to elect to repurchase goods. There is no need to not repurchase goods, but this provision option could be more cost-effective than staffing the distributorship until another distributor is found. In any event, the manufacturer should protect its intellectual property on termination of the contract.

17. REMEDIES. The parties acknowledge that they intend to establish a mutually beneficial relationship and that, to this end, they will strive to resolve any disagreements between them through amicable negotiations. Nevertheless, if a dispute does arise that they are unable to resolve otherwise, the parties will submit it to binding arbitration before the [*name of arbitration association*]. The arbitration will be conducted in [*place*], unless the parties agree otherwise at the time arbitration is demanded. Any arbitration award or determination will be final, nonappealable, and conclusive, and it may be submitted to a court with jurisdiction to enter a judgment. This clause will not limit the rights of the Manufacturer to pursue any remedy available for infringement of its exclusive rights in its Intellectual Property.

COMMENT: If arbitration is available within the local representative's country, it may be chosen as a means of resolving disputes. You should be cautious, however, in providing for arbitration because not all countries have such systems easily available. Moreover, arbitration is adversarial and usually involves more cost and delay than negotiation and compromise, although generally less than litigation. In some cultures, arbitration has the same stigma as court proceedings, both of which are viewed with suspicion and as personal insults.

18. MODIFICATION. This Agreement is modifiable only by a writing signed by both parties.

COMMENT: Always insist on written modifications to avoid any subsequent question of what was agreed. Proof of oral modifications may not be allowed in court to alter the terms of a contract that is otherwise definite and clear.

19. NOTICES. All notices that may be given under this Agreement must be delivered in writing to the other party at the address specified in this Agreement. A party must notify the other party of a change of address within [*number*] days after it becomes effective. Notices are deemed to be delivered on the date of receipt.

COMMENT: A notice clause is usually a wise provision to ensure that the parties understand the procedure for giving notice. This clause can prevent later disputes over what constitutes notice.

20. WAIVERS AND DELAYS OF PERFORMANCE. Neither party will waive any of the provisions of this Agreement with respect to its rights to seek remedies for breach or to demand strict conformance with the Agreement merely because the party has waived one or more of the other party's breaches in performance; has failed, refused, or neglected to exercise any rights, powers, or options granted by this Agreement; or has not insisted on strict compliance with this Agreement.

21. TERMS OF AGREEMENT. The Manufacturer and the Distributor have executed this Agreement to demonstrate their intent to be bound by its terms. The parties declare that this Agreement constitutes their entire agreement and replaces all of their prior negotiations, understandings, and representations. Each party has been encouraged and has had the opportunity to obtain the advice of independent professionals, including attorneys and accountants, and each has made an independent decision to undertake the obligations set forth. If any term of this Agreement is held to be unenforceable or invalid, such term may be modified to render it valid and enforceable. If modification cannot be made, the term will be deemed deleted and the remainder of the Agreement will remain in full force.

COMMENT: This standard clause is important and should rarely be eliminated from your contracts. It serves to establish the basic contractual notions of mutual understanding and intent. In international contracts, these clauses have added significance because each party's understanding of the contract terms could indeed be very different from that of the other party, given such invisible barriers as language, culture, environment, and inexperience.

Each party acknowledges that he or she has read and understood the terms of this Agreement, and accordingly sign below.

[*Name of Company*]
Distributor
By [*signature*]
[*name and title of person signing*]

[*Name of Company*]
Manufacturer
By [*signature*]
[*name and title of person signing*]

CHAPTER 20

Consignment Agreement

IN A CONSIGNMENT CONTRACT, the owner of products gives possession of them to another party, who sells them. Until the goods are sold, they remain the property of the owner (known as the consignor). Title to the goods never passes to the person selling them (the consignee). The risk that the products will not sell remains with the consignor because unsold or outdated products can usually be returned. Thus, the consignment contract differs from the distribution contract, where the goods are purchased by the distributor and resold, and from the sales representative contract, where the goods are sold on behalf of the manufacturer but usually are shipped directly from the manufacturer to the customer (and therefore are never possessed by the sales representative).

Sample Contract: Consignment Agreement

This Agreement is made on [*date*] between [*name*], [a/an] [*individual or type of entity and nationality or place of formation*] of [*address*] (the "Manufacturer"), and [*name*], [a/an] [*individual or type of entity and nationality or place of formation*] of [*address*] ("Consignee").

COMMENT: The agreement binds the parties who sign it, and these should be identified here. To ensure that there is no misunderstanding, the full name and business address of each party should be given. If a party is an entity (partnership, corporation, limited company, or otherwise), the type of entity should be disclosed here. In international contracts, the description of each party includes the party's nationality. Examples of descriptions: "a Société Anonyme organized and existing under the laws of France," "a partnership organized and existing under the laws of the State of California in the United States of America," or "an individual who is a citizen of Singapore."

RECITALS

A. The parties acknowledge that the Manufacturer produces and sells [*describe goods or* the goods listed in the Current Product List attached to this Agreement] and future products that are similar in nature and type (the "Goods").

B. The Consignee has requested to receive Goods on consignment from the Manufacturer for the purpose of stocking and selling the Goods as an authorized representative of the Manufacturer.

C. The Manufacturer desires to furnish Goods to the Consignee as an authorized representative in [*state and/or country*] ("Territory") on the terms and conditions of this Agreement.

COMMENT: The recitals are preliminary provisions that set out the intent of the parties, and sometimes definitions—such as of the goods—of terms used in the contract.

Therefore, the parties agree as follows:

AGREEMENT

1. RELATIONSHIP OF THE PARTIES. The Manufacturer agrees to furnish Goods to the Consignee in accordance with this Agreement, and the Consignee agrees to sell them in the Territory. The arrangement between the parties [is/is not] exclusive in the Territory. The parties acknowledge and agree that the Consignee is separate and independent of the Manufacturer. This Agreement is not to be construed as creating an employment, partnership, joint venture, fiduciary, or other similar relationship. Neither party is liable for the debts or obligations of the other. The Consignee is free to employ or engage any staff or independent contractors, and the Manufacturer has no power to limit, fire, or hire such persons. It is the Consignee's responsibility to ensure that all local law requirements for doing business in [*country*] have been met. The Consignee is further responsible for the payment of all taxes and fees arising from sales of the Goods in [*country*]. The Manufacturer will neither indemnify nor insure the Consignee against losses, claims, or other liabilities that arise in connection with the Consignee's actions with regard to sales of the Goods.

COMMENT: Exclusivity is a benefit to the consignee and may be particularly warranted in a relatively small market. This clause may be modified to provide for exclusivity, in which case the manufacturer will not have the right to sell goods there, whether by its own efforts or through other representatives. If exclusivity is provided, additional clauses should be added throughout the rest of the contract similar to the obligations set forth in the Distributor Agreement, such as prohibitions against the manufacturer selling to other parties and requirements that potential customers be referred to the consignee. The status of the consignee as separate from the manufacturer should be made very clear. Nevertheless, some jurisdictions may treat consignees in a similar fashion as employees and agents. There is a potential that the manufacturer will have to comply with labor laws regulating benefits and termination regardless of the attempt to include protective provisions.

2. TERM OF AGREEMENT. This Agreement commences on the date the last party signs it and expires after [*number*] years, unless it is terminated earlier as provided in this Agreement. At the expiration of this Agreement, the parties may negotiate a renewal or extension of the term, provided that the Consignee is in full compliance with this Agreement at that time.

COMMENT: You may agree to an indefinite term, with termination at will by either party on advance notice, but you should be cautious in agreeing to this type of term. In some countries, a consignment contract with an indefinite term may be considered as creating an agency relationship. The result would be to subject the manufacturer to agency laws, such as statutes that strictly regulate termination of agency relationships only for certain reasons and only on payment of significant separation packages.

3. STOCK ORDERS. The Consignee will submit all Stock Orders on a form supplied by the Manufacturer, specifying the types and quantities of the Goods that the Consignee desires to receive from the Manufacturer. After the initial Stock Order, the Consignee will submit a Stock Order no later than the [*number*] day of each month to reorder the type and quantities of Goods sold in the preceding month. Each Stock Order is subject to the Manufacturer's approval, which is final. The Manufacturer will review each Stock Order submitted by the Consignee and will approve or alter it within [*number*] days of receipt. The Manufacturer has discretion to change the types and quantities of Goods ordered. If a change is made, the order will not be shipped until the Manufacturer has given notice, written or oral, to the Consignee regarding the change and has received written or oral confirmation.

COMMENT: Given the delays inherent in overseas communication and transport, the monthly turnaround provided in this clause may be impractical. The order period should be negotiated to take into account standard communication and shipping times to the consignee's country.

4. DELIVERY TERMS. The Manufacturer will deliver within [*number*] days to the Consignee all Goods on an approved Stock Order, except when delivery is delayed because of the Consignee's fault or because it becomes impossible as provided in this Agreement. The Manufacturer will deliver the Goods by shipment to the locations designated by the Consignee within the Territory. The Manufacturer is responsible for procuring all export licenses and inspections and for complying with all export and import requirements within time to deliver the Goods, except that the Consignee must obtain any necessary licenses for importing and any other licenses or permits required by the Consignee's country.

COMMENT: The manufacturer commonly agrees to pay for most of the exporting and importing costs in a consignment contract because the goods continue to belong to the manufacturer until sold to the customer. The consignee is merely receiving a relatively small percentage of the price for making the sale. If the consignee is to be responsible for the shipping, transport, and importing costs, the percentage should be increased; otherwise, the consignee is likely to have no profit and no incentive to enter the contract.

5. TITLE TO GOODS. All Goods delivered to the Consignee pursuant to this Agreement will be held on consignment. The Goods will remain at all times under the ownership, direction, and control of the Manufacturer until they are sold to customers. The Consignee will not take title to the Goods at any time. Title to the Goods will pass directly from the Manufacturer to the customer.

6. PRICE TERMS. From time to time, the Manufacturer will supply a list of retail prices for the Goods. The Manufacturer reserves the right to change any of the prices for its Goods. The Consignee is authorized to sell the Goods only at the prices listed in the retail price list most recently received from the Manufacturer, or at amounts in the Consignee's discretion that are more than those prices. If market demand for the Goods declines in the Territory for any reason beyond the Consignee's control to such an extent that the Consignee's orders of Goods at the amounts stated in this Agreement are no longer commercially feasible, the minimum order requirements will not apply for so long as the condition continues.

COMMENT: In a consignment contract, the manufacturer may provide a mandatory price list without violating antitrust and price-fixing laws because the goods are still owned by, and therefore are being sold by, the manufacturer.

7. PAYMENT TERMS. Each Stock Order, except the initial one, will be accompanied with payment in full for the Goods sold in the preceding month, less the applicable discounts for the consignee on the sales. The Consignee will be allowed a discount [*specify, e.g.*, as shown on the Current Products List *or* of (*number*) amount for each of the Goods sold]. If the Consignee sells any Goods for an amount that is more than the Manufacturer's price, the Consignee will be entitled, in addition to the usual discount, to one-half of the excess amount. If the country of either party restricts the remittance of funds to the other party's country, the Manufacturer may instruct the Consignee to deposit sums due into an account in the Consignee's country but in the Manufacturer's name. This account must be held at a bank selected by the Manufacturer. When the Consignee presents the Manufacturer with documents that show the making of such a deposit, the Manufacturer will provide the Consignee with a receipt.

COMMENT: Presumably, by agreeing to a consignment, you have come to trust the other party. Therefore, you may agree to a less secure method of payment. This agreement requires the consignee to pay for the goods by the end of the month in which the goods are sold. The parties may find that the thirty-day turnaround for payments, reports, and orders is impractical because of the delays inherent in international transactions. You should also consider the rate of sales in the consignee's market when setting the turnaround time. If there is any potential for disharmony between the countries of the parties, it is wise to provide a means for payment in the event that a government restricts financial dealings after goods have been transferred but before payment has been received. This clause suggests one method for assuring payment—at least once the restrictions are lifted and assuming the account is still intact.

8. INVENTORY REPORTS. At the time the Consignee sends a Stock Order, the Consignee will also submit a monthly report stating the type and quantity of Goods sold during the preceding month. The report must be in the format as the Manufacturer directs. Every [*number*] months, or at any time the Manufacturer requests, the Consignee must submit to the Manufacturer a complete inventory of all Goods remaining in the consigned stock. If requested by the Manufacturer, the inventory must be taken by or under the direction of a representative of the Manufacturer, in which event the costs related to the Manufacturer's representative will be paid by the Manufacturer.

9. ADDITIONAL OBLIGATIONS OF CONSIGNEE. The Consignee agrees to do the following:

a. The Consignee will aggressively promote and sell the Goods to customers in the Territory. The Consignee will utilize, at its discretion, various selling strategies, including retail outlets, catalog, mail order, telephone, and electronic sales within the Territory.

b. The Consignee will not deal in any other goods, items, or parts that are not made by the Manufacturer and that serve the same or a confusingly or deceptively similar function as the Manufacturer's Goods.

c. The Consignee will not sell the Manufacturer's Goods to any other companies that are predominantly engaged in the sale, lease, or rental of the same or confusingly or deceptively similar goods.

d. The Consignee will be responsible for all costs of the business operation, including all taxes, labor costs, and penalties related to such operation.

e. The Consignee will be responsible for procuring and maintaining all import licenses, transport permits, business licenses, and other similar permits required for the import, transport, storage, and sale of the Goods in the Consignee's country. The Consignee will also be responsible for providing to the Manufacturer all documentation required for the import and transport of the Goods to the Consignee's destination. If the Consignee fails to provide this documentation to the Manufacturer within time for the Manufacturer to meet a delivery deadline, any delay in delivery caused by the Consignee will not be deemed a breach of this Agreement by the Manufacturer.

COMMENT: In many form contracts, a clause is included that prohibits the sale of competing products unless the company consents to such sales. It is recommended that the noncompetition clause be an absolute prohibition, unless the company really does have a good reason for allowing competing sales—which is probably unlikely. The noncompetition clause must be limited to sales of competing goods, as opposed to sales of all goods. Most jurisdictions will not enforce contracts that prohibit an independent operator from selling products that are not in competition with each other. Moreover, in some countries, you might find that the noncompetition clause should be eliminated because there are only a few entities (often government operated) that import and sell products or there are importers that specialize in certain types of products, such as cosmetic product lines or building supplies. If you want your product to gain a fast foothold on retail shelves, the importer who specializes may be your answer.

10. ADDITIONAL OBLIGATIONS OF MANUFACTURER. The Manufacturer will supply sales materials and technical specifications for its Goods to the Consignee as needed.

11. RISK OF LOSS. The Consignee assumes all risk of loss for all the Goods consigned. The Consignee will pay for all Goods damaged, destroyed, or stolen from the consignment inventory as if such Goods were sold.

COMMENT: This clause places the risk of loss on the consignee even though title to the goods remains with the manufacturer. This clause is intended to give the consignee incentive to operate its business with care and to avoid incurring losses. In reality, this clause could be overly burdensome in some countries, particularly where insurance coverage is limited or unavailable. Therefore, this clause may be a point of negotiation.

12. WARRANTIES. The Manufacturer will give a limited warranty for each of the Goods sold. The Consignee must furnish the Manufacturer's warranty to every person that purchases any Goods from it. The Consignee is prohibited from altering any terms of the Manufacturer's warranty. The Manufacturer will promptly repair or replace any Goods that malfunction, fail to operate, or are otherwise defective and that are covered under the warranty, regardless of whether the Consignee or the Consignor possess the goods at the time.

COMMENT: Manufacturers commonly extend warranties, particularly in overseas markets. Customer service and seller responsiveness are extremely important marketing features. Local products are often preferred if the buying public believes that customer service will be personal and fast. To gain market share, imports have to be offered with better service than the local suppliers. Warranties are one method by which this can be done. The manufacturer may agree to offer extended or limited warranties, or no warranties at all, as to fitness or quality of the goods. The exact terms of the warranties should be given in the contract. In some countries, the law will imply warranties unless the seller expressly disclaims them. Implied warranties also arise under the United Nations Convention on International Sale of Goods.

13. INDEMNITIES. The parties agree to the following mutual indemnities:

a. The Consignee will indemnify, hold harmless, and defend the Manufacturer against all claims and damages for injury to, or death of, one or more persons and for damage to, or loss of, property arising from or attributed to the conduct, operations, or performance of the Consignee.

b. The Manufacturer will indemnify, hold harmless, and defend the Consignee against all claims and damages arising out of any defects, failures, or malfunctions of any of the Goods, except those caused by the Consignee or otherwise arising out of or attributed to the Consignee's conduct, operations, or performance. At all times during the term of this Agreement, the Manufacturer will maintain product liability insurance covering all Goods sold to the Consignee in aggregate limits of at least [*currency and amount*] per occurrence, which policies will name the Consignee as an additional insured.

COMMENT: An indemnification clause is optional. In international contracts, the manufacturer will sometimes agree to hold the consignee harmless from damages that arise from specific causes, such as a design flaw or manufacturing defect, to encourage the consignee to debut the products in a new market. Product liability insurance is not available in all jurisdictions. The manufacturer should be certain to request advice on this type of insurance. Extension of it to the consignee is a voluntary gesture—after all, the defect or design flaw is the responsibility of the manufacturer, not the person selling the manufactured goods. Often, consignees in less-developed countries will be unable to obtain product liability insurance.

14. INTELLECTUAL PROPERTY RIGHTS. The parties agree as follows:

a. The Manufacturer owns valuable property rights in all of the marks, names, designs, patents, and trade secrets (the "Intellectual Property") connected with the Goods. None of these rights are being granted to the Consignee. The Consignee must not represent that he or she owns any rights in the Manufacturer's Intellectual Property, nor is the Consignee permitted to use the Manufacturer's name as any part of its own name. The rights to the Intellectual Property remain vested in the Manufacturer.

b. The Consignee is granted a right to use the Intellectual Property of the Manufacturer in connection with operating the distributorship and reselling, leasing, and renting the Goods. The Consignee has no right to use the Intellectual Property for any other purpose.

c. All advertisements, promotional materials, quotations, invoices, labels, containers, and other materials used in conjunction with the Goods must include a notice stating that the Manufacturer owns the Intellectual Property associated with the Goods. Such materials must also state that the Consignee is an authorized consignee of the Goods.

d. The Consignee is prohibited from altering in any way the Manufacturer's Intellectual Property used in connection with the Goods. All details, colors, and designs must be exactly as provided by the Manufacturer.

e. The Consignee may sell Goods only if the Manufacturer's Intellectual Property is used in connection with the Goods. The Consignee is prohibited from using the Manufacturer's Intellectual Property in connection with any products that are not furnished by the Manufacturer.

f. The Consignee will not duplicate or attempt to duplicate any of the Goods, will not make the Goods available to another person for purposes of duplication, and will not make or sell any products that are confusingly or deceptively similar to the Goods.

g. The Consignee undertakes not to do any act that would or might invalidate or dilute the Manufacturer's registrations of, or title to, the Intellectual Property. The Consignee will not attempt to vary or cancel any registrations of the Intellectual Property. The Consignee will not assist any other person in any of these actions.

h. Violation of this entire Paragraph will result in immediate termination of this Agreement. Further, both parties agree that violation of this Paragraph will result in the dilution or destruction of the Manufacturer's valuable rights in its reputation, goodwill, and intellectual property, resulting in substantial damages. These damages will be impractical or impossible to measure because of the difficulty in measuring intangible rights. Therefore, the parties agree that if the Consignee violates this Paragraph, the Manufacturer has a right to assess liquidated damages against the Consignee in an amount equal to [*number*] percent of the price listed on the Manufacturer's Current Product List for each of the Goods that is subject of the violation.

COMMENT: The value of intellectual property rights should never be underestimated. The manufacturer's goodwill and reputation are connected to its name and product markings, and the uniqueness of its goods are preserved through patent and design registrations. Foreign traders know the value of these property rights—which is why infringement is big business. Your reputation sells products, whether the products are legitimately your own or illegitimately copied. If you do not protect your intellectual property, you may lose not only sales but also the exclusive rights to that property. This clause will not on its own be effective. You should be certain that your trademarks, service marks, patents, and other intellectual property have been registered in the consignee's country, and you need to establish a system to monitor use of the mark in that country.

15. ASSIGNMENT. Neither party may assign this Agreement without the prior written consent of the other. Neither party may withhold consent unreasonably. The Manufacturer may withhold consent on any of the following grounds: the Consignee is in default of an obligation of this Agreement when consent is requested, the proposed assignee cannot financially perform the Consignee's obligations remaining under this Agreement, the proposed assignee refuses to assume all of the Consignee's remaining obligations under this Agreement, or the proposed assignee fails to meet the Manufacturer's standards for new consignees in effect at the time consent is requested.

COMMENT: The parties to a personal services contract are making the agreement based on characteristics that are unique to the parties. One party's assignment of the obligations under this contract would leave the other with an unknown partner. A prohibition against all assignments is usually not enforceable, but parties can protect themselves by demanding prior consent to any assignment.

16. TERMINATION OF AGREEMENT BY MANUFACTURER. The Manufacturer may terminate this Agreement at any time and for any reason by giving [*number*] days' advance written notice to the Consignee. This Agreement will terminate immediately without any advance notice, without affecting any other remedy that the Manufacturer may seek by law, if the Consignee becomes insolvent, a receiver is appointed for the Consignee's assets, or the Consignee assigns its rights or property for the benefit of creditors. If the Consignee defaults in performing this Agreement, the Manufacturer may give the Consignee [*number*] days' advance notice and demand to cure. If the Consignee fails to cure the default within the notice period, this Agreement will terminate, but if the Consignee cures the default, the termination notice will not take effect.

COMMENT: A common practice in business contracts is to allow for termination in several different ways, depending on the circumstances. For some events, immediate termination may be warranted, while for others, the party in default may be allowed to cure the default. It is not necessary to list every possible reason for termination by notice—you are bound to miss a few and therefore limit yourself to the ones you have listed. In deciding which events will give a right to terminate the contract, it is important to research the law of both the manufacturer's and the consignee's countries. Your termination rights could be subject to limitation by protective laws. Also, you should avoid using terms such as default of a "material" obligation because such terms are unclear. The parties may state certain defaults that are not grounds for termination, such as a delay in payment of only five days.

17. TERMINATION OF AGREEMENT BY DISTRIBUTOR. The Consignee may terminate this Agreement at any time and for any reason by giving [*number*] days' advance written notice to the Manufacturer and by returning all remaining consigned stock, collected payments, and accounts receivable. This Agreement will terminate immediately without any advance notice, without affecting any other remedy that the Consignee may seek by law, if the Manufacturer becomes insolvent, a receiver is appointed for the Manufacturer's assets, or the Manufacturer assigns its rights or property for the benefit of creditors. If the Manufacturer defaults in performing this Agreement, the Consignee may give the Manufacturer advance [*number*] days' notice and demand to cure. If the Manufacturer fails to cure the default within the notice period, this Agreement will terminate, but if the Manufacturer cures the default, the termination notice will not take effect.

COMMENTS: It is generally best to provide for termination rights that are the same or similar for both parties. The courts will usually allow mutual rights—if one party has the right, the same right may be implied for the other party. To make clear that both parties have rights of termination, two separate clauses are often included in the contract, one for each party.

18. TERMINATION OF AGREEMENT. If this Agreement is terminated, all Goods in the Consignee's possession on consignment must immediately be returned to the Manufacturer and will be accepted for full credit. Goods not returned will be presumed damaged, lost, or stolen, and the Consignee will be obligated to make full payment for them as if they had been sold. The Consignee will remit to the Manufacturer all money and accounts receivable from sales before termination. After the Manufacturer has collected the accounts receivable, the Manufacturer will pay the Consignee the applicable discounts based on the amounts actually received.

19. REMEDIES. The parties acknowledge that they intend to establish a mutually beneficial relationship and that, to this end, they will strive to resolve any disagreements between them through amicable negotiations. Nevertheless, if a dispute does arise that they are unable to resolve otherwise, the parties will submit it to binding arbitration before the [*name of arbitration association*]. The arbitration will be conducted in [*place*], unless the parties agree otherwise at the time arbitration is demanded. Any arbitration award or determination will be final, nonappealable, and conclusive, and it may be submitted to a court with jurisdiction to enter a judgment. This clause will not limit the rights of the Manufacturer to pursue any remedy available for infringement of its exclusive rights in its Intellectual Property.

COMMENT: If arbitration is available within the consignee's country, it may be chosen as a means of resolving disputes. You should be cautious, however, in providing for arbitration because not all countries have such systems easily available. Moreover, arbitration is adversarial and usually involves more cost and delay than negotiation and compromise, although generally less than litigation. In some cultures, arbitration has the same stigma as court proceedings, both of which are viewed with suspicion and as personal insults.

20. MODIFICATION. This Agreement is modifiable only by a writing signed by both parties.

COMMENT: Always insist on written modifications to avoid any subsequent question of what was agreed. Proof of oral modifications may not be allowed in court to alter the terms of a contract that is otherwise definite and clear.

21. NOTICES. All notices that may be given under this Agreement must be delivered in writing to the other party at the address specified in this Agreement. A party must notify the other party of a change of address within [*number*] days after it becomes effective. Notices are deemed to be delivered on the date of receipt.

COMMENT: A notice clause is usually a wise provision to ensure that the parties understand the procedure for giving notice. This clause can prevent later disputes over what constitutes notice.

22. WAIVERS AND DELAYS OF PERFORMANCE. Neither party will waive any of the provisions of this Agreement with respect to its rights to seek remedies for breach or to demand strict conformance with the Agreement merely because the party has waived one or more of the other party's breaches in performance; has failed, refused, or neglected to exercise any rights, powers, or options granted by this Agreement, or has not insisted on strict compliance with this Agreement.

23. TERMS OF AGREEMENT. The Manufacturer and the Consignee have executed this Agreement to demonstrate their intent to be bound by its terms. The parties declare that this Agreement constitutes their entire agreement and replaces all of their prior negotiations, understandings, and representations. Each party has been encouraged and has had the opportunity to obtain the advice of independent professionals, including attorneys and accountants, and each has made an independent decision to undertake the obligations set forth. If any term of this Agreement is held to be unenforceable or invalid, such term may be modified to render it valid and enforceable. If modification cannot be made, the term will be deemed deleted and the remainder of the Agreement will remain in full force.

COMMENT: This standard clause is important and should rarely be eliminated from your contracts. It serves to establish the basic contractual notions of mutual understanding and intent. In international contracts, these clauses have added significance because each party's understanding of the contract terms could indeed be very different from that of the other party, given such invisible barriers as language, culture, environment, and inexperience.

Each party acknowledges that he or she has read and understood the terms of this Agreement, and accordingly sign below.

[*Name of Company*]

Consignee

By [*signature*]

[*name and title of person signing*]

[*Name of Company*]

Manufacturer

By [*signature*] [*name and title of person signing*]

CHAPTER 21

Licensing Contract

LICENSING ARRANGEMENTS take a step beyond the mere sale of goods. These arrangements involve the sale of intellectual property to a local party who makes the goods in compliance with the licensing agreement. The licensing arrangement differs from a franchise in two major ways. First, the licensee makes the products sold, while the franchisee purchases the goods from the manufacturer. Second, the franchise involves an entire business structure, while a license allows the licensee more discretion over the business operation.

Sample Contract: Licensing Agreement

This Agreement is made on [*date*] between [*name*], [a/an] [*individual or type of entity and nationality or place of formation*] of [*address*] (the "Licensor"), and [*name*], [a/an] [*individual or type of entity and nationality or place of formation*] of [*address*] ("Licensee").

COMMENT: The agreement binds the parties who sign it, and these should be identified here. To ensure that there is no misunderstanding, the full name and business address of each party should be given. If a party is an entity—partnership, corporation, limited company, or otherwise—the type of entity should be disclosed here. In international contracts, the description of each party includes the party's nationality. Examples of descriptions: "a Société Anonyme organized and existing under the laws of France," "a partnership organized and existing under the laws of the State of California in the United States of America," or "an individual who is a citizen of Singapore."

RECITALS

A. The parties acknowledge that the Licensor owns exclusive rights in the intellectual property shown in the list attached to this Agreement ("Intellectual Property").

B. The Licensee desires to manufacture and sell [*type of goods*] ("Goods") carrying the Licensor's Intellectual Property in [*state and/or country*] ("Territory").

COMMENT: The recitals are preliminary provisions that set out the intent of the parties, and sometimes definitions—such as of the goods—of terms used in the contract.

Therefore, the parties agree as follows:

AGREEMENT

1. GRANT OF LICENSE. The Licensor grants to the Licensee the license and authority to use the Intellectual Property on and/or in connection with the

Goods made by or for the Licensee for sale in the Territory for the time that this Agreement is in force.

2. TERM OF AGREEMENT. This Agreement commences on the date the last party signs it and expires after [*number*] years, unless it is terminated earlier as provided in this Agreement. At the expiration of this Agreement, the parties may negotiate a renewal or extension of the term, provided that the Licensee is in full compliance with this Agreement at that time.

COMMENT: A license involves a substantial commitment of funds and efforts, and the term provided should be reasonably long to allow the licensee to grow a profitable business. You may agree to an indefinite term, with termination at will by either party on advance notice, but you should be cautious in agreeing to this type of term. In some countries, a license with an indefinite term may be considered as creating an agency relationship. The result would be to subject the licensor to agency laws, such as statutes that strictly regulate termination of agency relationships only for certain reasons and only on payment of significant separation packages.

3. INTELLECTUAL PROPERTY RIGHTS. The parties agree as follows:

a. The Licensor is the proprietor of valuable property rights in the Intellectual Property, having registered it in the Licensee's country and in many countries throughout the world. The Licensor has used the Intellectual Property in connection with its own products for [*number*] years continuously, has devoted substantial financial resources in advertising and marketing the Intellectual Property for its own high-quality products, and has established a reputation and goodwill in conjunction with the Intellectual Property in the trade and public worldwide.

b. This License being granted is limited to the Territory only. Any sales of the Goods outside the Territory or for export from the Territory must be negotiated separately.

c. The Licensee must vigilantly protect the Licensor's Intellectual Property from infringement and other improper use in relation to any goods, services, or advertising in the Territory. The Licensee will promptly report to the Licensor all information relevant to the infringement or threatened infringement of the Intellectual Property.

d. All advertisements, promotional materials, quotations, invoices, labels, containers, and other materials used on or in conjunction with the Goods must include a notice stating that the Licensor owns the Intellectual Property and that the Licensee is the authorized licensee of the Licensor. Further, all advertising and promotional material must first be approved by the Licensor as to content and choice of media.

e. The Licensee is prohibited from altering in any way the Licensor's Intellectual Property used in connection with the Goods. All details, colors, and designs must be exactly as provided by the Licensor.

f. The Licensee is prohibited from using the Intellectual Property in connection with any products that are not the subject of this Agreement or that are not otherwise approved in advance and in writing by the Licensor.

g. The Licensee will not duplicate or attempt to duplicate any of the Licensor's own products, will not make its own Goods or the Licensor's products available to another person for purposes of duplication, and will not make or sell any products that are confusingly or deceptively similar to the Licensor's products.

h. The Licensor undertakes not to do any act that would or might invalidate or dilute the Licensor's registrations of, or title to, the Intellectual Property, except that the parties will join their efforts in ensuring that the Licensee is registered as a user of the Intellectual Property in the Territory. To this end, the parties agree to complete, sign, and file all documents and agreements necessary to complete this registration. The Licensee will not attempt to vary or cancel any registrations of the Intellectual Property, and will not assist any other person in any of these actions.

i. If the Licensee uses its own intellectual property on or in connection with the Goods, the Licensee's use must not be such that it would create joint rights. The Licensee must separate its intellectual property from the Licensor's Intellectual Property by sufficient space and distinctive type.

j. Violation of this entire Paragraph will result in immediate termination of this Agreement. Further, both parties agree that violation of this Paragraph will result in the dilution or destruction of the Licensor's valuable rights in its reputation, goodwill, and intellectual property, resulting in substantial damages. These damages will be impractical or impossible to measure because of the difficulty in measuring intangible rights. Therefore, the parties agree that if the Licensee violates this Paragraph, the Licensor has a right to assess liquidated damages against the Licensee in an amount equal to [*number*] percent of the price obtained for each of the Licensee's products that is subject of the violation.

COMMENT: The value of intellectual property rights should never be underestimated. The licensor's goodwill and reputation are connected to its name and product markings, and the uniqueness of its goods are preserved through patent and design registrations. Foreign traders know the value of these property rights—which is why infringement is big business. Your reputation sells products, whether the products are legitimately your own or illegitimately copied. If you do not protect your intellectual property, you may lose not only sales but also the exclusive rights to that property. This clause will not on its own be effective. You should be certain that your trademarks, service marks, patents, and other intellectual property have been registered in the licensee's country, and you need to establish a system to monitor use of the mark in that country.

4. QUALITY OF GOODS. The Licensee will ensure that the manufacture of the Goods will meet the specifications set by the Licensor as set forth in the schedule attached to this Agreement. The specifications indicate the standard of quality to be observed by the Licensee for the production of all of its Goods. In furtherance of ensuring the quality, the Licensee will supply the Licensor every quarter with three random samples of the Goods on or in connection with which the Intellectual Property is being used so that the Licensor can verify the quality. The Licensee will abide by the Licensor's directions on the question of quality, which directions shall not be unreasonable in terms of practicality or financial cost. Within [*number*] months of the effective date of this Agreement, the Licensee will provide the Licensor with [*number*] free samples of the Goods. The Licensee will further provide the Licensor with a free sample whenever the Licensor so requests, provided that such request is not made more than [*number*] of times in any single quarter.

5. DESIGN AND COMPONENTS OF GOODS. The Licensee will prepare or will have prepared at his own cost a plan or design for the Goods that shows usage of the Intellectual Property and all packaging, advertising, marketing, and promotional materials and will submit the plan or design to the Licensor within [*number*] days after this Agreement becomes effective. The Licensor will supply suitable copies of the Intellectual Property and other items requested by the Licensee for the Licensee's use in designing the Goods. The Licensee will not vary the Intellectual Property in its design of the Goods in any manner.

6. PRICE OF GOODS. To preserve the standing of the Licensor's reputation in the trade and public, the Licensee will lower the price for its Goods only after obtaining the prior approval of the Licensor.

7. RELATIONSHIP OF THE PARTIES. This Agreement is nonexclusive. The parties acknowledge and agree that the Licensor is separate and independent of the Licensee. This Agreement is not to be construed as creating an employment, partnership, joint venture, fiduciary, or other similar relationship. Neither party is liable for the debts or obligations of the other, and neither has authority to bind the other to any contracts at all. The Licensee is free to employ or engage any staff or independent contractors, and the Licensor has no power to limit, fire, or hire such persons, except that all such staff or contractors must be required to sign an agreement not to use the Intellectual Property for any other purpose. It is the Licensee's responsibility to ensure that all local law requirements for doing business in [*country*] have been met. The Licensee is further responsible for the payment of all taxes and fees arising from sales of the Goods in the Territory. The Licensor will neither indemnify nor insure the Licensee against losses, claims, or other liabilities that arise in connection with the Licensee's actions with regard to resales, leases, or rentals of the Goods.

COMMENT: The status of the licensee as separate from the licensor should be made very clear. Nevertheless, some jurisdictions may treat licensees in a similar fashion as employees and sales representatives. There is a potential that the licensor will have to comply with labor laws regulating benefits and termination regardless of the attempt to include protective provisions.

8. PAYMENT OF LICENSE FEE. At the signing of this Agreement, the Licensee will pay to the Licensor [*currency and amount*], of which [*currency and amount*] will be a nonrefundable fee for the grant of the License and the remainder will be credited against Sales Royalties.

9. SALES ROYALTIES. For all sales of the Goods, the Licensee will pay to the Licensor [*number*] percent on all direct sales and [*number*] percent on all other sales calculated on the total Net Invoice Price. The Licensee will report Sales Royalties to the Licensor once every quarter by submitting a detailed statement within [*number*] days of the end of the quarter. The statement must set forth the quantity of direct sales separately from other sales, and it must be certified as correct by the Licensee's accountant. Payment of the Sales Royalties will be made at the same time the quarterly statement is furnished to the Licensor. The Licensor or its authorized representative will be permitted, at its request and during regular business hours, to inspect the accounts of the Licensee at the premises of the Licensee and to take any copies desired. At that time, the Licensor or representative may further request additional documentation supporting the records. The Licensee will keep its records for a minimum of two years after termination of this Agreement.

10. ASSIGNMENT. Neither party may assign this Agreement without the prior written consent of the other. Neither party may withhold consent unreasonably.

The Licensor may withhold consent on any of the following grounds: the Licensee is in default of an obligation of this Agreement when consent is requested, the proposed assignee cannot financially perform the Licensee's obligations remaining under this Agreement, the proposed assignee refuses to assume all of the Licensee's remaining obligations under this Agreement, or the proposed assignee fails to meet the Licensor's standards for new licensees in effect at the time consent is requested.

COMMENT: The parties to a personal services contract are making the agreement based on characteristics that are unique to the parties. One party's assignment of the obligations under this contract would leave the other with an unknown partner. A prohibition against all assignments is usually not enforceable, but parties can protect themselves by demanding prior consent to any assignment.

11. TERMINATION OF AGREEMENT. At any time after [*number*] months after the commencement of this Agreement and for any reason, either party may terminate this Agreement by giving [*number*] days' advance written notice to the other party. The giving of such a notice has no effect on any other remedy that the Licensor may seek by law for the infringement of the Licensor's Intellectual Property. If either party should be in default of an obligation of this Agreement, the other party may send a written notice of that breach and a demand for cure within [*number*] days. If the breach is not cured within the notice period, a further notice may be served to terminate this Agreement as of the date stated in the notice. Either party may notify the other in writing that this Agreement is immediately terminated on the ground that the other party is liquidating its assets, is insolvent, or is otherwise incapable of meeting its financial obligations.

COMMENT: A common practice in business contracts is to allow for termination in several different ways, depending on the circumstances. For some events, immediate termination may be warranted, while for others, the party in default may be allowed to cure the default. It is not necessary to list every possible reason for termination by notice—you are bound to miss a few and therefore limit yourself to the ones you have listed. In deciding which events will give a right to terminate the contract, it is important to research the law of the countries of both parties. Your termination rights could be subject to limitation by protective laws. Also, you should avoid using terms such as default of a "material" obligation because such terms are unclear. The parties may state certain defaults that are not grounds for termination, such as a delay in payment of only five days.

12. EFFECT OF TERMINATION. When this Agreement terminates regardless of the cause, all materials supplied to the Licensee and all materials used by the Licensee and its staff, contractors, or other representatives for making, packaging, selling, transporting, and otherwise handling the Goods will be kept by or delivered to the Licensor without charge. At the Licensor's option, these items may instead be destroyed, with evidence of destruction in the form of a certificate sworn by an authorized officer representing the Licensor.

COMMENT: The provision allows the licensor to order the destruction of the materials rather than their return. There is no need to return the goods, and this option could be more cost-effective than returning them. In any event, the licensor should protect its intellectual property on termination of the contract.

13. REMEDIES. The parties acknowledge that they intend to establish a mutually beneficial relationship and that, to this end, they will strive to resolve any disagreements between them through amicable negotiations. Nevertheless, if a dispute does arise that they are unable to resolve otherwise, the parties will submit it to binding arbitration before the [*name of arbitration association*]. The arbitration will be conducted in [*place*], unless the parties agree otherwise at the time arbitration is demanded. Any arbitration award or determination will be final, nonappealable, and conclusive, and it may be submitted to a court with jurisdiction to enter a judgment. This clause will not limit the rights of the Licensor to pursue any remedy available for infringement of its exclusive rights in its Intellectual Property.

COMMENT: If arbitration is available within the local licensee's country, it may be chosen as a means of resolving disputes. You should be cautious, however, in providing for arbitration because not all countries have such systems easily available. Moreover, arbitration is adversarial and usually involves more cost and delay than negotiation and compromise, although generally less than litigation. In some cultures, arbitration has the same stigma as court proceedings, both of which are viewed with suspicion and as personal insults.

14. MODIFICATION. This Agreement is modifiable only by a writing signed by both parties.

COMMENT: Always insist on written modifications to avoid any subsequent question of what was agreed. Proof of oral modifications may not be allowed in court to alter the terms of a contract that is otherwise definite and clear.

15. NOTICES. All notices that may be given under this Agreement must be delivered in writing to the other party at the address specified in this Agreement. A party must notify the other party of a change of address within [*number*] days after it becomes effective. Notices are deemed to be delivered on the date of receipt.

COMMENT: A notice clause is usually a wise provision to ensure that the parties understand the procedure for giving notice. This clause can prevent later disputes over what constitutes notice.

16. WAIVERS AND DELAYS OF PERFORMANCE. Neither party will waive any of the provisions of this Agreement with respect to its rights to seek remedies for breach or to demand strict conformance with the Agreement merely because the party has waived one or more of the other party's breaches in performance; has failed, refused, or neglected to exercise any rights, powers, or options granted by this Agreement; or has not insisted on strict compliance with this Agreement.

17. TERMS OF AGREEMENT. The parties have executed this Agreement to demonstrate their intent to be bound by its terms. The parties declare that this Agreement constitutes their entire agreement and replaces all of their prior negotiations, understandings, and representations. Each party has been encouraged and has had the opportunity to obtain the advice of independent professionals, including attorneys and accountants, and each has made an independent decision to undertake the obligations set forth. If any term of this Agreement is held to be unenforceable or invalid, such term may be modified to render it valid and enforceable. If modification cannot be made, the term will be deemed deleted and the remainder of the Agreement will remain in full force.

COMMENT: This standard clause is important and should rarely be eliminated from your contracts. It serves to establish the basic contractual notions of mutual understanding and intent. In international contracts, these clauses have added significance because each party's understanding of the contract terms could indeed be very different from that of the other party, given such invisible barriers as language, culture, environment, and inexperience.

18. INDEMNITY. The parties agree to the following indemnities:

a. The Licensor may withhold or cancel any or all rights granted by this Agreement on the ground that use of the rights is likely to infringe on the rights of third parties or to prejudice the Licensor. In such event, the Licensor will indemnify the Licensee against damages and costs that the Licensee may claim, and the Licensor will have the option to purchase the Licensee's stocks of materials and tools for production of the Goods and stocks of the Goods at cost plus [*number*] percent.

b. The Licensee will indemnify the Licensor against all damages, costs, and expenses incurred by the Licensor if the material and any design for the Goods are not provided by the Licensor but included in the Goods by the Licensee is the subject of a claim of infringement by a third party.

Each party acknowledges that he or she has read and understood the terms of this Agreement, and accordingly sign below.

[*Name of Company*]

Licensee

By [*signature*]

[*name and title of person signing*]

[*Name of Company*]

Licensor

By [*signature*]

[*name and title of person signing*]

CHAPTER 22

Glossary

FOR INCOTERMS 2000, refer to Chapter 5: Trade Terms and Incoterms. For a comprehensive listing of international trade, economic, banking, legal and shipping terms, we recommend the *Dictionary of International Trade* also by World Trade Press.

ABROGATION The cancellation of the part of a contract that has not yet been performed. For example, if parties agree to several deliveries of goods but, after the first delivery, war is declared in the buyer's country and no further goods can be delivered, the buyer must pay for the first delivery, but the contract is abrogated as to the remaining ones.

ACCEPTANCE An unconditional assent to an offer, or an assent conditioned on minor changes that do not affect material terms of the offer. See COUNTEROFFER, OFFER.

ACCOMMODATION An action by one party (the accommodation party) that is taken as a favor without consideration for another party (the accommodated party).

ACCOUNTING A remedy for a breach of contract that requires the breaching party to disclose financial records.

ACCORD AND SATISFACTION A discharge of a contract or cause of action pursuant to which the parties agree (the accord) to alter their obligations and to perform new obligations (the satisfaction). For example, a seller who cannot obtain red fabric to meet the contract specifications may enter into an accord and satisfaction to provide the buyer with blue fabric for a slightly lower price.

ACKNOWLEDGMENT See AUTHENTICATION.

ACT OF GOD CLAUSE See FORCE MAJEURE CLAUSE.

ADHESION CONTRACT A contract with standard, often printed, terms for sale of goods or services offered to buyers who usually have no power to negotiate any terms of the contract and who cannot acquire the products or services unless they agree to the contract terms. Also known as a "contract à prendre ou à laisser," or a "take-it-or-leave-it" contract.

AFFILIATED COMPANY A business enterprise that is directly or indirectly owned or controlled by another entity.

AFTER SIGHT A term in a financial instrument making the instrument payable a specified number of days after presentation or demand. Example: a bill of exchange payable 30 days after sight will mature and become payable 30 days after the person for whom the bill is drawn (the drawee) presents it to a bank (the payee).

AGENCY The relationship between one individual or entity (the agent) who represents, acts for, and binds another individual or entity (the principal) in accordance with the principal's request or instruction. In some countries, an agency is created only by written agreement or power of attorney. See POWER OF ATTORNEY.

AGENT An individual or entity who is authorized to act for and bind another individual or entity (the principal). See AGENCY.

AMENDMENT An addition, deletion, or change in a legal document.

À PRENDRE OU À LAISSER CONTRACT See ADHESION CONTRACT.

AS IS A contract term by which the buyer of goods takes them in the condition they are in without any warranties or guarantees for better or for worse.

ASSIGNMENT The transfer of rights, title, interest, and benefits of a contract from one party (the assignor) to another individual or entity (the assignee) that was not a party to the initial contract.

AT SIGHT A term in a financial instrument under which the instrument is payable on presentation or demand. Example: a bill of exchange that is payable at sight is payable at the time the person for whom the bill is drawn (the drawee) presents it to a bank (the payee).

ATTACHMENT The legal process for seizing property before a judgment to secure the payment of damages if awarded. Attachment may be sought before commencing a court action or during the action. This process is also referred to as sequestration. Example: a party who claims damages for breach of contract may request a court to issue an order freezing all transfers of specific property owned by the breaching party pending resolution of the dispute.

AUTHENTICATION The act of conferring legal authenticity on a written document, typically made by a notary public, who attests and certifies that the document is in proper legal form and that it is executed by a person identified as having authority to do so. Authentication is also referred to as acknowledgment.

AVOIDANCE Cancellation of a contract by law when an event renders performance impossible or inequitable, with the result that the parties are released from their obligations.

BAILMENT A delivery of goods into the possession of another (the bailee) under an express or implied contract and for a particular purpose related to the goods while possessed by the bailee, who has a duty to return them to the owner (the bailor) or to dispose of them pursuant to the bailor's instructions after the purpose has been accomplished. For example, a seller who delivers goods to a shipper with instructions to transport them to the buyer at a specified destination has created a bailment. In a bailment for hire, the bailor agrees to compensate the bailee. In a special bailment, the bailee is held to a greater duty of care for the safe transport and delivery of the goods.

BENEFICIARY A person or entity that is not a party to a contract but that will benefit from a contract made between other parties. Example: A sales contract may provide that, if the seller should die before the transaction is completed, the purchase price is to be paid to the seller's estate. The estate is a beneficiary of the sales contract.

BILL OF EXCHANGE A written instrument signed by a person (the drawer) and addressed to another person (the drawee), typically a bank, ordering the drawee to pay unconditionally a stated sum of money to yet another person (the payee) on demand or at a future time.

BOILERPLATE Standard contract terms usually printed in small type on the reverse of a pre-printed contract form. Also called fine print. Refers generally to the minute details of a contract. See FINE PRINT.

BONA FIDE In or with good faith, honesty, and sincerity. Example: A bona fide purchaser is one who buys goods for value and without knowledge of fraud or unfair dealing in the transaction. Knowledge of fraud or unfair dealing may be implied if the facts are such that the purchaser should have reasonably known that the transaction involved deceit, such as when goods that are susceptible to piracy are provided without documentation of their origin.

BOTTOM LINE (1) The last line in a financial statement indicating the profit of a company. (2) In a contract, the line upon which a party signs. (3) Pragmatic, realistic.

BREACH A violation of law or agreement.

CAPACITY TO CONTRACT A person's competency, as defined by law, to make a contract. Capacity to contract is typically determined by whether a person has attained majority age and is mentally capable of understanding the contract terms.

CHATTEL Personal property.

CHATTEL PAPER Documents that constitute a security interest in or a lease of specific goods for a monetary obligation.

CISG See CONVENTION ON CONTRACTS FOR THE INTERNATIONAL SALE OF GOODS.

CONFIRMATION A written contract or memorandum that sets forth the terms of an agreement that would otherwise have been difficult to prove and therefore to enforce. For example, parties who have agreed orally or through a series of letters to the terms of a sale of goods may formalize their agreement by signing a confirmation that contains all of the terms.

CONFLICT OF INTEREST A financial or ethical conflict between an official's private interests and official duties.

CONSIDERATION An item of value passed from one contracting party to the other as an inducement to make the contract and without which the contract is not binding. Consideration may consist of a right, interest, profit, or benefit that accrues to one party or a forbearance, detriment, loss, or obligation given, suffered, or undertaken by the other party. For example, the consideration in a sales contract is the price of the goods.

CONSIGNMENT CONTRACT An agreement by which a seller (consignor) delivers goods to an individual or entity (consignee) that will sell them. For goods sold, the consignee will remit the price to the consignor less a commission. Goods not sold may be returned to the consignor.

CONSULERIZATION An authentication by a country's consul or other similar government official.
See AUTHENTICATION.

CONVENTION ON CONTRACTS FOR THE INTERNATIONAL SALE OF GOODS (CISG) A United Nations convention that establishes uniform legal rules to govern international contracts for the sale of goods between nationals of member countries. If cross-border traders are nationals of countries that have ratified the CISG, their contracts for the sale of goods will be subject to the CISG unless the contracts specify otherwise.

COUNTEROFFER A reply to an offer that materially alters the terms of the offer. Example: a seller who accepts a buyer's offer on condition that the goods will be made of a different material has made a counteroffer.
See ACCEPTANCE, OFFER.

CROSSED CHECK A check that bears on its face two parallel transverse lines, indicating that it cannot be presented for cash. A bank that accepts such a check will pay the proceeds only to another bank, which will credit the money to the account of the payee of the check.

DAMAGES A monetary amount claimed and awarded to a person for loss or injury to the person or the person's property. Various types of damages may be sought depending on the circumstances of the injury or loss, including *actual* (compensation for amounts in fact incurred), *expectation* (compensation for amounts that a person could have reasonably anticipated receiving from a transaction had it not failed), *incidental* (expenses reasonably incurred in mitigating, or otherwise in association with, losses), and *liquidated* (an amount fixed by contract as reasonable compensation in the event a party defaults).

DESIGN A scheme, drawing, plan, or other depiction of a new pattern, model, shape, or configuration that is decorative or ornamental. In many countries, the rights to a design can be registered, allowing the registrant to claim exclusive use in that country.

DESTINATION CONTRACT A contract for sale of goods in which the risk of loss is passed to the buyer after the seller delivers the goods to the destination.

DOCUMENTATION The financial and commercial documents relating to a transaction. These documents may include a commercial invoice, consular invoice, customs invoice, certificate of origin, bill of lading, inspection certificate, and bill of exchange.

DOT THE "I'S" AND CROSS THE "T'S" To make certain that every detail of a document has been taken care of.

EXECUTION (1)The signing of a document, such as a contract. (2) A legal process for enforcing a judgment for damages, usually by seizure and sale of the debtor's personal property. Example: if a court awards damages in a breach of contract action and the reaching party fails to remit them, the party awarded damages may request the court to order seizure and sale of the breaching party's inventory to satisfy the award.

EXECUTORY CONTRACT A contract that has not been performed entirely.

EXHIBIT A document attached to a contract or agreement. For example, a document entitled Exhibit A listing product specifications attached to a purchase order.

FINE PRINT Standard contract terms printed in small type usually on the reverse of a pre-printed contract form. Refers generally to the minute details of a contract. See BOILERPLATE.

FORCE MAJEURE CLAUSE A contract clause that excuses a party who breaches the contract when performance is prevented by the occurrence of an event—such as a natural disaster, war, or labor strike—that is beyond the party's reasonable control.

GENERAL AGREEMENT ON TARIFFS AND TRADE (GATT) See URUGUAY ROUND.

GOODS Products, whether raw materials, semimanufactured components, or completed merchandise. Goods identified to a contract are all products designated by a contract or by the seller as sold to a particular buyer. *Consumable goods* are goods purchased for the buyer's personal, family, or household use. *Durable goods* are goods that last a relatively long time without being quickly dissipated or depleted during use, such as machinery. *Hard goods* are consumer durable goods, such as appliances or vehicles. *Soft goods* are consumer goods that are not durable, such as clothing or luggage.

GOVERNING LAW CLAUSE A contract provision that specifies the law that the parties have selected for the interpretation of their contract. Whether a court respects the choice of the parties is discretionary, since parties are not permitted to deprive a court of jurisdiction.

INTEGRATED CONTRACT A contract that states every provision to which the parties intend to agree. Parol evidence cannot be used to change or supplement the provisions of an integrated contract.

INTELLECTUAL PROPERTY Intangible rights that can be protected because of their novelty, uniqueness, and value to the creator. These rights include copyrights, trademarks, service marks, designs, and patents.

INVALID CONTRACT See VOIDABLE CONTRACT.

JURIDICAL (JURISTIC) ACT An action intended to have, and capable of having, a legal effect, such as the creation, termination, or modification of a legal right. Example: The signing of a power of attorney is a juridical act because it gives legal authority to an agent.

JURIDICAL (JURISTIC) PERSON An individual or entity recognized under law as having legal rights and obligations. Example: limited liability companies, corporations, and partnerships are entities recognized as juridical persons.

LEGALESE Language particular to the legal profession.

LEGALIZATION An authentication of a written document. See AUTHENTICATION.

LIQUIDATED DAMAGES A sum of money that contracting parties agree will be paid in the event of voluntary breach of the contract. The agreed sum must be a reasonable estimate of the damages that a party would actually incur because of the other party's breach. Liquidated damages are often included in contracts to avoid having to prove damages that are difficult to assess. For example, if goods are never received and the buyer is forced to obtain replacement goods at a higher price, damages may be assessed as the cost of replacement less the cost of the goods under the breached contract. However, if the buyer is unable to obtain replacement goods because the goods ordered had unique characteristics, the standards used to assess damages—cost of replacement or market value—do not apply. The parties may therefore choose to estimate what the reasonable damages of a breach would be and agree to the payment of liquidated damages on default.

MATERIAL TERMS Contract provisions that are so significant to the bargain made that the agreement would be substantially different if the terms were to be altered or eliminated.

MIDDLEMAN An intermediary acting as an agent or dealer between buyers and sellers.

MINIMUM CONTACT A person's connections to a jurisdiction, such as operating or soliciting business there, that are considered sufficiently substantial as to allow the person to come under the authority of the courts of that jurisdiction.

MITIGATION OF DAMAGES The duty, imposed by law, to use reasonable care and due diligence to minimize one's damages or to avoid aggravating an injury suffered or incurred because of another person's breach of contractual or other duties owed to the injured party. For example, if a buyer refuses to accept a shipment of goods that will quickly spoil if not immediately collected from the dockside, the seller has a duty to take reasonable steps to find another buyer or to move the goods into appropriate storage while the dispute is being resolved.

MUTUALITY OF CONTRACT The intent of both parties to a contract to become bound by the contract terms. Mutuality is essential to the enforcement of a contract. It is shown by the apparent intention of the parties as demonstrated by their actions relative to executing and performing the contract.

MUTUALITY OF REMEDY Contract provisions by which both parties are given the right to the same remedy or to remedies of equal effect.

NECESSARY TERMS Contract provisions for the goods, price, delivery time, and payment, without which terms a contract is generally considered unenforceable unless the parties have partially or fully performed it. Some jurisdictions may imply these terms from customary trade or financial practices.

NEGOTIABLE INSTRUMENT A written document transferable merely by endorsement or delivery. Example: a check or bill of exchange is a negotiable instrument.

NON SUI JURIS Strictly translated as "not of one's own right". This term is applied to persons who are underage or who otherwise do not have legal capacity to enter a binding contract. See CAPACITY TO CONTRACT.

OFFER A proposal that is made to a specific individual or entity to enter into a contract. The proposal must contain definite terms and must indicate the offeror's intent to be bound by an acceptance. Example: a buyer's order to purchase designated goods on certain delivery and payment terms is an offer. See ACCEPTANCE, COUNTER-OFFER.

OPEN-END CONTRACT An agreement by which the buyer may purchase the seller's goods at any time within a specified period without changes in the price or other contract terms.

OUTPUT CONTRACT An agreement by which the buyer agrees to purchase the seller's entire production.

PAROL CONTRACT A contract that is partly or entirely oral.

PAROL EVIDENCE Oral statements that are offered to prove the terms of a contract. In general, if the parol evidence changes, contradicts, or supplements the written contract terms, it is inadmissible to prove the intent of the parties. Thus, if oral statements are made during preliminary negotiations but are not incorporated into the final agreement, those statements may not later be used by one party to prove the meaning of the written terms.

PARTY (TO A TRANSACTION) An individual, group, or entity that represents one side of a question, contract, or dispute.

POWER OF ATTORNEY A written document by which one individual or entity (the principal) authorizes another individual or entity (the agent) to perform stated acts on the principal's behalf. Example: a principal may execute a *special power of attorney* (authorizing an agent to sign a specific contract) or a *general power of attorney* (authorizing the agent to sign all contracts for the principal). See AGENCY.

PRIVITY OF CONTRACT A mutuality of interest between the parties to a contract. Contracting parties are in privity if they have equal interests in the subject of the contract.

PRO FORMA INVOICE An invoice provided by a supplier prior to a sale or shipment of merchandise to inform the buyer of the kinds and quantities of goods being sent, their value, and specifications such as weight and size. A pro forma invoice is used as a preliminary invoice together with a quotation and for customs purposes in identifying the goods. Legally, it may serve as evidence of the contractual arrangement between the parties.

PURCHASE ORDER A buyer's written offer to a seller stating all terms and conditions of a proposed transaction.

REASONABLE PERSON STANDARD A test developed by the courts for determining whether a person's conduct within a particular situation is the same as what would be expected of another, reasonable person under identical conditions. In relation to contracts, courts may infer missing terms in accordance with what the parties would reasonably intend under the circumstances, i.e., in accordance with the common trade or industry practice.

REQUIREMENT CONTRACT An agreement by which the seller agrees to furnish all goods required by the buyer for a specified time and at a certain price, during which time the buyer agrees to purchase such goods from the seller exclusively.

RESCIND A contracting party's right to cancel the contract. For example, a contract may allow one party to rescind if the other party fails to perform within a reasonable time.

RESTITUTION A legal remedy for breach of contract by which the parties are restored to their original positions before the contract was made or the breach occurred. For example, if a buyer remits partial advance payment and the seller sends goods that fail to meet the buyer's specifications, the buyer may take legal action for the restitution of the payment to the buyer and return of the goods to the seller.

SEQUESTRATION See ATTACHMENT.

SEVERABILITY CLAUSE A contract term that provides that each provision of the contract is independent of all of the others so that if a court invalidates any of the clauses, the rest of the contract remains valid.

STATUTE OF FRAUDS A law that requires designated documents to be in writing in order to be enforced by a court. Example: contracting parties may orally agree to transfer ownership of immovable properties, but a court might not award damages for breach, unless the contract was written.

TYING ARRANGEMENT A condition of sale that a seller imposes on a buyer, requiring that if the buyer purchases one product (tying product), the buyer must agree to purchase a second product also (tied product), regardless of whether the buyer wants both products. The laws of some countries prohibit tying arrangements.

ULTRA VIRES An act performed without the authority to do so. Example: If a contract provision requires both parties to approve an assignment of the contract but one party agrees to an assignment without obtaining the other's consent, the assignment is ultra vires.

UNCONSCIONABLE Unfair or oppressive. For example, a contract with unconscionable terms favors one party and burdens the other to such an extent that a court may refuse to enforce the unconscionable terms because the result would be unjust.

UNFAIR COMPETITION Trading and business activities that are dishonest or fraudulent as against the activities of other traders. Unfair competition includes fraudulent advertising, counterfeiting, and similar illegal trade practices.

URUGUAY ROUND The eighth round of multilateral trade negotiations pursuant to the General Agreement on Tariffs and Trade (GATT). The meetings began in Uruguay in 1987 and were concluded in December 1993 with an agreement among 117 member nations. The major goals of this Round were to reduce trade barriers for goods, to strengthen the international role of GATT, to improve multilateral trading, to increase the responsiveness of GATT to the evolving international economic environment, to encourage cooperation in strengthening the interrelationship between trade and other economic policies that affect growth and development, and to establish a multilateral framework of principals and rules for trade in services.

VALUE ADDED TAX (VAT) A tax based on the value that is added to goods at each stage of production. These taxes can serve as indirect trade barriers to imports because the taxes are passed on to the ultimate consumer, making the imported goods more expensive than local products.

VOID AB INITIO Having no effect from the time of initiation. A contract that violates law or that is against public policy is void ab initio because, from the moment it is formed, it never takes effect.

VOIDABLE CONTRACT An agreement that is valid but that can be declared invalid at the request of one of the parties because of a defect or illegality in making it. For example, if one party made a fraudulent misrepresentation on which the other party relied in making the agreement, the agreement will be enforced against the misrepresenting party but the other party may seek relief by electing to void the contract.

VOID CONTRACT An agreement that has no legal effect and that cannot be ratified or otherwise made effective, such as a contract to perform an illegal act.

WAIVER (1) The abandoning of a claim or right. (2) The document acknowledging the abandoning of a claim or right.

WARRANTY A contract provision by which one party represents to the other that certain facts are true. For example, a seller might warrant that the goods will meet certain specifications and the buyer might be entitled to return nonconforming goods.

CHAPTER 23

Resources

Axtell. *Do's and Taboos of International Trade: A Small Business Primer*
John Wiley Publications.

Black's Law Dictionary
West Publishing, St. Paul, Minnesota.

Curry, Jeffrey E. *A Short Course in International Negotiating*
World Trade Press, San Rafael, California. 1999.

Digest of Commercial Laws of the World
Oceana Publications, Dobbs Ferry, New York.

International Law Digest
Martindale Hubbell. 1997. Revised annually.

Hinkelman, Edward G. *A Short Course in International Payments*
World Trade Press, San Rafael, California. 1999.

Hinkelman, Edward G. *Dictionary of International Trade*
World Trade Press, San Rafael, California. 1997.

ICC Model International Sale Contract: Manufactured Goods Intended for Resale
ICC Publishing, New York, New York.

Incoterms 2000
ICC Publishing, Inc. New York, New York.

The Legal Dictionary for Bad Spellers
John Wiley Publications.

Managing for Products Liability Avoidance: The Product Integrity Program
CCH Inc., Chicago, Illinois. 1994.

Mitchell, Charles. *A Short Course in International Business Culture*
World Trade Press, San Rafael, California. 1999.

Real Life Dictionary of the Law
General Publishing Group, Inc.

Retailing in the Single European Market
Office for Official Publications of the European Communities. 1993.
Available from Unipub, 4611-F Assembly Drive, Lanham, Maryland.

Schlicher. *Licensing Intellectual Property: Legal, Business, and Market Dynamics*
Wiley Law Publications, Colorado Springs, Colorado.

Simensky & Bryer, editors. *The New Role of Intellectual Property in Commercial Transactions*
Wiley Law Publications. 1994.

Sitarz. *The Complete Book of Small Business Legal Forms*
Nova Publishing.

Weiss. *Building an Import/Export Business*
John Wiley Publications.